Organizing Locally

Organizing Locally

How the New Decentralists Improve Education,
Health Care, and Trade

BRUCE FULLER
WITH MARY BERG,
DANFENG SOTO-VIGIL KOON,
AND LYNETTE PARKER

The University of Chicago Press
Chicago and London

Bruce Fuller is professor of education and public policy at the University of California, Berkeley. He is the author of *Growing Up Modern, Government Confronts Culture, Inside Charter Schools*, and *Standardized Childhood*. His writings appear in the *New York Times*, the *Washington Post*, and *Commonweal*.

The University of Chicago Press, Chicago 60637
The University of Chicago Press, Ltd., London
© 2015 by The University of Chicago
All rights reserved. Published 2015.
Printed in the United States of America

24 23 22 21 20 19 18 17 16 15   1 2 3 4 5

ISBN-13: 978-0-226-24640-6 (cloth)
ISBN-13: 978-0-226-24654-3 (paper)
ISBN-13: 978-0-226-24668-0 (e-book)
DOI: 10.7208/chicago/9780226246680.001.0001

Library of Congress Cataloging-in-Publication Data

Fuller, Bruce, author.
   Organizing locally : how the decentralists improve education, health care, and trade / Bruce Fuller ; with Mary Berg, Danfeng Soto-Vigil Koon, and Lynette Parker.
      pages cm
   Includes bibliographical references and index.
   ISBN 978-0-226-24640-6 (cloth : alkaline paper)—ISBN 978-0-226-24654-3 (paperback : alk.)—ISBN 978-0-226-24668-0 (e-book) 1. Decentralization in government—United States. 2. Community organization—United States. 3. Health services administration. 4. Community banks. 5. Charter schools. I. Title.
   HM766.F85 2015
   352.2'83—dc23
                                                      2014031547

♾ This paper meets the requirements of ANSI/NISO Z39.48–1992 (Permanence of Paper).

To Caitlin and Dylan, who teach me so much.

Contents

Preface ix

1 The Drive to Decentralize—After Hierarchies and Markets Disappoint 1
2 How Decentralized Organizations Work 47
with Danfeng Soto-Vigil Koon
3 Organizing Health Care from the Ground Up 73
with Mary Berg
4 International Banking Goes Local—Swedish Organizing in New York 105
5 The Four R's—A School Where Relationships Come First 129
with Lynette Parker
6 The Limits of Localism—Lifting Vets in Iowa 157
7 Learning from the New Decentralists—Cornerstones of Local Organizing 185

Methods Appendix 215
Notes 223
References 231
Index 241

Society and human fellowship will be best served if we confer the most kindness on those with whom we are most closely associated.
—CICERO, Athens, 44 BC[1]

If we are to have peace on earth, our loyalties must become ecumenical, our loyalties must transform our race, our tribe, our class.
—MARTIN LUTHER KING, Georgia, 1967

Deinstitutionalization is associated not only with the growing recognition that current institutional patterns are ineffective, but also with the development of a challenging alternative institutional logic.
—W. RICHARD SCOTT, Stanford, California, 2000

Preface

Organizing Locally, as the Center Folds

You may not recall—especially if under forty—that massive and vibrant institutions once animated modern society. American factories stamped out cars, magically wove elegant wardrobes, even crafted those cool stereo systems our parents coveted, tucked into sleek wooden cabinets. The efficiency of manufacturers, going back a century and a half, pushed prices lower for a breathtaking array of goods, from radios to washing machines. This, along with rising wages, would kindle a burgeoning middle class and seem to validate the wisdom of smug management scientists; human labor and social cooperation was best orchestrated by central engineers and leaders of public institutions, bent on standardized products, efficiency, and a tidy set of moral guideposts.

Modern government—eager to mimic the factory's humming routines and uniform products—built expansive school "plants," universities for the masses, huge hospitals, and a benevolent bureaucracy that lent order to economic and social life. A confident postwar America stretched out tentacles of interstate highways across the land, the grandest project ever undertaken by any civilization. You may even recall a nationwide network of spotless and well-staffed post offices? Through a child's eyes in the mid-twentieth century, Walt Disney's Tomorrowland was magically rising up around us, during this apex of modernity.

Almost two generations ago, top-heavy firms and feckless public institutions found themselves on the ropes, beset by lagging performance and fading legitimacy, now seen as potent only in eroding the human spirit. Our manufacturers suffered a first jolt of competition from East Asia in the 1970s, then from even lower wages in developing nations, falling into steady decline. America was no longer the marketplace at which the world shopped. Rust crept over the once shiny industrial machine, like an old engine discarded on a damp lot. Decrepit iron foundries that once cast and exported steel beams around the globe now sat empty. Cavernous auto plants lay abandoned on vast tracts, from Detroit to Los Angeles, enveloped by prickly weeds pushing up through cracked concrete, where rows of brightly painted cars with that scent of fresh Naugahyde once sat.

As the factory faltered, popular worry grew over the efficacy of creaky public institutions as well—first from the political Right, then from the Left—be it the nation's stumbling public schools or uneven quality and high cost of health care. This invited political leaders to attack (their own) state-run organizations, aiming to exact greater efficiency or less government spending. Central regulation of teachers or physicians, and single mothers on welfare, was to advance greater accountability for individuals and institutions alike— that tough love that Bill Clinton first doled out.

Better yet, why not infuse public institutions with a stiff dose of market competition; after all, it is a grassroots version of direct accountability between firm and client. The Reagan White House would embolden conservatives by awarding portable vouchers to parents to shop for allegedly better, even sectarian, schools, or for day care and housing in the 1980s. They brought price competition to health-care providers and even contracted with for-profit companies to run prisons. Civic spaces were no longer energized by social ideals and shared aspirations. Instead, the public commons became a contested ground for self-interested individuals or firms to pursue their particular interests; competition for clients was to magically lift the quality and productive efficiency of schooling, housing, or health care.

Corporate faith in hierarchy and top-down management waned as well. The factory model and its assembly-line jobs were packed up and moved offshore. Factories soon became an antiquated way to organize work stateside. California's sunny and sleek high-tech industry, powered by inventive thinkers and sandal-clad software writers, arose in stark counterpoint to stodgy manufacturers of the Rust Belt. The control of capital and major design decisions may remain centralized—as with Apple Computer or clothier Levi-Strauss—but the hierarchical organization chart and routinized labor made a steady exit overseas. And the value-added bonus now enjoyed by avant-garde companies stemmed from creative design and innovative code, bubbling up from down below, given shape by creative collaborators inside posthierarchical firms.

So it's no surprise that a variety of efforts to deinstitutionalize—to *decenter* who controls work, divvies up resources, and engages students, patients, or clients on the ground—have spread across public and private spheres over the past half century. Political and corporate leaders alike now rally around the idea of disassembling hierarchies, like a child eagerly toppling a castle of Legos only to piece together tiny yet colorful huts across the floor. Turns out that small may indeed be beautiful.

This book shares the lessons of decentralizing organizations—in the public and private sectors, along with an expanding territory in between—that energize their local practitioners and steadily lift their clients. We take you deep into a San Francisco charter school, where teachers experiment with caring roles and inventive pedagogies. We travel to central Pennsylvania to learn how a robust health-care company relies on house calls to learn about the support networks of aging or costly patients, even flattening power relations inside local clinics, long dominated by proud physicians. And we head to Manhattan, then Stockholm, to discover how one international bank grows more profitable by shipping loosely monitored chunks of capital to branch managers who call the shots.

These research forays—joined by three wonderful colleagues—were motivated by three basic questions. What forces have nudged public institutions and private firms over the past half century to decentralize authority, know-how, and who controls resources? Why have early efforts to decenter or marketize how we organize work—say, to lift learning, health, or trade—often fallen flat in terms of motivating local practitioners and the clients they serve? And how are the new decentralists—moving way beyond the rhetoric of breaking free of hierarchy or naively banking on market dynamics—proving more successful? These are the issues that spirit this book.

Top-Down Meets Get-Down

This is not simply a story about conservatives or so-called neoliberals who press unbounded faith in the wonders of market competition. Many political progressives and American intellectuals as well had become disaffected with centralized or homogeneous institutions a generation ago, pointing to the inability of public or private organizations to advance a fair and open society. The labor-led Left had long dueled with management, critical of the alienating effects of hierarchical authority and the deskilling of workers. Then the cultural Left, first spurred by the campus uprisings of the 1960s, would come to question the huge and impersonal universities that aging liberals once championed. Nearing a half century later a variety of proequity critics now argue that America's vast institutions seem unable to lift students, patients, or poor families—the idealistic missions for which they were designed. Rather than broadening opportunity for the disenfranchised, these bureaucratic behemoths appear to further alienate and simply legitimate widening disparities. Nor does our society's colorful array of tribes savor the bland cultural gruel still simmering in America's melting pot of old.

As Bill Clinton sought to move his party to the political center in the 1990s, Vice President Al Gore pushed to "reinvent government"—to dismantle the regulatory apparatus, define performance targets centrally, and free up local units to devise the inventive means for getting there. The eighteenth-century dawn of modernity had earlier seen European governments mimic newly hip industrial hierarchies, as the state chased popular legitimacy and public revenues. Mr. Gore's brave new world would now seek to copy the slim-center, local-innovation metaphor as advanced by high-technology firms that spurred robust growth. America no longer needed to make anything to compete in the global economy, or so it seemed during the dot-com boom. Instead, corporate managers oversaw the design of software, computers, and telecom tools—assembled overseas. And this burst in productivity was built on a more decentralized way of organizing work within postindustrial firms.

This widening critique of hierarchies and their pallid way of regulating human cooperation stemmed not only from restless managers or politicians eager to trumpet innovation. It was fed by a deeper *cultural* attack on graying forms of social authority—a humanist revival first sparked in the 1950s that questioned a meritocracy based on materialist benchmarks of status and white-collar conformity. It wasn't just the bureaucratic pyramid that began to crumble. The moral beacons that once lit a deep rut through life, that dream of an office job and ranch-style home in a leafy suburb, no longer shown so brightly. *Question Authority* was no longer simply an offbeat bumper sticker pasted on a pastel-painted Volkswagen: it became a core tenet held by many citizens across the land.

Books in the 1950s, like David Riesman's *The Lonely Crowd* and William Whyte's *Organization Man*, asked what Americans were sacrificing as they blithely pushed to get ahead materially, to fit into monochromatic shades of white-collar sameness. Blue-collar regimentation was simply being replaced with gray flannel suits, a bland postwar future that millions of youths had begun to question, even to reject. "The future is in plastics," the husky, martini-drinking executive told Dustin Hoffman in *The Graduate*.

This splintering of cultural ideals was followed by a material hit on America's dream of never-ending upward mobility; the upwardly sloping pulse of middle-class earnings went flat. The median American household today earns less than in the late 1990s. Playing by the old rules no longer yields a winning hand. Fewer and fewer citizens—even if they aspire for suburban nirvana—would ever experience the virtues of a well-paying job, that lush lawn, and two SUVs in every garage. Some 1.5 million college graduates under twenty-five years of age, are jobless or underemployed.[2] Many of our kids are still sleeping in, as their parents rush off for work, only to awaken to a pallid job market, a postindustrial economy that simply can't put our best and brightest to work, whether it feeds their souls or not.

Government of course wasn't immune from this steady erosion of centralized authority; it was a loss leader. Vietnam and Watergate sunk trust in the American state to new lows. Our highest public leaders misled the citizenry, even as they literally culled the next generation. As trust in the political center weakened, local ties grew more fulfilling, more authentic than the plastic roles promised by faceless organizations. And a rainbow of personal identities would arise from which to choose in a more pluralistic society—pressed first by African Americans, then Latinos, gays, evangelicals, and disabled Americans. Some groups articulated their shared identity and shared history, becoming forceful political actors, while others remained content with quietly affiliating in cultural enclaves, from rappers to rock hounds.

Sure, America had long stood for *political* pluralism, suspicious of centralized nodes of state power back in the Old World. But the likes of Thomas Jefferson or John Locke could never have imagined the *cultural* rainbow of ethnic pockets, tribal ties, and offbeat lifestyles that would bloom over the past half century. Now America's renewed commitment to localism—manifest in farmers markets, gentrifying neighborhoods, the share economy or yoga retreats—have largely displaced earlier faith in mass organizations.

Cultural icons from the 1960s forward still nudge us to "get real," to discard the roles imposed by waning forms, the unfulfilling and unsustainable excesses of materialism. The names of Baez and Lennon, Keith Richards or the Grateful Dead, still connote a hunger for authenticity and the visceral pursuit of human connection. "It was a time of awakenings," Erica Jong reflected, "that coalesced into movements. We could now read *Lady Chatterley's Lover* . . . without going to the locked rare book room at a university library."[3] Or think John Cage, performing scores filled with dissonant notes and disorderly percussion, even sitting at the keyboard with awkward periods of silence. So as nodes of central authority imploded, one domino effect has come to pass: Americans have devised a kaleidoscopic variety of local affiliations, fresh lifestyles that no longer seem "out there," but instead express what's deep inside, what's particular within my group rather than what's universally shared with others. "We are all multiculturalists now," as Harvard sociologist Nathan Glazer declared more than a decade and a half ago.

Simple categories no longer capture the centrifugal swirl of ideals and lifestyles that mark postindustrial society. Western civilizations have long experienced periods of far-flung diversity. Take, for example, how slowly uniting Christian leaders struggled mightily to stamp out a variety of pagan beliefs and festivals, as the Roman Empire was crumbling.[4] Or, how modernizing Parisians consolidated their nineteenth-century republics by incorporating parish schools into a uniform system, not to mentioning stigmatizing the local patois. But the contemporary pushback from the new localists is unprecedented on cultural and political fronts. It's impossible to encircle and categorize the dens of diversity that characterize cosmopolitan America. Sizing up an edgy sculpture by the twenty-something Columbian, Miguel Cárdenas, showing at New York's El Museo del Barrio, one reviewer wrote that for this young artist, "ethnic identity is an outfit to be lightly worn, mixed and matched with other identities and continually updated."[5]

Bringing Down Hierarchies

All organizations must adapt to shifts in their economic and ideological environs, particularly as the character and requisite tools of work evolve in postindustrial societies. So as rising shares of economic activity are tied to lifting the learning and health of our citizens—not simply to the production of foodstuffs and things—how firms design and coordinate labor and social practices must adapt as well. In a widening range of fields the "production process" is simply too complex and uncertain—whether to engage feisty students, move patients to healthier lifestyles, or lift the well-being of families—to be shaped by a distant front office. Classic bureaucratic principles of reducing complex projects down to routinized tasks, engineered and controlled from above, have become less sensible technically and less legitimate socially. This is especially true in fields where the task is to buoy or shift human behavior, as in organizations dedicated to lifting learning, health, or trade.

As these economic and cultural forces converge, once-modern edifices come crashing down, at times in quite dramatic ways. Skyscrapers that house the poor, once seen as the humane way to aid families, are now detonated with great fanfare, leaving nothing but mounds of concrete shards. Advocates of charter schools seek to break free of downtown education bureaucracies. Conservatives celebrate the spread of market dynamics and organizational competition, pressing for vouchers to fund public housing, child care, and sectarian schooling. Meanwhile, many on the Left applaud this disassembling of public hierarchies, seeking to fund local nonprofits and unfettered innovations, from building preschools and health clinics to seeding "empowerment zones" bent on gentrifying graying communities.

Early modernists were deeply suspicious of the local, the provincial, the parochial. Their revolutionary way of organizing modernity—after storming the Bastille in Paris and purging the British from the American colonies— would only be hampered by village affiliations, kinship, and religion. Instead, big and bold institutions would arise in London, Paris, and Philadelphia to standardize each nation's language, a common currency and unified postal system, even setting the uniform width of train rails to help integrate provincial economies. The secular head of state would now mastermind the integration of polities and regulation of social behavior, not the church or provincial landlords. Local authority—tied to the parish, old elites, and particular dialects—was to be stigmatized, tossed into a turbid civic cauldron, that same melting pot of modernity. The eighteenth-century advocates of the modern state and market relations promised to provide "an exit from tribalism," as political scientist Francis Fukuyama puts it, "We exit out of kinship."[6]

The individual's social bonds would now be situated in the grand and liberating universals of secular modernity: faith in science, a meritocratic way of getting ahead, a new social contract that promised individual property and civil rights for citizens—for those pledging allegiance to the constitutive rules of liberal capitalism. And the very notion of modern organizing and how individuals labor together would become tied to the magic of central engineering by the mid-nineteenth century, stamping out standard products through efficient routines. To this day many centralized reformers push for stiffer regulation of, say, the work of teachers in classrooms, or prescribe a twenty-minute diagnostic script for physicians with patients. Regulation of local work must trump the judgment of practitioners or the complexity of clients served.

Getting to Know the New Decentralists—Organization of the Book

Yet despite the sticky resilience of centralized firms and public institutions, why the rise of new localism, this yearning of postindustrial societies to decenter old ways of organizing work and rejecting a confining script for leading one's life? What forces have spirited this devolution of institutional authority at this particular moment in economic and social history? This is the opening question that motivates chapter 1. This opening section describes the declining relevance of hierarchical management in growing (yet not all) sectors of postindustrial economies. At the same time, as new decentralists adapt to shifting material and ideological climates, they hold little naive faith in markets alone, that is, engaging or incentivizing individual clients absent their own local context. In short, chapter 1 places the stiff economic and cultural currents—gaining force over the past half century—that now move public and private institutions to decentralize how they organize authority, know-how, and resources locally.

One key decentralizing force is the fact that few Americans grow or make anything for a living: just one in six, according to the Bureau of Labor Statistics. An already sizeable share of the labor force works to backstop or lift clients in some way—to advance their learning, pitch healthier lifestyles, to design new buildings or software, perhaps counsel the burgeoning count of retirees. Education and health care have shown the most robust growth of any economic sector over the past generation, now contributing one-third of the nation's gross domestic product (and largely staffed by women).[7] The cookie-cutter casting of standard products and top-down ways of organizing labor no longer match the kind of work that most Americans do.

In concert, the explosive growth of private firms and so-called nongovernment organizations (NGOs) to run public-minded endeavors—from healthcare firms to charter schools to supporting military veterans—has fuzzed the once crisp boundary between the state apparatus and textbook notions of pure markets populated by unregulated firms. More and more practitioners labor within mixed markets of local organizations, which are neither tethered to a bureaucratic center nor operating within a pristine market. Instead, everyday work is guided by dimly lit public oversight and shared logics for how to teach, provide medical care or financial services, and alike. The count of nonprofits registering with the federal government doubled to almost 1.1 million organizations between 1994 and 2010, as we detail in chapter 1.

Chapter 2 then turns to the empirical question of whether America's deepening experiment with decentralization has resulted in more effective schools, stronger health care, or robust private firms? What are we learning about this steady turn away from modern hierarchies and toward decentered firms and softly regulated markets over the past half century? Did the early forays into the decentralized coordination of work actually buoy local practitioners or lift their clients?

The jury is still out. Chapter 2 details how the evidence remains uneven and benefits vary across sectors of society. Yet the question is no longer whether to decentralize massive firms and public institutions, but *how* to devolve authority, resources, and tools in ways that embolden local practitioners. We examine how institutional history matters a lot, how particular sectors develop over time. Teachers, for example, opted to fit themselves into industrial forms of labor with the advent of public employee collective bargaining in the 1970s. Doctors still retain elements of their feisty professional guild, while adapting to federal rules and, of late, incentivized to move toward prevention and stron-

PREFACE

ger quality. Another case will take you into the world of international finance, where even radically decentralized banks must constantly read a complicated world of shifting regulation. These field-specific dynamics limit or enhance a firm's decentralizing tendencies in consequential ways.

Still, shared lessons continue to emerge from America's initial round of decentralized organizing following the 1960s. These first-generation decentralists focused on the political battle of breaking from central hierarchies, seeking liberation from bureaucracy in pursuit of market nirvana or neighborhood control. They invoked a rather dichotomous notion of "autonomy" versus central control—a black-and-white portrait first painted by eighteenth-century liberals, such as Adam Smith and Thomas Jefferson, or John Locke almost a century before. Chapter 2 describes the differing ways in which big institutions were disassembled, the extent to which local control implied market competition, and whether these surface-level structures proved sufficient to yield stronger results for practitioners and clients. We accent how this modernist dialectic—cast as organizational freedom or control—still distracts decentralists from the hard work of rethinking local practices and engaging clients in motivating ways.

Then, joined by my colleagues, we take you into four diverse organizations that are deeply committed to decentralizing authority, local discretion over resources, and the tools wielded by practitioners on the ground. "Ideas are no good without stories," says writer Lorrie Moore. "Stories are no good without characters."[8] So after sketching the overarching forces that inevitably drive decentralized organizing, we detail how these inventive social architects go about disassembling bureaucratic controls and redesigning work and social cooperation locally.

Case studies of four organizational settings are presented in two distinct pairs. The first coupling—a creative Pennsylvania health-care firm and an international bank in New York City—represents clear success stories, each displaying vivid signs of effectiveness within a competitive market. Each organization exhibits inventive central leadership that gently presses unifying ethical commitments, shares authority locally, and offers inventive tools (hardware and social innovations) that bolster practitioners on the ground. Each firm displays an intense curiosity over what's motivating their clients, a steady search for how to more tightly engage their patients or hardheaded clients. And each operates in a competitive field that offers material incentives and professional motivations for attending to clients' long-term interests, be it longer life expectancy or a stronger return on investments.

The second pair of firms—a private company that manages a network of inventive charter schools in California, and a modest set of NGOs that serves military veterans in northern Iowa—offer equally compelling cases of local organizing. But the consistency of results is less impressive when compared with the first pair of cases. This helps to illuminate specific organizational features that contribute to, or undercut, effective decentralization. It is these essential cornerstones on which *second-wave decentralists* focus their attention. This latter pair of firms host inspiring staff who engage clients—urban youths or military veterans who often face long odds of getting ahead. But indications are mixed on whether the Bay Area charter school or northern Iowa's fragmented alliance of local nonprofits truly lift their clients and nurture loyal practitioners on the ground. By contrasting the two pairs of organizations we see how the key cornerstones of social organization offer a firm or shaky foundation on which the work of the new decentralists depends.

We originally set out to identify decentralizing organizations that display signs of success. Quite early into our fieldwork we discovered a new generation of decentralists. Or, at least leaders and local practitioners that have moved way beyond the governance debates, no longer arguing over how to secede from a bureaucratic center or pitching the miraculous virtues of market relations. Instead, these inventive organizational architects have let local staff loose to experiment with novel practices, while becoming intensely curious over the motivations and human foibles of their clients. These reformers do not simply shrink their central office or preach the idealized magic of market competition. They have shred their parched, pyramid-shaped organization chart; they think deeply about everyday social relations between practitioner and client on the ground; they adjust roles and routines aiming to spark more robust engagement. They talk little of autonomy or opaque notions of power, while constantly taking stock of social ties, trust, and ethical commitments to one another. The new decentralists rarely see their expertise or knowledge as a "treatment" that's served up, delivered to a passive client. Instead, the student, patient, or customer must assume shared responsibility to learn, to engage more deeply, to pursue sustained relationships and social ties.

Overall, this book hopes to inform the perennial debate over who holds the legitimacy or economic power to structure how we work together. That is, when should we fight to preserve central rule-setting, say to enforce fuel efficiency for cars or raise the minimum wage? Or, when should government or corporate managers opt to devolve authority, expertise, and resources to local practitioners? And how might we move beyond the blinding dichotomy between central rules and market freedom—since it fails to get to the crux, as the new decentralists emphasize. This toggle switch between *freedom* and *control* fails to teach us how to better engage clients, or how to advance the

PREFACE

effectiveness of local practice across the nation's vibrant blend of public and private organizations.

I endeavor to forgo romantic interpretations of the decentering shift witnessed in postindustrial societies over the past half century. This book casts a constructively critical eye on the benefits and risks of disassembling large institutions. Scholars are beginning to test these gains and disappointing effects of decentralization in certain sectors. And this movement is unfolding in fits and starts, not in smooth progression, negotiated differently across various sectors and organizations within. Bennett Harrison published an influential book a generation ago, *Lean and Mean*, detailing how manufacturing was moving offshore, decentering production across a global panoply of smaller firms.[9] This helped to spur innovation in design, undercut labor unions stateside, and streamline production.

It also proved to exhibit "concentration without centralization." So Apple Computer's headquarters in Silicon Valley amasses huge chunks of capital and calls the major shots, while modest firms in developing countries churn out the components of our laptops and smartphones at low wages. While decentralization in some fields can be illuminating, a dark side is sometimes revealed as well. In short, the decentering of modern institutions or less fettered markets remains a work in progress—both risky in human terms and inevitable as economic and cultural drivers persist, maybe with intensifying force.

I do not argue that decentering all functions of government or disassembling all corporate hierarchies offer the optimal mix of institutions. To build sustainable forms of economic production, not to mention cooling down the planet, centrally set rules or governance will be required. Hierarchical firms help to ensure that our morning latte, or breakfast burrito, tastes exactly the same, whether dished out in L.A. or at JFK. Or, recall former New York mayor Michael Bloomberg's effort to regulate out of existence those obesity-inducing super-sized sodas. Still, across a widening range of fields practitioners aim to energize and move clients, young and old—moving well beyond formulaic treatments and insensitive uniformity. The mindset of civic and corporate leaders is already changing. As one deputy minister of education recently told me, "We can't regulate our way toward the type of learning that we are trying to see in our schools."

We distill lessons learned from each organizational case, and then clarify the shared organizing principles identified by new decentralists across the differing sectors. This must be weighed against the limits of generalizing from each case, a single organization that operates in a complicated field of firms. One success tells us more than a thousand failures, to paraphrase the late Columbia University sociologist Robert Merton.[10] On the other hand, the external validity of cases suffers, along with our ability to generalize, without identifying the organizational cornerstones, the key principles expressed by the new decentralists, across a variety of settings.

The book's final chapter distills lessons learned from the new decentralists as they work creatively across sectors and arrive at a shared social architecture for serving clients on the ground. The metaphor of essential cornerstones aims to highlight the social-organization features of decentralizing firms that explain their success or uneven efficacy. We endeavor to articulate how these core principles and social tools are advanced by the second-wave decentralists. Then, we consider how these organizational cornerstones offer testable pieces of theory, observable elements of decentralized management that may yield stronger benefits for clients and practitioners alike.

A Cooperative Effort

This book would not be in your hands if not for the work of three inspiring friends and intellectual soul mates—the royal *we* that I already have invoked. Each has worked as a skilled practitioner in local organizations, trained as a lawyer, physician, or teacher. Danfeng Soto-Vigil Koon helped to shape the book's overall argument and dug out much of the evidence on decentralizing reforms that appears in chapter 2. Her keen legal mind helped to clarify the core storyline and weigh competing claims.

Mary Berg guided our inquiry into the remarkable Pennsylvania healthcare firm explored in chapter 3. A family physician in her day job, Mary gently invited doctors, nurses, and central managers to detail how their reforms have reshaped relationships with many patients, raising the quality of care. Doctors and lawyers reason through arguments by reflecting on cases, building toward general principles of practice. In this way I learned much from Danfeng and Mary about how to dig into the human-scale dynamics of local cases, as one method for building a wider theory of local organizing.

Lynette Parker helped to lead our deep dive into the everyday culture of the San Francisco charter school. Her savvy ability to engage a feisty range of adolescents, always curious as to what we were up to, greatly enriched the education case that appears in chapter 5.

A heartfelt thanks is expressed to the front-stage characters that you will get to know across the organizational cases. This includes Pablo Alba, Daniel Allen, Mark Cleary, Kenda Danowsky, Roy Henagar, Danielle Johnson, Susie Kobylinski, Kim Marovets, Siv Nee, Allison Rowland, Monika Sandberg, William Stuflick, Janet Tomcavage, Magnus Uggla, and Rosetta Waychus. They

PREFACE   XXI

spent hours and hours fielding our questions, opening up their hearts and minds with remarkable candor. Most graciously they reviewed earlier drafts of the middle chapters, correcting factual errors and checking the validity of our interpretations.

Five funders have generously supported my research on the interplay among government, local organizations, and markets, going back two decades. Their unflagging commitment to learning about the ground-level effects of state policies and central institutions led me to the colorful range of firms and nonprofits that you are about to visit. Special thanks go to Susan Dauber at the Spencer Foundation, and to Mike Smith and Kristi Kimball, formerly at the Hewlett Foundation. They have long encouraged me to focus on the diverse range of schools that now populate America's cities, and hung in there when I wandered outside the education sector. The Haas families of San Francisco and the Packard Foundation generously supported my early work on nonprofit organizations, which still dominate the world of preschool and early education. The Spencer and the McCormick foundations have supported my time, along with stellar graduate students, to explore the interplay between centralized organizations, families, and local ethnic groups—where public projects meet tribal ties and culturally situated practices that hold enormous consequences for children.

I have benefited from invigorating colleagues and students at Harvard and Berkeley who have advanced my thinking. These fellow scholars include Ed Bein, Margaret Bridges, Luke Dauter, Eugene Garcia, Claudia Galindo, Alma Guerrero, Luis Huerta, Anthony Kim, Mike Kirst, Alice Kuo, Neal Halfon, Sophia Rabe-Hesketh, Susanna Loeb, David Plank, Judy Singer, David Stern, Elliot Turiel, and Anisah Waite. Special thanks to Jeff Henig and an anonymous reviewer for their generous and precise critiques of earlier drafts. Mario Small invited an early paper for a University of Chicago seminar that gave clearer shape to our core argument. Thanks go to Rachel Gordon, Don Huben, Naoshi Kira, Michael Neblo, and Vicente Reyes for asking me to lecture on parts of this work at Ohio State University, University of Illinois at Chicago, Tokyo University, and Singapore's National Institute of Education. The warm spirit of the late John Vasconcellos enlivens my perspective.

Elizabeth Branch Dyson offered candid coaching and warm encouragement when the project was nothing but a bright idea. She was everything that sustains a writer, an editor par excellence. Thanks to Dawn Hall for her meticulous copyediting.

The Institute of Human Development at the University of California, Berkeley, continues to offer a nurturing, stimulating place to hang my hat and plug in my laptop. Institute funding and medical school colleagues encouraged me to look across sectors and the converging discourse around decentralization and how to motivate and touch clients across organizational fields.

Finally, my long collaboration with Berkeley psychologist Susan Holloway still shapes how I think about the basic act of belonging, committed to and laboring with those we care about most. She taught me much about human motivation on a small canvas. My scholarly career began in the highlands of Mexico with Professor Holloway over three decades ago, examining how a modernizing government earnestly built pristine preschools and prepared kids for modernity, while largely ignoring the richness of social relations and the *cariñoso* homes from which they came. This simple discovery still kindles my intrigue with how well meaning centralists, no matter what their ideological stripes, often aim to fit kids, clients, or citizens into an imagined mainstream of the past, one that no longer speaks to the cultural pluralism and kaleidoscopic identities of the present. Our children, Caitlin and Dylan, teach me each day about joy and difference, about closeness and the challenge of human caring, together seeking a common good. Thank you all.

Bruce Fuller
Berkeley, California

1

The Drive to Decentralize—After Hierarchies and Markets Disappoint

You may have noticed. Purportedly mature grown-ups often resemble testy toddlers as they struggle mightily to cooperate, whether disparately laboring at work or haggling over contentious public issues.

We cling to our cars rather than hopping on the bus with others. Out in the suburbs we awkwardly hesitate to knock on the neighbor's door to fetch a cup of sugar. On a broader canvas our not-so-civil leaders routinely retreat into ideological caves rather than cooperating to squarely face pressing problems.

One way of nurturing more engaging forms of cooperation is to shift the authority and resources held by centralized institutions or corporate firms down to local actors. This book delves into America's blossoming yet rather unruly experiment with doing just that: decentralizing the power, capital, and know-how necessary for getting work done, long held by faraway managers, down to practitioners at the grass roots.

Indeed, colorful shoots of reseeded localism push up all around us. Take that newly sprouted farmers market in town, perhaps the inventive charter school down the street, or your local doctor who's joined a market-savvy health maintenance organization. Even the friendly nerd at the Apple Store who sports a bright T-shirt must signal not only being hip and expert but also that she comes from nearby.

Americans have long cast a skeptical eye on hierarchies—whether top-down ways of organizing work, setting moral precepts, or when central authorities try to dampen democratic discourse. Old World political and social hierarchies were soundly rejected at the nation's birth. Still, nineteenth-century America would fall star struck for the efficiency of modern factories, the humming of endless assembly lines, which delivered unprecedented levels of material comfort and stoked a burgeoning middle class.

But fast-forward to the last half of the twentieth century, as America experienced rising disaffection with large and faceless institutions and skepticism sank deeper over the flailing efficacy of government, along with the costly moral lapses of Wall Street, huge corporations, not to mention the Catholic Church. These currents would erode faith in centralized institutions and undercut aging renditions of social authority, a singular moral compass that now simply pointed toward a disaffecting destination.

Western thinkers—going back to Locke, Rousseau, and Jefferson—long argued for political pluralism and democratic vitality at the grass roots, favoring the individual's rights over the conforming prerogatives of centralized agents. But they could not have foreseen the colorful, decentered variability in how contemporary Americans now get work done locally, or the kaleidoscopic ways in which we find meaning in daily life. Nor could these early modernists—obsessed with the reified individual and stigmatizing "backward" communities—have envisaged how contemporary decentralists now aim to shape cooperative action across countless local commons, village by village.

We have witnessed a pantheon of big hierarchies breaking apart in recent decades—school bureaucracies, health-care institutions, telecom and high-tech companies—devolving their core remnants down to disparate communities, then ceding discretion over resources and tools to local practitioners. Civic leaders urge that we "think globally, act locally," progressives urge us to "buy local." Even multinational firms that exploit workers overseas, like those pitching smartphones and electronic tablets with cool adverts, must *look* local to gain legitimacy.

One initial question is why, after two centuries of modern hierarchy and routinized forms of work, have centralized organizations lost social authority and economic clout? And why at this point in Western history are we experiencing renewed vitality in localism—decentering how work is organized across wide slices of the economy, along with the centrifugal variety of social affiliations and lifestyles that now mark American society? These quandaries motivated our journey to the variety of organizations that you are about to explore.

The story unfolds in three parts, yielding the core thesis. First, I describe the stiff winds, the powerful economic and ideological currents, that continue to topple hierarchies and central nodes of social authority, which have anchored nation-states since the seventeenth-century dawn of the modern era. Second, I describe the differing ways in which massive organizations—be they public institutions or corporate firms—seek to decentralize, tracking the renewed interest in localism that's sweeping across many postindustrial societies. And third, we have corralled what is known about the (uneven) empirical results of first-wave experiments in decentralization, focusing on education, health, and technology sectors—where the urge to disassemble hierarchies has gained unstoppable momentum over the past half century.

Then we arrive at the question going forward: How might decentered ways of organizing social action or productive enterprise become more effective in lifting learning, health, and trade? And the flipside: How does the residue of modern hierarchy—in which capital, expertise, and authority remain lodged—still hamper labor or cooperative action at the grass roots? This requires uncovering the fine-grain social practices that lead to effective decentralization. So to learn about *how* decentered social action may pay off for clients and practitioners alike, we spent two to three years inside a wide variety of organizations spread across differing sectors, each experiencing varying levels of success.

This opening chapter details the contemporary economic and ideological forces, emerging in the 1950s, that prompted decentralizing forms of social organization, now sweeping across huge swaths of postindustrial economies. I begin with the contemporary arc of America's own rekindled fascination with localism—bubbling up from the Beat Generation as social criticism arose over the human cost of industrial routine and white-collar conformity. The 1960s of course fortified this multipronged attack on mass institutions, from huge universities that put undergraduates on alienating treadmills, to a national government that chose to lie about matters of life and death. The colorful forces of pluralism and diversity would stir the culture wars, channeling the old mainstream into a thousand rivulets of ethnic affiliations, sexual preferences, and lifestyles.

On material fronts, the evolving global economy and cheap wages overseas pushed manufacturing overseas, rendering hierarchical org charts less relevant to how work came to be organized stateside in postindustrial times. And one remaining myth—the American Dream of endless upward mobility—would be shattered more recently, as middle-class wages declined and inequalities worsened, a coarseness not seen since the Gilded Age of the 1920s.

These telling economic and cultural shifts now animate decentralization in public and private sectors alike, not to mention the vast organizational territory that lies in between. In fact, the new decentralists have left behind both the archetypal centralized hierarchy and textbook renditions of unfettered markets. Most of us now labor in organizations—from health care to education, the finance industry to design and trade—where faraway rules and dictates matter little for our everyday practice. Only the likes of roadside fruit vendors and rug dealers still operate in pure markets. Contemporary firms now compete and vie for legitimacy within mixed markets, characterized by light regulation and institutional habits of how work gets done.

Looking inside contemporary organizations, the industrial hierarchy has become a dying method for arranging human labor, jettisoned by many sectors while persisting in dusty corners of the welfare state. The factory model of breaking down complex production endeavors—from assembling cars to washing machines—into predictable and routinized tasks suffers from declining technical utility and alienating social effects. Contemporary work and postindustrial forms of human cooperation now involve lifting the learning or shifting the behavior of clients or patients, authoring design ideas or computer code, and inspiring the work of others. This means that the material tools and social agility required to improve one's practice can no longer be proscribed and controlled from above.

As organizational leaders and local practitioners began to adapt to these tectonic shifts, a *first-generation* discourse and strategy for devolving authority and resources first emerged about four decades ago. Old hierarchies and regimentation proved a deadly climate for technological innovation, as inventive managers in the electronics industry aimed to liberate their designers and software writers. The organizing notion of a slim and supportive center from which managers set free their local production units gained credibility in a widening array of corporate sectors, then migrated into the public sector by the early 1990s. Would not inventive schools, health clinics, or housing agencies find more effective ways to organize cooperation on the ground when severed from faraway bureaucracies, no longer hog-tied by rules and a deep-seated compliance mentality?

First-generation decentralists focused their battles on breaking away, to secede from the bureaucratic center or corporate headquarters. At times these first-wave pioneers were seduced by the idealized elegance of market theory, while rarely getting to the question of how they would better engage and motivate clients. Without a guiding and resourceful center, how would small-scale units stabilize revenues and enrich their grassroots practice, often struggling to survive in uncertain markets?

But I am getting ahead of the story. Let's back up and examine why the postindustrial desire to decentralize vast organizations first took root a half century ago and how a field of wildflowers did blossom, becoming a rather unkempt garden.

The Demise of Hierarchy

Everyday work and forms of human cooperation will continue to decentralize—to break apart from hierarchical nodes of capital and institutional authority—spurred by the postindustrial nature of labor and multiplicity of moral and cultural tenets that now variably guide our everyday lives. This is the leading edge of my argument. America's emerging position in the global economy requires work that aims to engage or lift human beings, not to churn out standardized widgets. It requires social cooperation led by thoughtful practitioners who aim to motivate learning or healthier behavior, lift the well-being of various clients, or perhaps sketch innovative designs or clever software. As macroeconomic forces reshape labor demand, how to get ahead in America and how to craft a meaningful life have already splintered into a variety of pathways.

This chapter first describes four stiff winds that have gained velocity and strength over the past half century—shifting the institutional landscape in which labor is organized and performed together, along with the tools and human agility required to get work done locally. These telling economic and ideological forces also open up space for the fresh generation of decentralists that you will meet in the middle chapters. These stiff forces set the environment in which organizations must seek legitimacy and resources, and cast how the work of individuals is coordinated and supported locally.

The new decentralists at times incentivize individuals to help move local practices; they are not averse to deploying economic carrots. But they are cultivating new forms of cooperative action and solidarity on the ground as well, not mechanically controlling their local staff or tossing clients into competitive, uncaring markets. A generation ago, sociologist Peter Evans claimed that the state and the market were the "master institutions of society."[1] I argue that this earlier reality has become a fading historical artifact, eclipsed by where work now occurs for most and lateral forms of social co-operation that have come to hold legitimacy in the eyes of clients, customers, and citizens.

Next, I briefly sketch the four major drivers of decentralized organizing in postindustrial societies. Then each force will be examined in greater depth, looking into the origins and consequences for the decentralization of institutions and authority over the past half century.

Blowing Out the Center

One gale-force wind that has flattened large hierarchies originates in America's shifting position in the global economy. The decline of manufacturers and their standardized production routines has received ample attention from management gurus and business writers. But it's the shifting *social organization of work*—recast in huge sectors, like education, health care, and white-collar services—that's most telling in accounting for the decentering of postindustrial firms. This is work performed by practitioners on the ground who must deploy their wits and knowledge in rather unpredictable ways. The motivations of local clients are equally variable and fickle—from students to patients and bank customers to serving our most disadvantaged citizens. Practitioners in decentralized firms must have expertise and resources at their fingertips to engage and motivate their clients, which can't be regulated by far-off hierarchies.

Closely tied to these macroeconomic shifts and the decentering of work are the faltering *fiscal capacity* and *legitimacy* of central government. And this exemplifies the wider demise of central beacons of social authority, which includes the dissolution of once-dominant, often monochromatic lifestyles and cultural guideposts. The unraveling of pyramid-like hierarchy stems not only from the plotting of conservatives and neoliberals. Faithful fans of the central state, critical of market remedies in the public sector, blame conservatives. But it's the cultural Left, going back to the Beats, that still wages unrelenting attacks on universal norms and social regulation from above. Pluralistic groups have largely succeeded in shifting once-private affiliations and identities—whether bounded by ethnicity, gender, language, disability, or sexual preference—into the civic sphere, as the late philosopher Richard Rorty pointed out a generation ago.[2] The personal has become political.

This cultural subversion of central authority interacts with the shifting sands of material conditions. One key example is declining trust in faraway Washington, witnessed since the Vietnam and Watergate eras. This acts to undermine government's fiscal strength, already battered by rocky economic shoals and treacherous levels of public debt, leading to a third force that makes matter worse for the central state: the *demographic graying of America.*

Even as postindustrial nations recovered (partially) from the financial collapse of 2008, still adapting to the long-running loss of manufacturing jobs, this third factor would undercut the state's fiscal resolve: the rising share of public spending required to buoy the health and pensions of aging boomers. If government and massive firms are to deliver on their promise of secure retirement, they now must shed other programs and public responsibilities. Central bureaucracies must pare back or offload other functions to local agencies or lightly regulated markets of nonprofit organizations. And meanwhile, collateral private sectors are stoked by demands expressed by aging retirees. Health care, social services, and the entire leisure industry now thrive, along with their local practitioners who engage and serve their graying clients.

These three forces, in turn, spur the fourth driver of decentralization: *the rise of nonprofit and for-profit firms* that pursue public projects. Government, in fact, doesn't run much anymore beyond the military and police services, not to mention riveting post offices and the department of motor vehicles. Instead, the state bureaucracy increasingly funds and softly monitors quasi-public organizations on the ground, including charter schools, health maintenance organizations, transport firms, even profit seekers that help run prisons and military campaigns. And the shift toward mixed markets of NGOs flows with the rise of labor that's dedicated to lifting students, patients, retirees, and white-collar clients.

The shifting economics of energy further fuels the creation of nonprofit firms and social enterprises. As energy costs climb, faraway management of production or human services becomes less sustainable economically. So instead we see the rise of locally rooted firms like Car Share in San Francisco, or the nonprofit Farmers Market Federation that helps New York City neighborhoods host marketplaces, all nascent elements of what Jeremy Rifkin calls "the collaborative economy."[3] Sharing is becoming both hip and profitable as household income slips and consumers look for less costly alternatives. A portion of the share economy is growing well beyond edgy and idealistic endeavors. Avis Rental Car moved in 2013 to buy Zipcar for a cool half-billion dollars. "We see car sharing as highly complementary to traditional car rental, with rapid growth potential and representing a scalable opportunity," Avis CEO Ronald L. Nelson said.[4]

Building from Theory, Not Faith

Let me situate the core thesis before detailing these four consequential forces. Many of my scholarly colleagues—working from Berkeley after all—blame old-line conservatives or neoliberal contemporaries for this decentering drift of postindustrial societies, including faith in market dynamics and the sanctity of private pursuits.

I am not so sure. Wider shifts in cultural mores and the structure of labor continue to unfold, rekindling America's commitment to localism. Sure, conventional economists and many on the political Right believe that public organizations would improve, becoming more responsive, if placed in the crucible of market competition. But not all forms of decentralized organizing are motivated solely by market faith, or a sacred tenet that lone individuals will compete to drive up quality. Charter schools and portable vouchers are far more popular in poor compared with affluent communities, since low-income parents worry deeply about unsafe and mediocre schools over which they have little power to change.

The decentering of institutional resources and authority also stems from the robust growth of nonprofit sectors across North America, Europe, and many developing nations. This creates a political and ideological wave—countering the bureaucratic state and the market—that lifts a variety of local organizations and decentered ways of running schools, health clinics, and related public endeavors. Even for-profit firms are becoming savvy to the power of particulars, as banks and burger joints hire bilingual clerks and sport signs in the local lingo. Would-be priests are now required to master Spanish in Catholic dioceses. Walkability has become a key tenet as city planners guide the rebirth of urban centers, from Silver Lake in Los Angeles to Columbia Heights in Washington, DC.

Or, think food when considering the diversifying array of local tastes. The food-cart movement offers a vivid alternative to Chicago's midwestern palette, where colorful chefs magically transform gray and abandoned lots into a celebration of cross-cultural cuisine, suddenly brimming with exotic delicacies and fine wine. Public health authorities may rightfully check in, but local variety is allowed to flourish. Even fast-food franchises now experiment with fitting meals to local preferences, like tweeting "secret" codes for personally tailored combos at In-N-Out Burger.[5] It's the appeal to particulars, to the myriad preferences of local tribes—even corporate caricatures of them—that holds appeal. Even for our taste buds we shake off the older script of modernity, where mass institutions once pushed efficient yet bland dishes, from frozen peas to chicken potpies.

This decentralizing drift may act to moderate the serrated edges of pure markets or rein in unaccountable managers of publicly funded enterprise. Once an idealized dream of Latin American dissidents, British Prime Minister Tony Blair by the 1980s would declare a Third Way—where local or private firms would run public endeavors with greater agility and direct accountability—as official national policy. Today, very little work or civic action occurs wholly within the state apparatus or idealized market. This duality has become a dusty relic of graying modernism. Instead, nonprofits or for-profit contractors now run most public projects. The education and health-care sectors alone host two-fifths of America's gross domestic product, delivered by private colleges, church affiliated hospitals, nonprofit HMOs, and the like.

I am not arguing that decentralized organizing is always preferable to central rule setting. Chapter 2 details colossal failures and disappointing results from first-wave experiments in decentering large organizations. These lessons are not lost on the new decentralists, as you will soon discover. And for the new decentralists, attracting clients is simply the first step; the real work of engaging and motivating students or patients then begins. Yet, it's difficult to see how we can cool down the planet or build sustainable economic means without stiffer rule setting by a forceful public authority. Elsewhere I have argued that radical decentralization in education can weaken the central state's capacity to equalize opportunity.[6] And even avant-garde firms like Apple Computer now rely on a decentered network of producers around the world while retaining capital and design decisions centrally, a topic to which we return in chapter 2.

Still, I do hope to convince you that the fading of centralized hierarchies, along with diminishing control over resources and guiding ideologies, has become unavoidable in key sectors of postindustrial societies. The decentering of big institutions has been quietly spreading, gaining devolutionary steam over the past half century, especially in how we organize schools, health care, finance, and human services. The efficacy of this widening range of decentered organizations—not to mention their legitimacy or market success—depends on how well these firms engage, how far they lift their clients. This requires moving authority, resources, and tools of the trade down to frontline practitioners.

Local Crafts and the Shifting Nature of Work

America's shifting position in the global economy spurs *decentered conceptions of work* and the *local coordination of everyday practice.* How the United States will cast its role in the global division of labor remains the topic of much debate. But the loss of manufacturing jobs and value-added production overseas—along with the end of bureaucratic means of controlling labor—bring two fresh challenges. First, how do managers structure job roles in ways that engage local staff and clients? And second, when postindustrial societies require fewer workers, what strains are put on government? For the state now suffers from diminished public revenues, along with the hangover of regulatory and standardizing habits—as colorfully pluralistic citizens question aging nodes of central authority and moral universals.

America's economic niche already requires greater attention to nurturing fresh ideas, technologies, and enriching the behavior of clients served in the public domain. From corralling inventive software designers to engaging feisty adolescents in high school, managers can no longer prescribe standard routines for getting the job done. Instead, those leading public or private organizations in postindustrial firms must coax and coordinate versatile practitioners engaged in highly cooperative work—not atomized individuals conforming to centrally specified tasks, nor lone wolves competing with one another in markets. It's this shifting nature of work that nudges the decentralized arrangement of social authority, resources, and more inventive tools of the trade.

America's shifting economic position does not necessarily imply a less lucrative spectrum of roles to play. It does imply that the nation's economy can grow with a stagnating count of firms and stateside jobs. Stateside-based factories have shed about one-third of their jobs just since 2000. We remain the second largest manufacturer in the world, but this role doesn't require much human labor within our borders, or anywhere for that matter, thanks to the unrelenting march of robotics. The United States is the third largest agricultural producer in the world, yet just 2 percent of American workers make a living as farmers.[7]

Long before the Great Recession the US economy was hemorrhaging jobs, not to mention widening disparities in wealth between rich and poor families. The unprecedented irony is that total output per capita continues to tick up each year, even as the number of jobs nosedived after the 2008 financial crash, then recovered at a pallid pace. Almost one-third of GDP growth in the United States since 1990 has come from rising output by multinational corporations that require little additional labor inside the United States.[8]

The average family in America—the true middle class—has watched their annual wages steadily decline over the past generation. The US Census Bureau tracks mean earnings of the middle quintile of the nation's households, the one-fifth of all Americans that hover around the average level of yearly income. This middling slice earned just over $50,700 in 1990 (inflation adjusted 2012 dollars), rising to $56,300 in 2000, as the nation's high-tech boom sparked robust economic activity. But average earnings for this same group fell to $51,200 by 2012, a decline that began seven years before the 2008 collapse of financial markets.[9]

The shrinkage of manufacturing jobs sent many workers over this economic cliff. Yearly earnings for the median male worker have fallen by over one-sixth in the past four decades (constant dollars).[10] The recession killed off one in every six blue-collar jobs in machine operations, repair work, and skilled crafts, stateside occupations that still suffer from softening demand. One in twelve middle-class jobs in nonmanagerial office posts was lost in the wake of 2008. To return to full employment, defined as unemployment dipping below 5 percent, the US economy must rebound by adding back twenty-two million new jobs, many of which will not likely return from overseas. Only a half million manufacturing jobs returned to the domestic economy between 2010 and 2014. The overall count of employed Americans had returned to prerecession levels (about 138 million workers). But the working-age population had grown by fifteen million, and millions more have exited from the labor force.

Gender, Work, and Cooperative Practice

This painful jolt to the nation's workforce not only determines the count of employed Americans, or those who exit the labor market; it also shapes the kinds of work that we do each day. And this holds direct implications for the decentering of large organizations, whether publicly funded or for-profit. Gender differences offer an intriguing case in point, as a rising share of workers labor to buoy clients rather than stamp out things. Manufacturing, as recently as 2001, employed as many people within our national borders as did the education and health-care sectors combined, about sixteen million in each set. Yet since then, the human service sectors—mostly employing well-educated women—added another four million positions. In contrast, manufacturing firms, mainly employing men, lost an equal number of job slots.

Between 1990 and 2008, just prior to the economic avalanche, the number of Americans employed grew from 122 to 149 million. And about 98 percent of this growth sprouted in the so-called nontradable sector, meaning workers who directly serve clients or customers rather than laborers who grow or make something. The two biggest job generators in the US economy are now government (twenty-two million jobs in 2008) and the health-care industry (sixteen million). Occupations that involve cultivating crops or crafting goods were essentially flat over the same three decades.

Three in four workers in education and health care—the sectors that require decentralized practices and cooperative action with clients on the ground—are now women. And job demand will grow in the latter sector as Americans age. The count of baby boomers turning sixty-five will almost double from forty-seven million to eighty million over the next two decades in the United States.[11] For the first time ever, a bare majority of women overtook men in terms of professional and management jobs economy-wide in 2010, according to the Bureau of Labor Statistics.[12] Together, our evolving place in the world economy and demographic shifts, are reshaping the nature of work and the decentered forms of cooperation required to engage and motivate clients.

Rising Inequality, Eroding Trust in Central Authority

Not everyone's economic stake has been uprooted by these remarkable economic events. Wealthy Americans, for example, have became more deeply invested and richly rewarded over the past two generations. Widening inequality made national headlines once again as the Occupy Wall Street movement swept across the country in 2011, from Manhattan to the Port of Oakland, fueled by disparities felt by allegedly 99 percent of the citizenry. Rising inequality serves to further erode faith in private firms and the (not always) competitive market relations in which they work. The fading legitimacy of these hierarchies further feeds a renewed interest in human-scale forms of cooperation.

The numbers remain sobering: the share of personal income nationwide held by the richest 1 percent doubled over the past half century, from 10 to 22 percent. The top 1 percent received 36 percent of all new income generated in the past three decades. Put another way, the wealthiest 300,000 Americans (the top one-tenth of 1 percent) now take in annual incomes that equal the wages of 180 million workers combined (the bottom 60 percent).[13]

How do leaders of massive corporations expect to retain much authority when they alone benefit from such inequality? And ditto for political leaders who fail to muster any discernible movement toward fairness? When President Obama proposed to raise income taxes on millionaires in 2012, a CBS News poll found that just under two-thirds of all Americans supported the idea, including two-fifths of rank-and-file Republicans.[14] The Congress promptly killed it. Beyond political alienation among the nation's citizenry, rising cynicism over central authority likely represents collateral damage.

Corporate profits promptly bounced back from the Great Recession, reaching an all-time high, rising $1.8 trillion after the 2008 crash. Profits rose in late 2010 at the fastest clip since this statistic has been calculated, going back six decades.[15] These massive profits continue, despite the nation's sticky jobless rate and after millions of Americans have given up looking for work. As the US economy recovered at a glacial pace between 2009 and 2012, the income of the nation's richest 1 percent grew by 31 percent, compared with an uptick of less than half a percentage point among everyone else.[16]

Less discussed is how the waning of unifying ideals further accounts for America's buckling economic foundations, especially when weighed against our competitors. One reason that Chinese businesses are beating US firms at their own game—as did Japanese firms in the 1970s—is the high rate of personal savings found in Asia. Chinese households stashed away almost two-fifths of their disposable income in 2009, compared with just over 5 percent among American households. We spend over 70 percent of our personal income each year on average, relative to the Chinese, who spend only 34 percent.[17] Despite our alleged Protestant work ethic and affection for pulling up our bootstraps, Asian wage earners take more seriously the virtues of tough discipline, self-sacrifice, and Spartan living. Such guiding ideologies, and the comparative social cohesion they may offer, hold direct economic consequences as well.

Chinese leaders now even publicly goad Washington, to "cure its addiction to debts . . . to live within its means."[18] After all, the federal government is now in hock to Chinese bond traders. It's an ironic reminder, now coming from Beijing, of our nation's earlier religious commitment to thrift and hard work—universal moral tenets that once guided individual behavior and social cooperation. Beijing currently holds $1.7 trillion of US debt in the form of federal bonds.[19] So our central government finds itself on even shakier economic ground. In this context it's not surprising that Washington aims to off-load organizations and obligations to local government and the lightly regulated mixed markets that increasingly characterize the fields of education, housing, and health care.

These unrelenting economic forces mean that government's fiscal capacity becomes ever more brittle. And its declining fiscal punch becomes interwoven with eroding public authority as well. Let's turn next to these interwoven dynamics, powering the second force that makes decentralized organizing ever more attractive.

The State's Declining Capacity

Unless you are a glutton for sobering statistics, I don't need to belabor America's economic transformation and the evolving character of work. It's the institutional consequences of these global pressures that become most pertinent. The state's *declining fiscal strength* has come to recursively shrink its *popular legitimacy* as well. Central government, just like a corporate headquarters losing revenue, must begin to scale back, identifying ways to cut costs, off-load tasks to the locals, or eliminate public efforts altogether. One way to cut central costs, spur innovation locally, and perhaps better engage clients is to decentralize resources and authority—at least that's the theory of action that has gained widespread appeal.

The Congressional Budget Office warns that unless Washington shaves back spending, public debt will rise from 62 percent of the nation's annual output (GDP) in 2010 to above 80 percent by 2035.[20] These fiscal strains are interwoven with public worries over cutting social security checks, or whether government bureaucracy can run anything effectively outside of the IRS and the military.

Good intentions have gone terribly awry in sectors where costs spiral upward—as benefits to clients remain flat or falter. Across the nation's schools per pupil spending tripled between the 1970s and 1990s (in constant dollars), before leveling off.[21] But test scores inched up ever so slightly. Similarly, government spending on health care equaled 4 percent of GDP in 1950. Today this sector eats up 17 percent of the nation's annual output and continues to rise, despite cost-control efforts by every president since Ronald Reagan.[22] The United States spent $2.9 trillion on health care in 2012, exceeding the size of the French economy. Average health-care premiums paid by individuals or employers have tripled over the past three decades. Yet hospital quality and health outcomes sink lower when compared with European nations that spend far less.[23] And pension costs threaten to break the treasuries of many state governments; they have watched unfunded pension liabilities climb from $197 billion in 2001 to just under a trillion dollars in 2011.[24]

The state's fiscal capacity now grows even thinner at our contemporary *demographic moment*, as baby boomers age and retire across postindustrial societies, replaced by a shrinking and often less well-educated urban workforce—laborers who must now fund old-age benefits. Almost seven workers contributed earnings to support pension funds for every one retiree in 1950. But by 2010, just two and one-half individuals labored to sustain each retired American, and this number will continue to fall through 2030.[25] It's this "slow march of demographics," as historian Niall Ferguson puts it, that condemns Washington to mounting debt in the absence of entitlement reform.[26]

Asian and Latino immigrants now fill job slots left behind by shrinking white populations. This ranges from skilled high-tech engineers in Silicon Valley to those who can barely read (in any language). So unless government redoubles its investment in education, faltering worker productivity will further erode the state's fiscal capacity. In urban centers like Chicago new entrants to the labor force show declining job skills on average. One recent analysis by DePaul University's John Koval revealed that three out of five new entrants into the metro-area labor force over the past decade were Latino, according to the 2010 census. Most are US citizens yet poorly educated.[27]

Across Europe and North America, "economies have been growing too slowly, for too long, to pay for the coming bulge of retirees," writes David Leonhardt. "They have promised themselves benefits that, at current tax rates, they cannot afford."[28] This will hog-tie government's fiscal clout and popular legitimacy for decades to come. Britain's public debt runs even higher than America's as a share of GDP. One in five British citizens hold government jobs. Or take Greece, where mass demonstrations recurrently express frustration over severe cuts in government salaries and pension benefits. Before the European Union marked down this nation's accumulated debt, Greece was approaching a half-trillion dollars worth of IOUs—this in a country of just eleven million people.[29]

The Fleeting American Dream

As upward mobility stalls, the *unifying ideals* that long spurred the next generation to get ahead—encapsulated by the American Dream, fueled by that Protestant work ethic about which Max Weber wrote—lose credibility as well. The central institutions that once delivered mobility and social status with reasonable regularity—strong public schools, labor guilds, and robust employers—also suffer from eroding legitimacy. One recent poll of teenagers revealed a 50–50 split on the question, "Does the cost of college outweigh its importance for getting ahead?" The American Dream has simply become more elusive, more dreamy.

Our citizens have begun to question the nation's old ways of getting ahead, as defined by central authorities. The Pew Research Center began asking a question in 2002 that in itself signaled a crumbling faith in America's constitutive rules. Members of core Western nations were asked if they agreed or disagreed with the statement, "our people are not perfect but our culture is superior to others." Do Americans themselves believe that we are "chosen by God and commissioned by history to be a model to the world," as George W. Bush once claimed? Not really. Just 49 percent of respondents agreed in 2011, down from 60 percent a decade earlier. Just over one-third of young Americans, age eighteen to twenty-five, concurred with the superiority of the American way.[30]

Citizens have not soured on the importance of ambitious public projects. But fewer trust that the central state can tackle problems or invest their tax dollars effectively. In the wake of the Watergate affair, the fall of 1973, public confidence in government hit an all-time low: just 26 percent of respondents to a Gallup poll said they were satisfied with "the way the nation is being governed." This rose to 58 percent early in the Reagan administration, then steadily diminished, falling to 27 percent by fall 2010, with joblessness still above 8 percent and the Congress immobilized by partisan jockeying.

Cynicism over corporate leaders now competes with skepticism over government's inefficiency and its lack of palpable efficacy locally. Even 64 percent of grassroots Republicans agreed with the statement, "The job of a Wall Street banker is to get a good return on their investment, and they have taken those skills to Washington," in one 2012 survey.[31] Back in 1979, only about one-quarter of Americans polled said that more than half of every federal dollar was "wasted." By 2009 that share had climbed to 45 percent. One year later, half of those polled, when asked, "how much confidence (do you) have in the Congress," said, "very little" or "none."[32]

Still, Americans retain strong affection for *local* government. In June 2009, 51 percent of those polled said they had a "great deal" or "quite a lot of confidence" in the (Obama) presidency, while a markedly higher share, 69 percent, expressed this level of "trust and confidence" in their "local government in the area where you live."[33] The pattern is similar when the Gallup organization each year asks citizens about public schools. A majority believes "the school system" is beset by many ills, but *their* local school is just fine.[34] This holds direct implications for discerning politicians and civic leaders who argue that returning authority and taxpayer dollars to local authorities will yield stronger results, whether the evidence warrants such a claim or not.

Government Struggles to Look Effective

Under attack from the voters, government leaders struggle mightily to demonstrate that public institutions can work. But this requires sufficient fiscal capacity and effective means of lifting organizational quality. And regulating our way toward more engaging services on the ground shows little promise. In a sense, one element of Jean-Jacques Rousseau's eighteenth-century social contract does remain intact: government's protection of the individual's civil and property rights. But the state's preservation of atomistic freedoms is far different from nurturing more effective forms of social cooperation—from fostering the spread of renewal energy, to more potent public schools, to providing robust health care.

So government searches for better ways to organize or incentivize effective practices on the ground, hoping to advance shared interests and rekindle trust in the commonweal. Good progressives like Bill Clinton or Barack Obama push to hold educators accountable, that is, raise pupils' scores on standardized tests. The state reverts to its regulatory habits as it struggles to display its own efficacy. Medicare reimburses physicians for patient visits that don't exceed 20 minutes, allegedly sufficient to diagnose the patient's condition (and now press preventive care). Don't count on any premium for bedside manner. Or, take how Washington encourages medical "protocols," procedures that are linked to evidence of effectiveness, just as many states bet heavily on tying student test scores to the evaluation of teachers.

When rules alone seemed insufficient, government has tried to cultivate "mixed markets" of public and private firms over the past generation, aiming to spur innovation and efficiency through local competition. This strategy has swept across education and Amtrak, not to mention the struggling US Postal Service. The logic of action is not unlike how high-tech managers try to surgically regulate local work units, but otherwise set them free to devise creative means of production. Just as Apple Computer outsources the production and assembly of Macs and iPhones, the state now outsources to private hospitals, or voucher-supported landlords who house poor families. State-level health insurance exchanges, created under President Obama's legislation, host a space in which insurers face competitive pressure to lower prices, based on variable forms of coverage and levels of public subsidy. This has succeeded in creating downward pressure on prices. Average premiums in the first year fell below the average $450 premium forecast by the Congressional Budget Office.[35]

Trumpeting his enthusiasm for charter schools, former Los Angeles mayor Antonio Villaraigosa titled a speech "A New Contract," to focus his local government on "less regulation and more innovation."[36] It's a refrain President Kennedy first voiced, as his White House directed fresh funding to a new generation of community action agencies mostly situated in black neighborhoods. Vice President Al Gore, three decades later, would push to "reinvent government," hoping to shift Washington bureaucracy from its obsession with rules to offering incentives and decentralized innovations, like charter schools, price competitive health clinics, and appealing carrots for taxpayers who buy solar panels or hybrid cars.

Even strong-state hawks are coming to realize that rules alone can't motivate children to learn or move patients to lead healthier lives. This spurred first-generation affection for decentralization and market medicine—embraced by conservatives and then progressives—during the Reagan and Clinton eras. "It used to be, when we wanted to use public policy to nudge private behavior, we poked people with a stick," wrote *Time* magazine columnist Nancy Gibbs. She and a youthful bevy of behavioral economists celebrate the successful use of public incentives for prosocial behavior. Escalated taxes on cigarettes have helped to reduce the incidence of smoking. Washington's $3 billion Cash for Clunkers program in the wake of recession was hugely successful in jolting the auto industry back to life and killing off old gas hogs.

Doling out juicy carrots to trainable individuals has demonstrated that government can make a difference, that civic action can fill carpool lanes, encourage home ownership, or boost the supply of livers for transplant patients. But can monetary incentives alone motivate practitioners or clients on the ground? The state, of late, delivers rewards to teachers who raise pupil test scores, or doctors who trumpet the virtues of preventive health care. But how to engage a working-class youth on the edge of leaving high school, or truly alter behavior of an obese parent? Or, in the private finance sector, how to build trusting relationships with new clients?

We have looped back to the key question posed in the organizational cases that we soon explore: *how* can managers or policy makers decenter authority, resources, and tools in ways that animate and equip frontline practitioners? Neoclassical bunches of carrots may nudge simple, even prosocial behavior, but they cannot alone strengthen social engagement between clients and practitioners, or demonstrate what's going to work across wildly varying local conditions. So managers of hierarchies—situated in the public or private sector—search for new ways of organizing work that nurture effective practice. They aim to lift clients and demonstrate to voters, clients, or customers that effective ways of laboring together are close at hand. But their first attempts relied on naive hopes for incentives or proto-theories of motivation, like Bill Clinton's penchant for "personal responsibility," as if virtue and carrots alone would spur practitioners and clients toward richer cooperative action.

Let's next move to a third swift current that further prompts America's contemporary break from centralized hierarchy and atomistic markets: rising disaffection with mass institutions, universal moral strictures, and plain-vanilla lifestyles. As we search for meaning and human connection in uncertain economic times, secure moorings seem difficult to find within the graying institutions and markets in which many citizens have lost faith.

Splintering Ideals, Authority, and Institutions

The debate over where to lodge social authority and concentrate economic capital has long riled human societies. Harking back to the early Greeks, political and commercial leaders built centrally run institutions to civilize the masses, inspire ethical norms of cooperation, and tax the people to ensure peace and protection. The modern state, cohering by the late eighteenth century, began to advance the social and material infrastructure necessary for integrating local economies, for inching toward a unified nation-state. This widening of the secular civic sphere would legitimate the centralized press for a common national language, uniform secular schools, and webs of highways to integrate disparate provinces.

Modern notions of progress would soon be powered by mass production, designed centrally by engineers who reduced complex tasks into standard routines, easily monitored and controlled from above. This yielded remarkable levels of efficiency, falling consumer prices, and, by the 1920s, a burgeoning middle class. How we thought about the management of human labor below—from stamping out automobiles to churning out high school graduates—implied crisp production goals, providing uniformly cast tools to largely deskilled workers, and following repetitive routines. Hierarchies would devise the standard steps of production, ensure the steady inflow of raw materials, and track the productivity of workers.

Modern government would come to mimic and legitimate the factory's regularity and constitutive social forms in which individuals cooperated to produce both things and human services. As Max Weber argued a century ago, "The operation of large-scale capitalist enterprise depended on the availability of the kind of order that only a modern bureaucratic state could provide."[37] Indeed, government enjoyed widespread legitimacy for much of the modern period, from postrevolutionary America through the 1950s. Most schools ran well, at least those in middle-class suburbs. New hospitals spread across the land. When unions arose to resist dismal working conditions inside factories, textile mills, or slaughterhouses, the state stepped in to enforce labor rules and codified protections. Modern government was dedicated to ensuring the necessary order and infrastructure that aided capitalist expansion. For markets to thrive, the liberal-capitalist state must protect the worker's ability to move freely in the labor structure and hold property and corporate rights as sacred, a close cousin of the individual's civil rights. The sufficiency of these moral tenets, of course, still depends on the economy's capacity to deliver, and whether the individual gains meaning from playing by these rules.

Beyond the secular state, centralized religious institutions sustained conforming moral signposts as well, offering well-marked pathways for how to behave, what to believe. And for wayward disbelievers, the modern state's allegiance to secular ideals offered a cosmopolitan alternative—an ideological frame trumpeting transcendent values around the sanctity of family, literacy, fairness, and certain forms of marriage and sex. Sure, families came from many lands, at first abiding by disparate creeds. But wide and gradually more inclusive civic space helped to deliver upward mobility for most groups through the first half of the twentieth century. Until recently the glue of Christian-lite mores and secular tenets for getting ahead would offer sufficient social cohesion across most of America's modern period.

The Moral Center Fails to Hold

This harmony met with a series of discordant ideological and economic notes beginning in the 1960s. A series of ethical lapses at the political center—deceit in Vietnam, the Pentagon Papers, Watergate, Bill Clinton's odd notion of stately behavior, and George W. Bush's befuddled notion of leadership—sustained cynicism over the state's efficacy and underlying moral integrity.

Corporate scandals, from Enron's corrupt implosion to Wall Street's massive greed, of course, undercut trust in huge firms and unrestrained markets. Or take the example of how Catholic hierarchies protected high priests for generations, dodging accountability for the dastardly abuse of young followers—yet another case of central authority going terribly awry.

The sputtering capacity of postindustrial economies to deliver on the promise of upward mobility would further erode the state's popular legitimacy by century's end. It's not simply that the materialist American Dream has lost appeal among youthful generations since the 1960s—that suburban home, wandering about shopping malls, or melting away one's ethnic or linguistic identity in that bland cultural cauldron. In addition, the steps required to climb up the mobility ladder are becoming too steep and unaffordable. The private cost to families of sending a child to college has climbed from just 5 percent to over one-third of median household income since 1970.[38] Our graduates—when lucky enough to find a job—now opt to buy a cramped condo, or rent forever, given the high cost of homes relative to leveling wages.

Aspirations and lifestyles logically splinter as the main line into the mainstream becomes ever more elusive. And the centralized institutions that once delivered on mobility via meritocracy—public institutions and corporate employers—suffer from declining legitimacy as they fail to meet their promises. This is no longer a Nietzsche-inspired academic debate over whether the center of modern liberalism will hold. It's become a stark reality that rusting bureaucracies that once churned out new cars and fired up coal-powered plants, ran massive school systems and vast hospitals to deliver health care have stumbled badly. These centralized firms and institutions now host fewer jobs and offer less inviting pathways for young people, whether they are searching for mobility or everyday meaning. Baffled urban planners now speak of the "hodgepodge structure . . . the improvised order" of postindustrial cities, one literal analogue to the loss of modal ideologies, nodes of social cohesion that once guided everyday life.[39]

Just half of those surveyed in 2011 still believed that they or their family could "achieve the American Dream," even as the nation's economy displayed upbeat vital signs. One-third of the 2,188 adults queried no longer believed that the American Dream was even a reality.[40] A second poll found that barely two-fifths of all adults believe that "their kids will be better off than they are."[41] Notably, when the pollsters ask respondents whether the American Dream pertains mostly to "achieving material goods, or is it more about finding spiritual happiness," 40 percent went with the traditional economic indicator, while 38 percent now preferred lifestyle returns. As the promise of economic benefits fades, a diversifying search is underway for fresh ideological anchors, a new order by which to live.

Personal Pluralism

As centrally cast moral codes melt away, even norms regarding our most intimate relationships continue to shift. Nearly four in five adult Americans were married in the 1960s, falling to just one in two by 2009. More than half of all births to women under thirty now occur outside of the institution of marriage, according to the 2010 census. "It used to be called illegitimacy," writers Jason DeParle and Sabrina Tavernise point out. "Now it is the new normal."[42] The rate of out-of-wedlock births among white women with some college has been climbing most rapidly of late. And among Catholics worldwide—a population that grew by seventeen million over the past four decades—marriage rates fell by almost 60 percent. The loss of manufacturing jobs in the US context, followed by climbing rates of family poverty, likely plays a role in shaping fertility behavior. But cohabitation rates are up sharply in tony white communities as well, like the Bay Area, the Miami metro area, and once culturally staid New England.[43]

Nor is the proliferation of colorful lifestyles restricted to hip, cosmopolitan regions. Gay residents help to spark the gentrification of inner cities; upwardly mobile Latinos seek to recover Spanish for their children; Washington Heights in upper Manhattan, has become a polyglot of Dominican old timers, middling blacks, and young white professionals starting new families. These diversifying tribes, old and new, engage in fresh forms of cultural production and economic activity—from indie music and festive farmers markets, to scanning and producing an exploding array of YouTube videos.

The multiplicity of local communities and fine-grained affiliations breeds tolerance for other groups as well. Cultural relativism is coming to define America's mainstream. Even private firms advance the whatever-spirit of the times. One nationwide health club sports a motto over its front door, reading "Judgment Free Zone." So the contemporary liberation from hierarchy is not so much about becoming a lone individual seeking detachment from conforming institutions or moral dictates. Instead, it speaks to decentering out to local social organizations and particular ties as they host jobs and everyday affiliations.

The revival of localism alters the nature of social organization on the ground, new categories for defining close and supportive camaraderie. It's this fresh power and cohesion that stems from particulars, veering away from modern and moral universals, that is coming to characterize postindustrial societies. "There are no facts, only interpretations," Nietzsche argued in the late eighteenth century.[44] The colorful blossoming of political and cultural pluralism now hosts a rather postmodern fracturing of social interpretations, such as how meaningful jobs and lifestyles are defined with unprecedented variety.

Even government seeks to regain legitimacy by expanding hyperlocal organizations, from charter schools to vouchers for sectarian education, or seeding neighborhood health clinics and urban gentrification. Modernity initially aimed to stigmatize the "backward" ways of local associations. Civilization implied allegiance to formal roles and contributing to the productivity of hierarchical firms. Yet now reformers seek to "personalize" schools or build "professional learning communities" inside local branches. Medical staff members aim to understand the patient's social context, while nudging her toward healthier behavior. It's power to the particular, no longer to universal remedies that ignore the client's local situation. Family-like gemeinschaft is fighting back against utilitarian and impersonal gesellschaft, to flip sociologist Ferdinand Tönnies argument a century ago.

Shaking the Modern Duality—Hierarchy, Markets, and the Individual

The new decentralists, who you will soon meet, shed another artifact from the modern era: the old duality between hierarchical control and individual freedom. The new decentralists instead begin with notions of social cohesion, belonging, and membership—situating the individual within his or her immediate milieu. This leads to strategies to engage and motivate clients within their social context, which offers both enabling assets and constraining risks. Still, persisting assumptions about cooperation in organizations, along with the wider civic discourse, cling to this aging dialectic, setting the reified and calculating individual against the rules and conformity pressed by central authorities and their hierarchies.

Backing up, Western societies have long been torn between loyalty to particular tribal ties—to family, faith, class membership, or local village—and the ideal of a context-less free and feisty individual. After all, the modernity script itself replaced the ancien régime, firmly established by European aristocrats and the landed class. Only after the bloody revolution in Paris, with the rising proletariat and middling classes storming the Bastille in 1789, did modern liberal tenets come to define the individual as sacred, now free to move in labor markets and incrementally liberated to enjoy shared civil rights.

The central authority of the aristocracy and the church—along with the caste imposed on indentured workers—would be violently challenged, displaced by a secular state that promised to integrate disparate classes and groups. And this novel political institution was to sharpen and protect the newly drawn boundaries and rights of the sacred individual. Membership in this inventive space called *civil society* was extended to men of various social classes, who now enjoyed the right to roam across, and presumably rise up within, industrializing labor markets. The individual was no longer penned in by class origins or ascribed characteristics, but was now a free citizen who could work hard, prove his mettle in universal institutions like schools and factories, and enjoy upward mobility. "The idea that the moral worth of a person does not lie in his inherited gifts or natural talents, but in the free use he makes of them is a notion which Christianity gave to the world," writes the Sorbonne philosopher Luc Ferry.[45] But industrialization of Western societies meant that factories and commercial hierarchies would become the secular proving grounds for the individual's display of merit.

Six centuries earlier the Vatican had broken from nearby emperors, struggling to establish its own autonomy from civil authorities, a treaty sealed by the Concordat of Worms. But modern government would bring this full circle, following the American and French revolutions, "the state becomes a church," as Francis Fukuyama puts it. The rise of modernity in the eighteenth century "called for the liberation from all the ties which grew up historically in politics, in religion, in morality," wrote sociologist Georg Simmel in 1903.[46] The central state would proceed to weave together a nation-state, to define modern ways of believing and getting ahead via meritocratic pathways carved out by central institutions, engineered far from local villages, from those backward tribal ties. The display of merit and worthy performance, of course, increasingly occurred in centralized hierarchies: schools, factories, and steadily emerging white-collar jobs.

This was the rub. As the industrial and commercial revolutions fostered the growth of mammoth hierarchies—firms that expanded way beyond early grain or textile mills set in pastoral rural scenes—the hierarchical control of work, often deskilled and regimented, would diminish the individual's celebrated freedoms by the late nineteenth century. While modern political reform celebrated the sanctity of the individual and his Epicurean-inspired pursuit of happiness, these Enlightenment ideals would be undone by the industrial control of atomized workers. So the modern duality came into focus: hierarchical rules and routines set against the individual's freedom and expressive fulfillment. The lone and powerless individual had become liberated to pursue work in a free market, only to enter a dark and dreary production line, the iron cage of organizational rationality, as Max Weber would call it.

To mediate this divisive duality, modern philosophers like Rousseau had looked to the state—the only collective actor with sufficient heft to protect the sanctity and rights of the individual. In place of aristocratic control Rousseau proposed a "social contract" in 1762, by which the individual would pledge allegiance to a secular state, which in turn would protect one's civil and property rights. What he dubbed the "general will"—individuals cooperating in the civic space to serve public interests—would enable the people to regulate and govern itself, a form of human virtue, going back to Seneca's search for commonly held ethics, which Rousseau trumpeted as the basis of social integration.

The modern social contract required that political freedom from the elite oligarchy (and moral liberation from the Vatican) be balanced with individual engagement in civil society, the notion of citizenship still taught in civics textbooks. It was a simple yet wildly pluralist bundle of social ideals: fusing the modern argument for a centralized government with the (eventual) Jeffersonian ideal of local activism exercised by a wider range of citizens. "Every motion not produced by another can come only from a spontaneous, voluntary action," Rousseau wrote. "The principle of every action is in the will of a free being."[47]

Rousseau took the radical step of claiming that only a paramount state could protect the sanctity of the individual's civil rights. A forceful political center was necessary to combat the inequalities tolerated by the Church and landed elites, tracing injustice to the first man who fenced off his property, sacrificing the village commons. Rousseau would come under blistering attack from Catholic leaders and Parisian aristocrats and was chased to England at one point. He would die in disrepute among European officialdom.

But he had the last laugh. Five years after the populist assault on the Bastille, with the rise of the first French Republic, Rousseau's universal ideals would be resurrected—his body exhumed and carried through the streets of Paris during a three-day celebration. It dramatically accented the new constitutive rules of the secular civic sphere. The individual's liberty was juxtaposed to government's responsibility to build a nation's infrastructure, advance secular rationality, and provide due process for the now sacred individual. And Rousseau had cast the underlying dialectic. It still frames our political discourse, how we think about managing individuals in firms, even casting control against freedom when parenting our kids. The reified and context-less person was set against controlling agencies, be they exploitive factories or religious dogma. And conflicts between the individual and the institution must be mediated by a vigorous state.

Yet America's rekindled faith in localism, stoked in contemporary times, helps to reveal the blinding limits of this duality. Freedom versus control. The ability to choose one's faith or one's job. The right to exit from a repressive institution. These constitutive rules, of course, are just, they challenge mind-numbing regimens that still characterize factory-like models of organization. But the modern duality leads contemporary reformers to assume that liberation from hierarchy or cultivating market dynamics will alone improve how work gets done, how practitioners motivate clients to lift the organization's performance. If central bureaucracy is the problem, let's free local units from the hierarchy, even let them compete for clients or customers. Sure, this thread helps to weave a more colorful array of decentered organizations within economic or social sectors. But it only opens up new possibilities, new conditions under which more effective practice and cooperative human engagement may flourish or not. This is a pivotal discovery by the new decentralists.

White-Collar Conformity and Cultural Pluralism

To unearth the roots of America's contemporary break with hierarchy and moral doctrine we must look back to the 1950s. Early social critics began to sketch a dark side of the postwar economic boom, often focusing on the conforming suburbanization of society. Men in suits and ties, filing into corporate skyscrapers, now animated unprecedented levels of material comfort, appliances for all occasions, and rows of identical homes set alongside pristine tree-lined streets. But would this unprecedented affection for materialism feed the soul, motivate a young generation that often seemed to want much more?

From the Beats in San Francisco to folksingers in Greenwich Village, a range of bearded dissidents questioned the rise of white-collar conformity. Rather than complying with the modernization script—where the individual was seeking his fortune in corporate hierarchies of untold scope and size—a range of writers, artists, and academics seemed to have their ear out for a different drummer. American workers had lost touch with any feeling of efficacy or meaning in their craft. They were becoming cogs in the industrial machine, or of late, trapped in white-collar bureaucracies. The cheerful suburbanite of the 1950s was materially better off than before, critics argued, yet had become alienated from his or her identity, now rootless in a corporate world overrun by sleek bureaucracies. That unsettling experience of disconnection was brought forward, amplifying the desperation that tore at Willy Loman, the alienated suit in *Death of a Salesman*, first performed on Broadway in 1949.

Many of these cultural critics would be caricatured and lampooned. Think, Maynard G. Krebs, the irreverent protobeatnik in the popular television sitcom *The Many Loves of Dobie Gillis*, which ran from 1959 to 1963. But these idealistic writers, harking back to the humanist ideals of the Enlightenment, would soon be joined by Harvard professors, magazine editors, even midwestern parents that would mobilize against the Vietnam War. The fledging questioning of corporate values—whether faith in markets or hierarchical ways of organizing work—would inform and frame the debates of the 1960s, soon defined by civil rights activists, feminists, and the peace movement. The search was on to devise forms of cooperation that manifest richer meaning and authentic human connection—beyond enforcing regimented roles and satiated consumers.

These critics reached back in social history, grasped the modern duality, and placed it back on the civic mantle to debate once again. The individual's freedom and expressive capacities were being squashed by corporate hierarchy and the moral stricture pressed by central authorities. Or, in terms Karl Marx first articulated, the first-person self (or subject) was still being bound by the factory or white-collar bureaucracy and its unrelenting rationalization of cold, impersonal work life. This harked back to Weber's "iron cage" analogy in the early twentieth century, not to mention Enlightenment-era humanists who combatted the Church's uniform moralism. For Weber, the ample material benefits of efficient factories had come with a high price: the subordinated individual, whose aspirations were now locked away, grew more alienated from one's craft, from one's own self.

Of course not everyone read the subversive poetry of Allen Ginsberg or Gary Snyder in the 1950s. Yet when middle-age sociologists at NYU and Harvard began to echo the Beats, the soul searching sunk deeper into the American psyche. In his haunting book *The Lonely Crowd*, David Riesman invoked analytic renditions of Willie Loman, the alienated salesman who came to feel little of anything, other than disorientation. Then came William Whyte's, *Organization Man*, and later *The Feminine Mystique* by Betty Friedan. Each argued persuasively, pulling forward humanist ideals, that white-collar hierarchies threated to squash one's identity, the individual's wider and deeper aspirations in life.

This was no longer a recalcitrant labor movement that talked of exploited factory workers, or a tribe of offbeat critics appearing at San Francisco poetry readings. Now Ivy League professors and national magazines, surfacing amid the diffuse tranquility of the 1950s, were asking whether corporate hierarchy and that plain-vanilla lifestyle—awash in appliances, new cars, and stereo systems—came close to nurturing the human spirit, the telos, the expressive or caring potentials of everyday life.

Less than a decade later, by 1968, a youthful generation seemed hell bent on questioning all renditions of authority, any form of control or mindless conformity. It was a year bookended by San Francisco's Summer of Love and the violent response of Chicago police to antiwar protestors at the Democratic National Convention. Even before Vietnam, the free speech movement at Berkeley focused in part on providing undergraduates smaller classes, a more deeply human setting in which to learn. A breathless variety of experiments in how to organize work and everyday life blossomed, from communal settlements and alternative schools (like freedom-inducing Summerhill), to free clinics and church-run preschools.

Cultural criticism, not to mention subversive sarcasm, went mainstream. The comedy duo the Smothers Brothers became widely popular, before being kicked off the air by CBS for antiwar commentary. Or take *M*A*S*H*, the satirical antiwar series that first debuted in 1972, adapted from Robert Altman's original film. The irascible, wise-cracking medics stationed in the Korean jungle, played by Alan Alda (in the TV series) and Elliot Gould (in the film), seemed to channel America's rising distrust of government authority, not to mention exposing the bloody horrors of war. The critique of corporate hierarchy had spread to the state, yet another node of central authority that would suffer from crashing legitimacy.

Searching for Authenticity and Local Membership

The theme of authenticity emerged from the 1960s as well, stemming from worries that corporate hierarchy and public institutions required us all to play a role, to constantly conform to others' expectations. Life was theater, a series of performances that rarely came from the heart. The book *Games People Play*, by psychiatrist Eric Berne, became a bestseller in 1964. "Question authority" was no longer an edgy bumper sticker plastered on the back of Volkswagens—it became a sentiment that would sink deep into a skeptical American culture.

Or, remember that iconic scene in *The Graduate* (1967) where a disaffected Benjamin, played by boyish Dustin Hoffman, is cornered at a cocktail party and told "there's a great future in plastics," by an earnest Mr. McGuire. More pointedly, the likes of Bob Dylan, Joni Mitchell, and the Rolling Stones would shatter the flat, gray facets of bureaucratic firms, along with the cold and rational social relations found within. Volumes have been written about the 1960s and the rebirth of humanist ideals in Western societies, advanced by cultural icons, from Allen Ginsberg to Joan Baez, Daniel Ellsberg to Cesar Chavez, not to mention the subversive comedy of a George Carlin or Jon Stewart. Getting real—pushing past the ritualized, impersonal behavior required inside large firms and public institutions—would become an ethical imperative as well.

This distinctly American thread of authenticity not only subverts central authority and exposes phony scripts, it also moves individuals to find *real* human connections locally. The Great Rationalization Project, as Stanford sociologist John W. Meyer calls it, had organized work and much of social life into regulated sectors and formal institutions. And these hierarchical authorities simply assumed that the errant individual must be ruled, guided through labor routines and unambiguous moral codes. Instead, humanistic psychologists—like Rollo May and Carl Rogers, who sold millions of books into the 1980s—assumed that the individual naturally engaged the social world, seeking the intrinsic benefits of belonging, competence, and felt experience.

Breaking down hierarchical power relations—even at the interpersonal level—was key to nurturing more open and authentic lives. The personal became political in the wake of the 1960s, as feminist Robin Morgan coined. Gordon Allport in 1955 observed a "healthy and contrary trend in America," pointing to "the liberalizing of child rearing practices, more humane treatment of workers in 'the industrial economy,' and the rising popularity of therapy."[48] So authority figures now went beyond distant college presidents or corporate executives; the quite local deconstructing of social hierarchy was pressed daily between women and men, students and professors, customers and sales clerks. The aim was to devise more lateral and transparent relationships, to shed ritualized roles that tacitly served to preserve power differentials.

This unrelenting probing of authenticity—steadily seeped into the arts and popular culture—now percolates into work settings and formal organizations as well. Bruce Springsteen found himself under this microscope after relying on a teleprompter to remember the lyrics, even to his classic tunes. The *Washington Post*'s reviewer asked whether such "kinds of fakery violate the implied contract between a performer and concert-goer," cutting The Boss no slack for his age.[49]

Today it's hard to find an emperor who remains fully clothed. The Vatican is pushing to take control of the Leadership Conference of Women Religious, the US association that represents Catholic nuns in four-fifths of religious orders. Some have vocally questioned the church's prohibition on women serving as priests and opposition to birth control. "We have a differing perspective on obedience," said Sister Pat Farrell, president of the conference.[50] Their challenge to central authority stems in part from a book by Fordham University theologian Sister Elizabeth A. Johnson, who reports how God is talked about and perceived differently between men and women, Latino groups, the poor, even among Holocaust survivors. Catholic bishops protested, saying, "The book does not take the faith of the Church as its starting point."

So America's new decentralists scrap a key page from the aging script of modernity, what sociologist Robert Wuthnow calls "the humanist agenda of emancipation."[51] You will see how contemporary decentralists are no longer obsessed with breaking free of hierarchy, or somehow liberating their staff or clients in the neoclassical sense of becoming a lone actor. Instead, they seek to organize work through means that pull together local practitioners and clients in motivating, engaging ways—to lift learning, shift behavior, collectively tackle problems. The break from hierarchy is motivated not by an ideological desire to be free as a context-less individual. Instead, today's decentralists voice the post-1950s desire for human connection, that is, forms of human cooperation that offer membership, a feeling of mutual support, and the possibility of learning from one another. The new decentralists are leaving the old Western duality behind—less obsessed with finding liberation from bureaucratic centers and more keenly focused on engaging social relations on the ground.

In this light we are witnessing a revival and elaboration of local affiliations, tribal ties across many postindustrial societies. Whether such local associations serve only to fracture the wider civil society has long preoccupied modern theorists. Charles Darwin argued that the moral contours acquired by the individual stems from "social instincts, including under this term family ties."[52] Yet French sociologist Émile Durkheim, also writing in the nineteenth century, believed that only the state could deliver a modern, secular morality, advocating that Paris should take control over parish schools throughout France and stamp out the local patois to ensure that all youngsters would learn "proper" Parisian French. The secular nation-state would be committed to cultural assimilation, filing down the sharp edges of tribal differences.[53]

But contemporary decentralists punctuate a telling reversal of Hegel's hope that government would incorporate and rationalize control of organized players in civil society. Instead, the contemporary state has reversed the flow of authority and capital back out to this decentered panoply of community organizations and for-profit firms that now carry out public projects. Rather than seeing the central state as striking a bargain with the reified individual, à la Rousseau's social contract, some analysts now argue that the Western polity is better viewed as "an association of associations."[54] If public projects are increasingly carried out by networks of decentered firms—from education and health care to postindustrial enterprise—then cooperative work comes to occur in networks of practitioners and clients now understood as being embedded in their local contexts.

What remains unclear is whether this will result in postmodern tribalism, an archipelago of cultural islands that are tolerant of one another in cosmopolitan fashion. No doubt members of a coherent tribe express stronger loyalty to fellow members than to others who live outside the group. They gain more affection and feel more efficacious with like-minded compadres. But tribes can also be highly flexible and respectful of other tribes, as philosopher Stephen Asma argues.[55] We see this cosmopolitan pluralism among the new decentralists—this array of well-educated practitioners laboring in human services, along with local civic activists, tied to what the optimistic sociologist Richard Florida calls the "creative class."[56]

Still, concern over tribal segmentation recurs, as when rioting and violence swept through immigrant communities on the segregated edges of London in mid-2011. "Under the doctrine of state multiculturalism, we have encouraged different cultures to live separate lives," David Cameron, Britain's prime minister, said. "Europe needs to wake up to what is happening in our countries." The home secretary, David Davis, said that European liberals had permitted "people of different cultures to settle without expecting them to integrate into society."[57] The debate that ensued was not unlike America's recurring culture wars—waged over what language(s) should be spoken in classrooms, must the institution of marriage be reserved for heterosexual couples, should secular rationality always trump religious faith?

Reconceiving the Individual in Context

By the close of the twentieth century intellectual currents, too, had come to undermine the modern postulate that the bounded individual makes decisions and works markets absent any social context. The 1960s reminded civic leaders that children are born into social classes, advantaged or stigmatized by race and language. The individual enters into tribal memberships and affiliations, and these enclaves hold varying access to firms, jobs, and institutions. Popularized notions of *social capital* also clarify how the individual blends into social ties that manifest differing degrees of trust, reciprocity, and behavioral norms, like a sugar cube melting into hot molasses.

Indeed, the torrent of ideals and contention that swept across American society in the final third of the twentieth century dealt in part with individual freedoms and whether to tolerate out-there forms of expression. But also pulled forward, from the Enlightenment and the Beats, was the question of how to create humanistic forms of community, of cooperation, that offered the warmth of membership and a sense of belonging. It wasn't simply that bureaucratic conformity or market options failed to feed the soul. Entirely new forms of local community would be required. More fulfilling organizations must be devised, lent order by decentered ideals and authentic commitments to one another.

How to conceive of the individual's "rights" and boundaries when the person remains embedded in local collectivities has long preoccupied modern thinkers. Even the neoclassical liberal, Adam Smith, argued in the mid-eighteenth century that "both pleasure and pain are always felt so instantaneously, and often upon frivolous occasions, that it seems self evident that neither of them can be derived from any such self-interested consideration."[58] He would later define the individual as capable of lone rationality, at times pursuing calculated utility within a market. But this pursuit of one's utility is built atop a foundation of shared "moral sentiments" in which the individual was deeply embedded. This included a variety of tacit virtues and expressions, from enjoying mirthful company, as quoted above, to the "the pleasure of mutual sympathy."[59]

Smith argued how "a climate of mutual trust has to be cultivated and fostered" to nurture great unity in his modernizing England, as paraphrased by economist Amartya Sen. These commonly enacted virtues were seen as either awarded at birth or, more likely, socialized as the child and young adult sought membership and meaning within intermediate collectives: the family, peer groups, or local parish. Yet for Smith a more cosmopolitan framework was required, ensuring that the individual would gain distance from his surroundings, achieve an eye-opening perspective. "We can never survey our own sentiments and motives . . . unless we remove ourselves from our own natural station, and endeavor to view them as at a certain distance from us," he said.

What's so contemporary about Smith's early struggle to define the universal motivators that animate the individual, as central authority now fades, is how he situates the person in his or her local context, where shared sentiments and human ties are tacitly learned. Then these attachments or sentiments are expressed with spontaneity, not necessarily stemming from a self-interested, rational calculus, as modern-day economists would have it. So we see the modern duality already being questioned: the individual's behavior and expressiveness is couched in immediate contexts. There is no lone individual pursuing her selfish interests in a social vacuum, constantly trying to escape from constraining structures.

Nor did formal hierarchy always serve as the predictable foil pitted against the atomistic, volitional individual. Even the ancient Greeks struggled with when to look toward Athens, versus when to follow the dictates and tacit norms of the local city-state or family. Foundational ideals of Greek philosophy emphasized how the individual must express his virtue by conforming to the moral virtues defined by the city-state. Elite civic leaders, like Cicero, pitched universal dimensions of personal character, mirroring the social foundations of Greek culture and cooperative norms, prior to the rise of Christian forms of morality.

Soon after Julius Caesar's assassination, Cicero articulated the moral tenets of mutual obligation to each other, how the individual must seek knowledge to serve the commonweal. The virtuous citizen was to learn about natural, underlying "forms" or structures that organized human and material physics. Abstract knowledge of the forms, captured by mathematics and astronomy, gained precedence over everyday understandings. Plato accented that "in the best soul, its best element—reason—will regulate its passion and bodily needs," writes James Miller.[60] The individual was to dedicate learning and ethical understanding to advance civil society, not to simply produce as a lone individual, a busy bee within the amoral market.

Contemporary decentralists in a sense agree. They avoid sharp dichotomies that assume that decentered organizations must choose between tighter rules from above or unleashing free or "autonomous" action by the unencumbered individual. These new social architects are not simply obsessed with shaking free of an immutable organizational center. Instead, they are rethinking how headquarters might devise the tools and practices necessary to truly engage and motivate clients. The new decentralists think deeply about what makes the individual client tick, how their organization might scaffold up from the everyday contexts and tribal ties that envelope the client. It's the client's particular local context that must first be understood before the client can be engaged and motivated. This inevitably leads back to the socializing power of intermediate collectives—kin, peers, church, and village settings—that reinforce or nudge the client's aspirations and behavior.

The splintering of central authority and universal ideals, along with the shifting nature of work, has spurred the rise of organizational pluralism as well. A widening array of decentralized institutions, be they nonprofit or for-profit, now carry out a dizzying range of public endeavors. This includes charter schools and online teaching, HMOs that operate in local markets, portable vouchers that help poor families pay for housing and transport, or recycling firms that serve us all. Let's turn next to how the search for more local and responsive organizations fosters growth of a third sector in society, which now challenges, even subverts the market and the central state.

Nonprofits and Mixed Markets for Public Good

> Just as a family is an immature kind of state, so civil society is also a kind of state. When men realize that the cleavage between universal and particular ... is only an appearance, they realize the concrete unity of universal and particular in their own nature.
> —HEGEL, *Philosophy of Right*, 1821[61]

It turns out that Hegel was wrong. The particular affiliations and local organizations that thicken civil society have not been incorporated into, or homogenized by, a monochromatic state. Sure, essential questions must be tackled by the official political apparatus, debated and settled in codified laws. Government still offers a sturdy civic stage on which the theatrics over pressing issues play out. How else could society move toward renewable energy sources or cool down the planet? When does life begin? Should widening inequality in wealth be tolerated or remedied? Civil society must tackle a few core issues centrally.

But central government's authority and fiscal clout to steer the aims and character of public institutions—to serve pluralistic impulses within a neatly bounded town square—is on the decline. Our case studies reveal that private firms increasingly respond to diverse clients and local conditions through decentralized ways of organizing work on the ground. I have argued that the shifting character of work, our aging demographic structure, and the cultural renewal of tribal ties act to subvert central nodes of authority, be they government leaders or corporate executives. The appeal of particulars and decentered forms of cooperation continue to overtake the fading modernist faith in universals, centrally set rules, and moral guideposts.

The remarkable growth of nongovernment organizations (NGOs) over the past half century, chartered to run public endeavors, further reveals the state's keen interest in decentralizing its functions and forms of human cooperation. And private firms, large and small, are now largely financed with taxpayer dollars while serving public interests in (variably) regulated markets. The middle chapters detail how this works for health care and charter school companies, even for international banks and firms paid to backstop military veterans. Let's first review government's recurring interest in creating and watching after NGOs that organize locally and run a variety of enterprises, touching our everyday lives.

Community Organizing, Local Efficiency

Washington's unprecedented support for nonprofits emerged early during the Great Society. Presidents Kennedy and Johnson aimed to spur organizing on the ground, to advance the well-being and opportunities afforded black families. This was a centrally engineered effort to decentralize political authority and public resources, in contrast to the bottom-up organization of craft guilds during the Renaissance, or settlement houses founded by the likes of Jane Addams and Dorothy Day in the early twentieth century.

The federal government had never attempted to aid hundreds of ethnic activists and community groups, directly bypassing the politics of state and municipal governments. The widening civil rights movement inspired Mr. Kennedy's advisors to rethink how infrastructure could be built inside neighborhoods to lift poor families, from registering voters and constructing better housing, to running preschools. Reform minded foundations—ironically carrying the names of Carnegie and Ford—came to believe that predominately white local governments in the South (and North) would act to subvert local organizing inside black and later Latino communities. A shift in the political economy of urban centers was required, antipoverty advocates argued. So the Kennedy White House would create and fund an expansive constellation of neighborhood development agencies, which proceeded to build Head Start preschools and health clinics, devise housing-finance initiatives, and attract private investment into the central city. These federally funded hubs became known as community action agencies.

Fresh dollops of funding also bolstered the efforts of charitable organizations that had long struggled to lift the poor, already numbering over 50,000 back in 1953, according to the Internal Revenue Service. By 1978 the IRS reported that over 730,000 nonprofits were either running community services or acting as a foundation and qualifying for tax-deductible contributions.[62] By 2010 the National Center for Charitable Statistics reported that over 1.5 million organizations filed as tax-exempt nonprofits. This included just under one million charities or NGOs that provided direct services to individual clients locally, about 118,000 gift-giving foundations, ranging from the humongous Bill and Melinda Gates Foundation to local families or charitable societies, along with 453,000 civic groups or activist organizations not offering social services.[63]

The entire nonprofit sector reported $1.3 trillion in total spending in 2010, which aided a colorful array of enterprises from religiously affiliated hospitals to private universities to local child-care centers. The sector, employing

13.5 million paid staff, accounted for just over 8 percent of all wages and salaries paid across the US economy.[64]

The highest count of nonprofits—firms that either provide funding or operate direct programs—falls in the education sector, numbering over 64,000 organizations. The second biggest subsector is health care, including nonprofit research shops, in total numbering over 44,000 separate tax-exempt firms.[65] Overall, two in every five dollars of revenue enjoyed by NGOs come from government. Another half stems from client fees, including tuition for private colleges and payments to nonprofit health-care firms.

Not all nonprofits operate as authentically rooted inside neighborhoods, or sprout from particular local priorities. Catholic Relief Services operates internationally, as does the Quaker-founded American Friends Service Committee. Fully 137 nonprofit "education management organizations" (an acronym rhyming with HMO) now run one-third of the nation's charter schools, funded by taxpayers and private foundations.[66] The highly praised Knowledge Is Power Project (KIPP) out of Houston runs eighty-three schools nationwide, a franchise firm of sorts—drawing criticism as an "astroturf organization," not truly sprouting from the grass roots.

Helping to sustain local NGOs and civic organizations, one-fourth of all Americans over sixteen years of age now report volunteering during the week, a vivid signal of social cooperation at the local level. If volunteer labor were to be monetized, it would have cost nonprofits over $80 billion in 2010 by one estimate.[67]

A parallel development is government's growing reliance on private firms to advance public endeavors. This includes the spread of charter schools, HMOs, and a variety of social or psychological supports, as we explore in the middle chapters. And over the past generation political leaders of various stripes and colors have realized that the state can recover legitimacy by chartering-out previously public functions. Sure, conservatives still press market dynamics, even privatizing management, as key to boosting the overall performance of public transportation, schools, or health care. But it's the shift toward relying on local nonprofits, smaller-scale collective actors, that now defines the moderate center when it comes to organizing public projects. NGOs—whether nonprofit or for-profit—have come to be seen as more nimble, innovative, and responsive to diverse communities, whether there's evidence to warrant these claims or not.

The density of nonprofits may offer a dab of social glue within neighborhoods, thickening civil society. Debate persists over whether social ties across segmented groups and classes are thinning out in America, where suburban sprawl and mall crawl spread unabated. So the growth of NGOs may offer a counterforce, advancing cohesion through civic activities, festivals, human-scale markets, and political activities. Local variation in the vitality of nonprofits is associated with familiarity among residents and reciprocal social relations in some cities, which sociologist Robert Sampson terms *collective efficacy* (a conceptual cousin of *social capital*). Tracking the lives of hundreds of Chicago nonprofits between 1970 and 2000, Sampson found a strong degree of organizational stability and sustained civic activities, ranging from annual cultural celebrations to unifying protests over local and national political issues (one in six of all recorded events arranged by the average nonprofit).[68]

Sampson also discovered that variability in the level of services provided—tied to budgets and client engagement displayed by nonprofits—helped to predict a neighborhood's level of collective efficacy, the shared expectation that neighbors watch out for each other and pull together to lift parks, schools, and civic spaces. A variety of reputable nonprofits operated in poor and middle-class communities alike, ranging from tenant associations and welfare agencies, to volunteer groups, the Elks, and Rotary Club. These robust nonprofits act to socialize and mentor successive generations, nurturing solidarity locally.[69]

Government's interest in nonprofits goes back to Latin American activists in the 1970s, as they began to define the sector as a third institutional stage on which to organize social action, whether delivering human services in poor communities or spurring political protest. Grossly unequal societies, from Mexico to Argentina, had weathered centuries of exploitive economy relations, typically protected by plainly repressive political regimes. The budding nonprofit sector was to be closer to the people, more responsive and authentic. It aimed to thicken civil society to counterbalance the power of plantation owners, foreign companies, and government elites. The political economies of western Europe and the United States have certainly traced differing histories. But similar skepticism deepened in the 1980s from various corners over what many felt had become a feckless bureaucratic state unable to confront the market's disinterest in worsening inequality.

The Left Leans into Markets

British Prime Minister Tony Blair advanced what he called the Third Way, a phrase borrowed from Latin America, aiming to shrink the state's administrative tentacles and array of nationalized organizations, shifting public responsibilities and programs to decentralized NGOs. Blair would impart key principles of Vice President Gore's effort to reinvent government in the 1990s as well, funding nonprofits to train teachers, take over health clinics, and rebuild vast swaths of old industrial cities. By the decade's end nearly half of all Washington's own spending on goods and services was produced by private organizations, nonprofit or for-profit, according to one estimate.[70]

For Blair the Old Left had remained too ideological, too dominated by Labour and self-serving bureaucrats. Blair argued that career politicians didn't get how the average citizen doesn't care about policy debates. Busy families "worry about the kids, the parents, the mortgage, the boss, their friends, their weight, their health, sex and rock 'n' roll," he once mused.[71] Government would regain its popular legitimacy and organizational efficacy only after shedding its regulatory habits and instead cultivating agile, grassroots firms that responded to local preferences with greater efficiency. Presidents Clinton and Obama would toe this line as well, pitching charter schools, expanding preschool through myriad nonprofits, and spurring market competition among local health maintenance organizations.

The Third Way tacitly revives the warmer, personalized facets of those intermediate collectives that modernists have tried to erode over the past two centuries. NGOs are to offer more family-like settings for toddlers and preschoolers. Charter schools are supposed to be small and cozy, devising inventive ways of engaging kids and boosting learning. Health-care reform now funds hospice care, nurse practitioners, and family physicians that try to shift patients toward preventive care—all methods for making local institutions less formal, more familiar and inviting. In these ways the central state is no longer the direct agent that civilizes or cultivates the masses toward a shared cultural frame, what Immanuel Kant termed *erziehung* in German. Or, consider the Spanish word *aprender*, from the Latin: to be enlightened. The Third Way diminishes this modernist presumption of the state's universal authority, giving way to a colorful array of local organizations, privately run to advance shared public interests.

Similarly, as the Soviet empire imploded and the Berlin Wall fell in 1989, the Czech leader, Václav Havel, and fellow east European democrats convinced the United States to fund nascent NGOs to thicken civil society and keep the market and hierarchical state in check. Nelson Mandela and his African National Congress did the same as apartheid came unglued, prior to the 1994 free elections, trusting neither government nor the market to spur social action down below.[72] Even the market-worshipping World Bank created a "civil society group" in 1995, and then invested heavily to bolster the capacity of NGOs in developing nations. The bank reported that over $2 billion was allocated to these small-scale firms in 2009, and four in five country projects involved "civil society organizations" that work alongside governments.[73]

Even good Democrats in the United States have long deployed market mechanisms—widening family or parental choice—to move financing from monolithic bureaucracies to leaner, local NGOs. Senator Claiborne Pell in 1972 expressed greater trust in the choices made by college entrants than university administrators, as he sent aid out through voucher-like Pell Grants rather than funding colleges. The first experiment to channel education funding through parents, via vouchers, was initiated by Lyndon Johnson's advisors in the mid-1960s. A Democrat-controlled Congress voucherized federal child-care funding in 1990. These demand-driven finance mechanisms have brought untold revenues to private organizations and local nonprofits, provided they attract clients and families.

What's remarkable is how the state hopes to advance its legitimacy by shaving back its own bureaucratic apparatus, then chartering private organizations to serve public interests. By directly funding NGOs, or indirectly through portable vouchers, government hopes to sustain a colorful panoply of local organizations, which presumably match the range of family and client preferences—shaking off modernity's affection for standardization and regulated routines. In short, government now nurtures mixed markets of public and private firms, hoping to renew its own organizational efficacy. Then publicly funded institutions must vie for clients by playing the new competitive game the state itself devised.

Overall, these four stiff winds now howl through vast institutions, setting them on a tack to decentralize resources, authority, and the tools of their particular trade. America, like its postindustrial peers, must reconsider its position in the global economy and recognize that only a tiny slice of the labor workforce is still subjected to factory-like routines and the top-down control of everyday work. Central governments suffer from diminished fiscal capacity as the world flattens economically and aging populations exercise a growing purchase on public budgets. In turn, the nonprofit sector flourishes as the state seeks efficiencies, a responsive fit with kaleidoscopically diverse communities, along with voter pressure to show results—to somehow fix schools, health care, public transportation, and an energy-hungry economic system. These forces, in short, rekindle America's renewed faith in localism.

Other accounts try to explain the contemporary decentering of authority and institutions, not only among postindustrial societies but spreading worldwide as well. Each theory is illuminating yet incomplete. Critics of neoliberalism emphasize resurging faith in market dynamics as capitalist expansion intensifies globally.[74] This involves the migration of market mechanisms and material incentives into public sectors under the European banner of

New Public Management. This perspective assumes that surface ideology drives the organization of work and the state's political calculus, not shifts in the structure of labor or deeper cultural developments as detailed above. The neoliberal argument also highlights the agency of promarket advocates, while largely ignoring how pivotal actors within the political and cultural Left have long battled against centralized nodes of authority.

The intensifying impulse to decentralize stems from the tandem desire for stronger institutional effectiveness (boosting learning, lifting health outcomes) *and* freeing up local practitioners to puzzle through situated remedies—"accountable autonomy," as political scientist Archon Fung puts it.[75] It's actors on the Left—civil rights groups, Democratic mayors, neighborhood activists—pushing to detach from the regulatory center, not simply neoliberal elites. These constituencies aim to hold firms and public institutions stiffly accountable *and* enable local actors to craft inventive, culturally consonant solutions.

A second explanatory account—stemming from neoinstitutional thinking in sociology—claims that the decentralization of mass organizations, like government-run schooling, merely manifests the spread of a mythology, a logic of action that gains legitimacy, often pressed by international agencies, like the World Bank or the Organization for Economic and Community Development (OECD). Yet two generations of neoinstitutionalists argued that Weberian-like rationalization was the dominant social form seeping out from the West into every nook and cranny of the third world. Organizations across sectors were allegedly becoming isomorphic in their Weberian form. Now some of these same theorists argue that the new religion swivels around not homogenous rationality but decentralized diversity of organizational forms.[76] Which is it?

This socially constructed account of decentering tends to ignore its material manifestations, including the sprouting of novel organizational forms—locally controlled firms that don't operate in markets per se—whether situated in the education, health-care, or nonprofit sectors. The neoinstitutional account usefully highlights how decentralization has come to symbolically legitimate certain organizations in various fields, but fails to acknowledge how decentering of authority and institutions spawns novel forms of social organization and cooperation across a breathless variety of local settings.

Decentralists, Old and New

As decentralized organizing becomes inevitable across a widening range of sectors, we better learn about how these social relations unfold. How do the new decentralists go about their work, aiming to better engage clients and fellow practitioners? What are the specific organizational mechanisms they forge to effectively lift their clients—to buoy learning, health, and trade? And do these mechanisms help to explain when decentralized organizations fail to lift those they serve? What's so new about America's revival of localism? To begin, let's meet these inventive organizational architects, these decentralizing reformers, old and new.

Human settlements have long struggled over who can best coerce or coordinate their members to produce goods and services, or to mount public endeavors. The question still besets hierarchies and markets, especially among the civic leaders and central managers who search for motivating rules, norms, or incentives that spur effective cooperation on the ground. The option of decentering authority and know-how down to local managers or practitioners has long tempted organizational leaders. I will argue that contemporary decentralists are getting better at engaging their clients, motivating their local staff, and rethinking how the center can help. But let's take a brief glance back to illuminate what's truly new.

Sixteen centuries before the outbreak of modernity, first-century Rome was contracting with small firms to collect taxes out in the provinces, an early case of a privatized public project. When the shenanigans played by these tax collectors raised the dander of elites in far-flung provinces—arbitrarily levying higher tax rates and pocketing portions of their collections—policy makers back in the capital shifted operations to their own civil servants, directly answerable to Rome.[77] The lack of accountability inherent in this early privatization of a public service threatened to undercut Rome's credibility.

Or take the pluralistic cultural currents that flourished in the decades leading up to Constantine's swerve toward Christianity in the fourth century. Competing faiths spread across diverse populations throughout Europe and North Africa. Many still followed pagan rituals and totems, challenged largely by the ideals of classical humanism "in a spirit of mingled rivalry and absorptive tolerance," as Stephen Greenblatt writes.[78] Both the Jews and Christians "did not doubt that other gods existed, but those gods were without exception demons, fiendishly bent on luring gullible humanity away from the sole and universal truth." Thus the Roman state—soon pulled asunder by such divisions—had to be enlisted by the Christian minority to sanctify and legitimate their particular version of universal truths.

Still, the center of empire would not hold—unable to manage the centrifugal forces of plural languages, customs, and political unrest. Disenchanted by decay and corruption inside the empire's capital, provincial landowners now resisted the tax collectors and instead advanced civic development outside Rome's authority. Uprisings grew among the empire's noncitizens, stigmatized in Latin as backward *gentes* (tribes). The resulting notion of a federal republic that distributes central state control over core ideals and public functions, while sharing authority and public capital out in the provinces, would become a key balance wheel as the modern state took shape following the French and American revolutions. The likes of Thomas Jefferson and fellow federalists would argue against a forceful central government, instead reviving Rome's earlier conception of a federalist republic and retaining considerable authority out in the young states.

So what's new about America's revival of localism? Are we simply replaying an ancient debate over where—inside what institutions or local collectives—we should lodge authority and public resources? Or, do contemporary decentralists, perhaps learning from their institutional forebears, go further in crafting novel social relations, ways of shaping human cooperation on the ground?

A New Architecture for Local Organizing

America's contemporary story of decentralization, unfolding over the past half century, is unprecedented. Never before has a Western civilization placed so much hope and capital in nonprofit or for-profit organizations to advance public endeavors. Nor has such a colorful array of firms been harnessed within lightly regulated markets to blend private and public pursuits. Yes, Alexis de Tocqueville detailed the young nation's lively array of civic groups and small town volunteerism in the 1830s. But he could never have predicted that the nonprofit sector would contribute $1.3 trillion in economic activity and employ almost one-tenth of the nation's labor force. There's no precedent for a society to dedicate a third of its economic output to education and health care, increasingly carried out in mixed markets. It's the mere scope and formalization of local institutions, aiming to meet their clients or customers in largely decentralized units that marks the past half century in the United States and other postindustrial societies.

This prompts a second novel feature of the contemporary debate over localism. We are no longer simply debating whether Washington or local governments should run our schools, watch after health care, or regulate marriage and interstate commerce—the narrower terrain in which federalist battles are fought. Today's debate pushes into deeper questions of how local organizations can deliver higher quality, less costly public goods and services, while being held accountable when they fail. The current conversation is not over *whether* to decentralize but *how* to create social organizations that encourage clients and practitioners to cooperate with greater care and efficacy.

First-wave decentralists, emerging from the 1970s took several steps forward, especially as they exposed the shortcomings of hierarchy and its compliance mentality. Pioneering decentralists on the political Left demonstrated how agile nonprofits could stimulate urban redevelopment, organize direct services inside poor neighborhoods, and offer a training ground for urban activists. A variety of inventive reforms have come from decentralists on the Right as well, spurring the creation of charter schools and education options for parents, making college aid portable (just like vouchers), and infusing market dynamics into various sectors.

Firms in less fettered markets, like Hewlett-Packard or Levi Strauss, sparked fresh thinking about how a surgical center can set clear performance targets and monitor progress, while otherwise liberating local units to innovate and discover productive efficiencies. Now even progressives experiment with market-like incentives to advance public endeavors. Overwhelmed by mountains of trash, Mexico City residents can now schlep recyclable materials down to a monthly market where they receive tokens in return—redeemable when buying locally grown fruits and vegetables. This innovation advances an environmental ethic, while spurring farmers markets and gains in the purchasing power of low-income families.[79]

First-wave decentralists focused on the mechanics and politics of breaking away from the bureaucratic center in the wake of the 1960s—the necessary but insufficient struggle over how to move authority, capital, and know-how down to local units. But these early localists often failed to touch or animate their clients any better than the centralized bureaucracies they hoped to dislodge. Chapter 2 details the reasons underlying such failures of first-generation decentralists. It's their second-wave descendants that now show impressive results, as we explore in the organizational cases.

And finally, the new decentralists are no longer stuck in sociologist Wuthnow's "humanist agenda of emancipation," introduced above. Factory-like ways of organizing work—so central to the industrial revolution, then mimicked by public institutions—forged the dusty duality between command-and-control versus individual freedom. Ever keen on polarizing dichotomies, Western philosophers and scholars set the two forms of cooperation—hierarchy and market—as diametrically opposed to one another. Neoclassical liberals, like Adam Smith and John Locke, then set lasting connotations of each: tying hierarchy to the aristocracy and the Vatican, while equipping the sacred individual with novel rights over property and civil action. This commitment to liberties in the public square was, in fact, advanced by the modern state.

Of course, the extent to which the individual experienced freedom and opportunity remains situated in their group, class, or cultural tribe. Still, the simplifying duality stuck, and it framed the liberationist obsession of first-wave decentralists over much of the past half century.

Second-generation descendants get it, and they now move beyond such a binary understanding of the interplay between center and local, hierarchy and individual. They are thinking as organizational leaders and situated practitioners, not so much as political strategists. And second-wave decentralists see little utility in being confined by notions of archetypal hierarchies or textbook renditions of the utilitarian individual maneuvering through a market. You will see how the new decentralists are more social in their orientation, sensitive to how local context conditions motivation. They keenly get to know the individual, understood as situated within a thick milieu. And the new centralists are steadily rethinking the role and resources of managers situated at the center of an otherwise lateral organizational network.

Meet the New Decentralists

Telegraphing the book's punch line, we uncovered four organizational cornerstones, essential principles on which the new decentralists depend, "floating [them] out as a proposition rather than advancing [them] as a polemic," to borrow a phrase from art critic Holland Cotter.[80] These social foundations support the pursuit of deeper, more inspiring relationships between local practitioners and a variety of clients, at least across the diverse sectors on which our fieldwork focused: education, health care, and finance banking.

First and foremost these organizational designers exercise *intense curiosity about their clients*, steadily learning what makes them tick. Just ask Pablo Alba, a thin blue-collar kid with dark, Bolivian features. After finishing middle school, Alba's parents checked out a small charter school in the outer Mission District of San Francisco. His new teachers figured out what made Pablo tick, a blend of curiosity about computers and a passion for Brazilian drumming. Alba's teachers scaffolded up from his own interests, finding internships and campus jobs that fed his interest in music and technology. "The teachers know me by my first name," Alba told me one day, "and what I'm interested in."

The new decentralists serve as resourceful managers as well, articulating how *a lean and surgical center can bolster local staff*. This stems from strong data about clients and ground-level practices that work, that motivate clients. The new managers keep their ear to the ground, learning from their practitioners, as they reciprocally share data and inventive ideas. Take Buck

Strozzi. He literally shot himself in the foot during a rather humbling hunting accident, which this big-rig driver refused to discuss. His leg often swelled to twice its normal size, the blood and fluids blocked between his shin and foot by the circulatory damage. His personal nightmare was shared by his insurance company, as Strozzi pulled into emergency rooms again and again to reduce the edematous fluids in his leg.

Sitting in a patient review session in his Pennsylvania clinic, a half-dozen doctors, nurses, and case managers brainstormed about Strozzi's own social context and what remedies he might find motivating. Strozzi's case manager, Kenda Danowsky, did much of the talking (not his physician), since she knew the most about his context, his surrounding network of social support. He would never quit being a trucker, Danowsky reported. So to help Strozzi take charge of his costly condition, the medical team found a small pump that would reduce fluid in his leg as he cruised the interstate.

Those who guide second-wave decentralization—whether posted centrally or locally—advance a rich *ethical focus*. These leaders may materially incentivize their frontline staff to attend to what motivates their clients. Yet the word *ethics* is derived from the Greek terms signifying manners and customs, the underlying social forms that signal membership and competent action within one's tribe. It's an ever-burning ember that glows within these decentralized firms. Envision Charter Schools, the parent firm of Alba's campus, hires principals who are deeply committed to nurturing relationships. Geisinger Health System, the Pennsylvania firm caring for Strozzi, offers bonuses to doctors who implement preventive strategies for patients with chronic health conditions, eased through behavioral change.

Second-wave decentralists experiment with *new job roles* as well. The former nurse, case manager Danowsky, visits patients at home, talks with their spouses and friends—whatever motivates them to improve their diet or to exercise more. Through this novel role Danowsky gets to know patients who suffer from chronic (and costly) conditions—diabetes, obesity, congestive heart failure—and then nudges healthier behavior. Her role resembles how teachers in the San Francisco charter school display unrelenting curiosity about their students, or how a profitable international bank shifts chunks of capital to branch managers, then returns a year later to check on progress. In each case, the organization chart is no longer sacred, vertical relations flatten, and novel roles are tried—constantly asking how to better engage and motivate clients, young or old.

These new roles bring purposeful informality to the organization and serve to motivate richer dialogue between client and practitioners. A flatter organization ensures that information flows smoothly across a more *horizontal set of roles*, no longer stymied by pulling rank, by pyramid-like forms of authority or status. The ancient elements of intermediate collectives—family, kin, peer relations—are pulled into these formal, yet decentering organizations. Crisp goals and performance remain inside the hearts and minds of local practitioners. But the means for engaging clients draw on informal and trusting social ties as well.

It's tempting to call this quiet revolution in organizing, Decentralization 2.0, although a technocratic metaphor would be antithetical to the ethical mission and social foundations of these inventive managers. The new organizational architects are not simply letting a thousand flowers blossom. They go way beyond the surface-level tussles of shifting authority and capital down to local units. Much of their work now focuses on figuring out how local staff can spark novel learning or agile behavior of clients, in turn lifting the firm's overall effectiveness.

"The primary good that we distribute to one another is membership in some human community," political philosopher Michael Walzer argues.[81] The new decentralists make this pivotal break as they build from—rather than discount, as modernists would have it—the respectful and trusting ties that characterize activities inside their locally rooted organizations. The new decentralists eagerly inquire about, then scaffold up from, what I call *tribal ties*, the immediate social bonds and associations that lend meaning and support to our everyday lives. The decentering of institutional authority, resources, tools, and know-how sets the condition for building these more engaging relationships. But we will see it's not a guarantee. It's a necessary but insufficient condition for nurturing more compelling forms of human cooperation.

*

Without doubt the central regulation of work and social relations found inside organizations will persist as long as capital or engineered expertise, is concentrated and doled out from above. Still, the cost effectiveness of state-funded organizations and the profitability of firms in postindustrial sectors will increasingly rest on the capacity of local staff to engage and motivate clients and customers. We cannot contain health-care costs without altering the behavior of patients with preventable maladies. Nor will the nation's stock of human capital improve until we create schools that energize a diverse range of youths and impart strong character and social agility. Decentering the work of organizations may begin with breaking from a center that demands regimentation, or an impersonal market that erodes human cooperation. But then the real challenge of enriching local practice and motivating clients only begins.

Next, we review lessons learned from the early decentralists, empirically surfacing over the past generation. Then we arrive at the everyday work of their second-generation descendants, exploring their locally situated organizations, which are spread across four diverse sectors. How do these organizational architects go about decentralizing authority, resources, and technical know-how? Beyond the forces that spark this unrelenting press to disassemble big institutions and central authority, how does the decentering of human-scale units unfold on the ground? Our desire to account for America's renewed faith in localism and how it's reshaping formal organizations motivates this book.

2

How Decentralized Organizations Work—
Early Lessons from Early Pioneers

WITH DANFENG SOTO-VIGIL KOON

> To find a form that accommodates the mess, that is the task of the artist.
> —SAMUEL BECKETT

A strange set of eventual bedfellows—policy activists and corporate leaders—began to date almost a half century ago. It was a blind date at first. Upstart black leaders in New York City sought to wrestle control of their neighborhood schools from the downtown bureaucracy. Nascent high-tech firms puzzled through ways to stimulate design innovations without sacrificing production schedules. President Nixon pushed through a novel organization—the health maintenance organization—that would subject physicians to market competition. Congressional Democrats eagerly fought to break up AT&T, a public monopoly that had grown sleepy and inefficient. Student leaders pushed Congress to yank control of college aid from university bureaucracies, then create voucher-like Pell Grants.

These unlikely abettors came to share a hopeful romance with breaking from or disassembling massive hierarchies and central authority in the wake of the 1960s. Conservatives aimed to subject public institutions to market dynamics, predicting gains in quality and efficiency. Progressives had long mistrusted corporate monopolies as enemies of consumers and lower prices. And small "d" democrats now conspired to empower black and, soon, Latino communities, hoping to shift social authority, public capital, and know-how down to village-level schools, child-care centers, health clinics, housing and community action agencies. Yet a shared suspicion of hierarchy and unchecked markets held this political ménage together, not any clear vision of *how* decentralized organizations might do better.

These interests would coalesce through the Reagan era, as moderate Republicans and leading Democrats aimed to inject market principles into public institutions, or nurtured diverse forms of organizations that were to spur innovation, quality gains, and direct responsiveness to parents or clients across diverse communities. Government's own legitimacy came to rest on becoming more effective, or at least looking inventive and dynamic, less bureaucratic. George H. W. Bush in 1990 doubled federal support for childcare centers after convincing Democratic leaders that the funding should go directly to parents in the form of portable vouchers. Presidents Clinton and Obama followed suit, telling governors to lift caps on the count of charter schools or lose dollars; backing nonprofits that run Head Start preschools; and nudging the consolidation of doctors and medical staff into HMOs, now subjected to price competition. Neoliberal principles thrived on the promarket Right. Yet the push to decentralize cumbersome hierarchies intensified from the political Left and high-tech progressives as well.

Learning from First-Wave Decentralists

The first generation of contemporary decentralists—pulling away from centralized hierarchies and authority during the final third of the twentieth century—remind me of those on both sides who brought down the Berlin Wall. They tacitly assumed that a rainbow of democracy and prosperity would magically rise after the towering regime was toppled. The political strategy for breaking away from bureaucracy or infusing market principles into established institutions was somehow sufficient. Less frequently discussed was the next step: rethinking the social organization of decentered firms, how to support diversifying populations of organizations, or what more effective kinds of labor and human cooperation must be crafted to truly lift the firm's efficacy.

Claims about the comparative benefits of decentralized firms and mixed markets of organizations continue to outpace hard evidence. Does the decentralization of authority, capital, and know-how spur greater motivation among frontline staff? Are clients more engaged—be they students, patients, or customers—when local practitioners gain more discretion and professional flexibility? Does a colorfully varied range of organizations lead to more responsive and tailored options for clients?

This chapter discerns what lessons have emerged on these empirical questions, what the first-wave decentralists have taught their second-generation disciples. Overall, the evidence is quite mixed that decentralizing reforms benefit clients more strongly than earlier institutional forms. Yet recent findings point to when and how decentered firms and lightly regulated markets do yield gains for local staff and clients alike. Empirical work is thicker in particular sectors, especially education and health care, which share long traditions of careful evaluation. And while hard evidence from the public sector accumulates more steadily, we also find parallel lessons that have emerged from the private sector's efforts to decentralize management.

Consequential lessons are leading to adjustments in the strategies of second-wave decentralists. To get ahead of the story, for instance, the first generation expressed great faith in demand-side forces, a postulate about which second-wave reformers are less sanguine. Awarding dollops of purchasing power to the ultimate client or customer would naturally lead to higher-quality and more productive organizations, as earnest economists argued. But it soon became clear that so-called supply responses at the grass roots failed to meet the robust expectations of armchair theorists. The staggering growth of HMOs failed to lift quality or patient outcomes; the kaleidoscopic array of new charter schools led to uneven achievement gains and fiscal rip-offs; the vibrant mixed market of child-care providers was failing the youngsters of middle-class families due to gaps in quality. The middle chapters amplify such lessons, still being learned by naive decentralists.

We begin with a preview of the punch line, taking stock of the evidence on *whether* decentralized organizations effectively lift clients or the local practitioners that serve them. This leads to a second, more illuminating question about which much less is known: What *organizational practices* or *social mechanisms* inside decentered firms lead to stronger benefits?

As the nation's decentralizing drift gains momentum, we better figure out *how* these local organizations work inside, and how they could become more effective on the ground. It's this formative question that first animated our fieldwork inside four differing sectors. Along the way, we discovered that first-wave experiments now give way to a clearer organizational architecture, founded on discernible cornerstones shaped by a second generation, the new decentralists.

We limit this empirical review to the fields of education, health care, and high-tech electronics—in which heftier evidence has emerged in recent years. This also serves to frame our case studies. So, here is what's been learned in recent years about whether decentered firms work better, and if so, through what inventive mechanisms and social relations. We begin with empirical lessons regarding the *diverse populations* of decentralized organizations proliferating across differing fields over the past half century—

- First-wave reformers remain focused on detaching local organizations from a bureaucratic center or seeking regulatory relief. But alone, this break from hierarchy—or rush into an imagined market—does not necessarily lead to higher quality across the diversifying population of local organizations.

- Similarly, shifting the finance of public endeavors to portable grants to families or clients rather than directly funding institutions—as with vouchers or tax credits—may spur the creation of diverse organizations, but it will not necessarily result in more effective firms. Quality stems from the available workforce, the social organization of work inside decentered firms, and persisting norms and rules in lightly regulated fields, not simply from purchasing power.
- When a robust supply response *is* observed—be it a colorful variety of charter schools, health-care providers, or software designers—a wide and sometimes unequal distribution of organizational quality and performance can emerge. This may harden disparate opportunities afforded to differing groups of families, clients, or customers.
- Decentering authority, resources, and know-how to local units does not necessarily alter the count or quality of local practitioners available to work in local organizations. The availability of stronger, more agile practitioners—from teachers to medical staff to high-tech programmers—depends on collateral organizational fields, including guilds and higher education to produce a rich workforce.

In short, we are learning that public policy and corporate strategy can reconfigure governance and grow a more diverse array of organizations within a field. But the surrounding environment will enhance or constrain the vitality and social technology inside decentralized organizations. So faith in localism must be tempered by how organizational populations evolve alongside other fields and within persisting norms and rules regarding how cooperative work gets done, now situated within lightly regulated markets.

Accumulating knowledge also informs our understanding of the *internal workings and social relations* found inside decentralizing organizations, especially the inventive architecture that better engages and motivates clients on the ground—

- Decentralizing firms vary in their capacity to attract the resources necessary to mount a high-quality and effective enterprise. These resources include a versatile and stable set of local staff, a secure stream of clients and revenues, and the capacity to innovate with social practices that engage and lift clients or customers. Take, for example, that charter schools often suffer from high teacher turnover, physicians complain of diminishing time with patients, and the failure rate of start-up firms in the electronics field remains high.
- First-wave decentralists speak little about *how* detaching from bureaucracy or centralized authority will shape higher quality services, improve practices

inside, or equalize the uneven distribution of capital available to power decentering firms. These theoretical linkages remain mysterious and largely unspecified, yet they invite advances in organizational design now pressed by second-generation decentralists.[1]
- After decentralizing organizational authority, resources, and know-how—providing local staff greater discretion and responsibility—these practitioners often stick with implicit assumptions of how work gets done, institutionalized routines, and logics of action. Breaking free of hierarchy is a necessary but insufficient step in thawing out entrenched roles and tacitly expected ways of getting work done, engaging clients.

Consider these claims as working hypotheses, inferences in progress as our empirical knowledge continues to grow within and across differing sectors. We will see how second-wave decentralists reflect on what their elders have learned, recognizing that breaking free of hierarchy or embracing raw market competition in wide-eyed fashion has yielded a muddy mix of effects on the ground. Taking stock of the evidence—on *whether* and if so, *how* decentralized organizing has worked for clients or practitioners—informs a more durable social architecture and points to human-scale relations that might better engage and lift clients inside.

Decentralizing Bland and Bureaucratic School Systems

The front page headline in the *New York Times* sank the spirits of eager decentralists in the summer of 2004: "Charter Schools Trail in Results, U.S. Data Reveals."[2] Well into the second decade of radically localizing who and how schools were run—bankrolled by taxpayers—the news sounded rather dismal. "The first national comparison of test scores among children in charter schools and regular public schools shows that charter school students often do worse than comparable students in public schools," wrote *Times* reporter Diana Jean Schemo. This based on a one-shot look at the performance of about 3,400 students attending one of 150 charter schools, participating for the first time in federal testing.

By the mid-1990s President Clinton had decided to support and shift federal largesse to local charter schools—one emblem of how he and Vice President Gore aimed to "reinvent government" and move Democrats toward the political center. Gore's management guru, David Osborne, boldly claimed in 1999, "Those who invented charter schools . . . want to improve all 88,000 public schools in the country, [and] empirical studies have demonstrated, indeed, competition works just as reformers predicted." Similar optimism rang out in Wisconsin governor Tommy Thompson's 2001 state-of-the-state address, alleging that, "Nowhere in America does a parent have more choices than in Milwaukee . . . and it's making all the difference."[3] President George W. Bush would trumpet how charter schools offered market competition to poke a bland and bureaucratic school system, requiring that perennially lifeless schools be handed over to charter companies under his No Child Left Behind Act signed in 2002.

Over 6,100 of these human-scale schools would sprout by 2013—publicly financed yet run by site principals and teacher-leaders—serving 2.3 million students nationwide.[4] But this early assessment showed that just one-quarter of fourth graders attending charter schools were proficient in reading and math, compared with almost one-third of their peers enrolled in regular schools.[5] "A little more tough love is needed for these schools," said Checker Finn, a high official in the first Bush administration. Bemoaning the failure of naive deregulation—the loss of an organizational center to hold local units accountable—Finn told the *Times*, "Someone needs to be watching over their shoulders."

Yes, researchers inside one of the nation's two teachers' unions had conducted this first empirical study. Yes, an important scientific debate ensued over how to statistically take into account the confounding, prior effects of children's family background.[6] Yes, the charter lobby purchased a full-page ad in the *Times* eight days later, sporting testimonials from notable scholars attacking the study. Still, when the official Department of Education analysis emerged two years later in 2006, the findings remained quite similar. This second research team carried out more careful estimates of the benefit of attending a charter school. They showed lower performance of fourth graders enrolled in charter schools nationwide, and no discernible advantage for eighth graders.[7] Had this popular movement to blow up the central regulation of public schools, spawning a variety of human-scale counterparts, proved to be all for naught?

Do Charter Schools Lift Students?

National studies in more recent years generally confirm this original finding: the average student attending a decentralized charter school at best just slightly outperforms his or her peer attending a traditional public school. Yet local studies reveal more promising benefits of charter schools under certain organizational conditions, drawing on stronger data and more rigorous analytic methods. Only a vague understanding of these contextual features has come into empirical focus, including the local economic, demographic, and policy environs that condition the efficacy of charter schools. But the flurry of recent scholarship is getting us closer to the questions of *whether*, and through what *organizational mechanisms*, the decentralizing of school management pays off for students and teachers alike.

Margaret Raymond, a Stanford University economist, ambitiously tracks students moving through charter schools in many states. She estimates achievement effects for these charter pupils relative to comparable peers attending traditional public schools, net the prior influences of family background. Raymond initially collected data on 1.7 million students attending 2,400 charter schools situated in fifteen states and the District of Columbia, accounting for 70 percent of the nation's students that attend charter schools. She reported in a 2009 report that charter attendees failed to outperform their regular-school peers, actually falling behind on average when attending a typical charter high school.[8]

Yet certain types of charter schools and those situated in certain regions did show notable gains for kids, especially those from poor families. Now the plot thickened and moved the debate beyond the summative question, does the radical decentralization of schools work, yes or no? Secondary questions—soon pressed by second-wave descendants in education and neighboring sectors—began to emerge. What distinguished effective from pallid charter schools? Did central agencies—either school districts or charter management organizations (CMOs)—play key roles in learning about their clients, sharpening ethical principles, or advancing more effective practices on the frontlines, inside classrooms?

Scholars are just beginning to delve into how local conditions matter, offering the rich or depleted soil in which charter schools take root. Ron Zimmer and colleagues at the RAND Corporation in Santa Monica tracked several thousand charter students in a handful of California cities. They found no average differences in achievement levels between charter school pupils and peers who remained behind in traditional public schools. But Zimmer dug deeper to compare spending levels and the cost of instruction, finding that California charter schools were producing the same results at significantly lower costs, due in part to reliance on younger, less costly teachers. So from a policy standpoint the benefit-cost ratio for investing in charter schools was discernibly stronger.[9]

Encouraging findings also emerged from a 2009 study that tracked students whose parents had applied to one of New York City's growing count of charter schools, at least those that were unable to admit all comers and maintained waiting lists. Economist Caroline Hoxby, along with colleagues Sonali Murarka and Jenny Kang, tracked the performance of kids who won a seat through a random lottery (required by law), comparing them with lottery losers, following about 37,000 students over six years. Most of the city's charter schools, forty-two of forty-seven, were oversubscribed, although the length of waiting lists varied. This elegant design created a near-experimental situation, minimizing worries that charters were "creaming off" students with parents who were more committed to education, even within low-income communities.

Two weaknesses marked this otherwise upbeat study. First, findings can only be generalized to savvy parents who worked the education market and applied to a charter school.[10] And second, the scholars' took into account baseline test scores after, rather than before, charter lotteries determined who won admission after grade four and which students remained in a traditional public school.[11] With those cautions in mind, Hoxby's team found significant, at times moderate, differences in the growth curves of charter students, compared with peers attending a regular public school. The magnitude of these benefits is notable, equal to lengthening the school year by about one month. Charter attendees in grades three to eight enjoyed stronger gains; the majority of charter students in the New York context were of African American heritage. The investigators detailed how achievement benefits varied dramatically among different charter schools—opening up the question of how funding levels, organizational features, or social relations inside charter schools explain their widely varying effects.

Modest yet discernible benefits for charter students in Los Angeles have been estimated by Raymond's team as well during the 2010 to 2012 period.[12] The first generation of charter schools in L.A. served to further stratify children along lines of race and class, and small "mom-and-pop" charters versus those created from existing public schools ("conversion charters"). And no detectable learning advantages could be detected for charter students over the 2002–08 period, according to my research with Luke Dauter and Doug Lauen.[13]

But Raymond's more recent data, stemming from an expanding set of charters in L.A., revealed that Latino pupils from poor families may enjoy the strongest benefits, relative to comparable peers in traditional public schools (one-sixth of a standard deviation in math scores). This is a notable advantage, equaling the benefit of dramatically lowering class size for poor children. Los Angeles sports more charter schools than any other district in the nation, serving one-seventh of all students in public schools. Charters yielded no achievement advantage for white students. Schools run by charter management organizations (CMOs) outperformed unaffiliated mom-and-pop charters. Raymond failed to control on children's achievement level prior to switching into a charter school, perhaps upwardly biasing achievement benefit. This more conservative technique would thoroughly control for unobserved confounding factors (for example, whether parents nudge children to complete their homework, or watch less television) before they enter the charter school treatment.

Encouraging results also appear for charter students in Boston and San Diego, and particular charter school companies, such as the Knowledge Is Power Program (KIPP). Mathematica Policy Research conducted a careful evaluation that revealed impressive gains for KIPP students, gaining about 1.2 years of schooling for each year attended by a matched comparison group of children from low-income families attending traditional public schools.[14] Still, the KIPP school day runs from 7:30 to 5:00 and often includes Saturday classes. About one-third of the firm's funding has come from private foundations and other nonpublic sources.[15]

So while local studies and evaluations of particular kinds of decentralized schools demonstrate promising results, it's not clear what can be generalized to the average charter school across the wildly mixed market of these small-scale institutions. It does appear that when mayors or civic leaders cap the number of allowable charters and nurture them carefully—cultivating these gardens of blossoming schools—stronger effects on learning can be observed. This includes evidence from New York City's wider shift to small high schools, beyond charters.[16] But this requires unrelenting oversight and greater public investment, rather than assuming that market competition alone will raise all boats. There's no evidence that relying on liberalized parental demand and market dynamics alone lifts students in the absence of determined efforts to raise organizational quality.

Raymond's research team continues to track the performance of charter schools across a growing count of states. She reports in a 2013 paper—not yet peer reviewed—that achievement gains enjoyed by charter students are inching upward. The policy conditions, including how lightly regulated markets of charters are culling lousy schools, remain unknown. But by tracking students over time in twenty-six states, Raymond found that charter students gained the equivalent of eight days of instruction in reading or English language arts, on average, relative to peers attending traditional public schools.[17]

Just one-fourth of Raymond's school sample yielded learning gains that were significantly higher than regular-school peers; three-quarters of the charter schools displayed no advantage or lower performance than nearby traditional schools. And mean achievement differences between charter students and peers in traditional public schools remained quite small.[18] Raymond did control for baseline test scores, which accounts for some confounding effects.

But she failed to focus on students switching into charters and to control on their "pretreatment" achievement levels. These concerns illustrate how methodological complexities must be considered as we discern the comparative advantages of decentralized organizations, carried out in a politically charged environment.

That said, market competition may play a role: the rising average performance of charter students was tied to states closing down about one-tenth of their charter schools between 2009 and 2013, schools that performed at discernibly lower levels, compared with those charters still operating.

Diversifying Populations of Decentralized Schools

We have gone deep into the evidence on radically decentralized schools. Yet charters now operate within a diversifying population of alternative schools in many metropolitan areas, including magnet programs, so-called career academies, and small high schools. This prompts the question of whether the driving force of charter expansion spurs positive spillover effects, as the decentralized model and dynamics within lightly regulated markets now press traditional public schools to do better. It assumes that competition either moves practitioners to work harder, keeping their nose closer to the grindstone, or that fresh resources will spark innovative pedagogies and organizational features, such as a longer school day. It also assumes that, newly detached from central bureaucracy, charter schools will allocate resources more efficiently and reduce operating costs, as when they rely on twenty-somethings to build their teaching staff.

But evidence is quite uneven on such positive externalities. Sound methods are slippery to apply, given that a nonrandom array of parents are more likely to select charter schools compared with those who lack the time, knowledge, or wherewithal to work this education marketplace. Indeed, the theory of action emphasizes that higher quality charters will magnetically pull kids out of neighboring public schools, likely leaving behind less motivated kids and families. So charters may operate as yet another sorting mechanism and not necessarily raise kids' learning curves through richer practices.

Julian Betts, an economist at the University of California, San Diego, examined the competitive effects of charter schools on student performance in traditional schools, concluding that district officials or principals do respond to emerging competition, but their adaptations at best lead to modest achievement gains.[19] Survey results suggest that neither charter nor regular school principals have the time or inclination to share innovative practices. And it's not clear that charter leaders actually know empirically what features of their organizations or teachers pay off, relative to conventional peers. Market theorists often ignore such institutional stickiness. Skeptical findings emerged from New York City, where economists Sean Corcoran and Henry Levin found—under liberalizing parent choice—that low-income parents tended to select schools with students achieving at higher levels than their child's current school. But better-off families push for entry to the most selective schools, squeezing out access to many schools to which poorer parents aspired.[20]

We don't really understand why the benefits (or disadvantages) stemming from charter schools vary so dramatically across local conditions, across cities and states. We do know that prior features of a region's economic and policy environment serve to cultivate or starve the spread of decentered organizations. Linda Renzulli, a University of Georgia sociologist, found that communities with greater counts of private schools tend to generate more applications to open charter schools.[21] And demand for new charters runs stronger in bigger school districts, along with those employing higher counts of administrators. This suggests that mixed markets do spur a wider array of schools, as wealthier parents help spark wider demand, and the bureaucratization of urban schools kindles interest in options among parents, rich and poor.

Ron Zimmer, after moving to Vanderbilt University, corralled achievement records for students attending charter schools across seven cities or states. His team hoped to identify local conditions that mediate the varying effects that children experience in a charter school.[22] For example, charter effects may be weaker in states that have few entry barriers or regulatory protections, or fail to invest in quality improvement. Arizona has long been known as the wild west of charter schools: state officials embrace new charter schools with almost no entry barriers, assuming that market competition will separate the chaff from the wheat. Some states allow private schools to convert to charter status; many districts liberally allow existing public schools to convert into a charter organization, free of state rules and labor contracts. Zimmer's own review found that charter effects, while nil overall when averaged across the five states, did vary for specific states and grade levels. This between-state variability suggests differing organizational conditions, either in terms of which kids enter charters or how internal practices differentially lift students or fail to do so.

A colorful spectrum of schools is coming to populate the education field, prompted by the steady growth of charter and similarly decentralized schools. An intriguing historical analysis conducted by Richard Buddin—published by the conservative Cato Institute—details how charter schools are sucking students out of private and Catholic schools. Tracking local enrollments between 2000 and 2008, Buddin found that one-third of charter elementary schools pulled children from private schools in urban centers. This share equaled one-sixth of total enrollment in charter high schools nationwide.[23] Such costly competition among alternative schools hits parochial schools particularly hard, punctuated by the Catholic diocese's decision in Washington, DC to shut down most of their schools. Even modest tuitions placed them in a losing position relative to free and publicly funded charter schools.

Research into early experiments with school vouchers yielded less encouraging results, compared with the locally conditioned benefits of charter schools. Even when promarket scholars have tracked students over time in Milwaukee and Washington, DC, the results have been tepid at best. As Patrick Wolf, a disciple of Harvard University's voucher enthusiast, Paul Peterson, summarized for Milwaukee, "At this point the voucher students are showing average rates of achievement gains similar to their public school peers."[24] Wolf's parallel evaluation of the DC voucher experiment yielded more upbeat results. Kids sent to Catholic or other private schools after their parents won a voucher in the DC lottery (creating a quasi-experiment) showed small, statistically insignificant gains. More hopeful, voucher participants were 24 percent more likely to graduate from high school, compared with peers whose parents had applied but not won a voucher. But remember that school options in DC are shrinking as charter schools cannibalize children who once attended parochial schools.

After taking stock of this past decade of empirical results, Fred Hess, a seasoned policy analyst at the American Enterprise Institute, accented a huge lesson for first-generation decentralists. "Only by stepping back from the notion that 'choice' itself is a panacea, and instead embracing the contingent nature of choice's impact, can we make sense of when and why choice 'works.'"[25] That is, all the political bloodletting over parental choice, vouchers, and charter schools—going back to the 1970s—did yield remarkable governance reforms in terms of who runs schools, how they are financed, and the power of local principals to hire strong teachers and fire lousy ones. At times, these human-scale and largely deregulated schools have devised inventive pedagogies and lifted children's learning curves.

Still, for all this policy talk and contention, the surface-level governance change often fails to yield a deeper conversation over how relationships and expectations change inside the guts of these local organizations, whether students or teachers become more energized, more adept at engaging their clients. First-wave decentralists in the education field went into battle to secede from a bureaucratic center and break free of union rules, rebels with a cause.

But their rallying cry focused on becoming liberated from hierarchy, escaping into competitive markets. Voucher advocates rushed to create a textbook rendition of pure markets, which never came to pass. Yet less discussed was how a diversifying rainbow of schools would reshape pedagogy and social relations deep inside. These enthusiasts seemed to argue, if we could just tear down the Berlin Wall, educational nirvana, just like market liberalism, would naturally flourish. In retrospect this seems so naive, a lesson not lost on the emergent second generation of decentralists.

Next, let's turn to the neighboring sector of health care, where a less regulated guild of physicians once wielded plenty of professional clout, compared with teachers and the bureaucratic governance of schools. But the medical guild would cede considerable authority and regulatory power to government under the Great Society. The pendulum then shifted back toward decentralizing innovations, like the advent of health maintenance organizations (HMOs), along with market competition and, of late, the consolidation of physicians and small practices into bigger firms, spurred by the Obama administration's press for greater efficiency. Still, the steady drift from defining medicine as managing illness to preventing disease requires a shift in human-scale relationships locally, tackling the question of how to get patients to alter their behavior, their everyday lifestyles. So what's being learned in this sector when it comes to decentering medical practices—couched in a mix of central regulation of costs with nudging physicians and patients to focus on prevention? This requires human-scale change inside clinics, hospitals, and nursing homes—innovative behavior and fresh norms that can't simply be legislated and controlled from above.

Guilds, Markets, and Intimate Practice—Who Runs Health Care?

Faced with escalating costs and uneven quality, the Reagan White House administered a stiff dose of market dynamics to the health care field in the early 1980s. This spurred the spread of HMOs—aiming to contain costs through competition among these local firms, and by shifting away from expensive specialists and diagnostic testing, moving toward primary and preventive care. Rather than spending more on treating disease, *managed care* promised to lower the incidence of preventable maladies that stem from smoking, obesity, or the lack of exercise. And with federal stimulation of HMOs in local regions, along with consolidating small medical groups, lively price competition was to ensue.

But this would require shifting age-old routines in local clinics and hospitals, and nudging patients to break unhealthy habits and alter their own behavior. This insinuated the traditional authority of physicians, whose discretion and everyday practices became scrutinized by government regulators and fellow medical workers who filled novel roles, including nurse practitioners, case managers, and business directors. This shift also sparked new lines of organizational research inside local clinics and hospital settings, briefly reviewed below and detailed in chapter 3, as we delve into one healthcare company that aggressively reorders authority and know-how inside local clinics while rethinking the center.

The Kaiser Industrial Company pioneered with managed care in 1945, stemming from a makeshift insurance pool for the firm's construction workers, eventually moving into well-off suburbs. HMOs like Kaiser devised a decentralizing alternative to hospital-based networks of physicians, bureaucratic institutions that by the 1970s displayed variable quality, including high infection and low mortality rates. HMOs—eventually including the Mayo Clinic, Geisinger Health System in Pennsylvania, and university-based companies—promised higher quality at lower costs, achieving economies of scale that were not possible for small clusters of physicians in private practice. These larger and regionally based clinics began to emphasize regular check-ups and preventive measures (for example, mammograms, colonoscopies, information about proper nutrition). This shift to a localized and proactive strategy could reduce the incidence of chronic disease, minimize expensive testing downstream, and reduce the aggregate cost of high-paid specialists. And these largely decentralized firms, now playing in competitive fields, would certainly face central regulation over high-cost procedures, yet would otherwise innovate locally to lift quality, responsiveness to patients, and efficiency.

A Surgical Center That Shifts Local Behavior?

This remarkable change in organizational strategy—emerging with greater force in the 1980s—has been further legitimated and pressed forcefully within President Obama's health-care reforms, approved by Congress in 2010. Several institutional shifts resemble the policy frame that charter school advocates deployed. Customers would enjoy liberalized choice among a diversifying range of health-care firms, provided that affordable health insurance became available. As this (regulated) market became populated by a variety of clinics, HMOs, physician groups, and hospital-based plans—and potential customers gained purchasing power—more robust competition would raise quality, while containing the cost burden shouldered by patients, employers, and government. These decentralized and market-sensitive firms would seek to innovate and be rewarded when their medical services became more responsive to clients, offering higher quality care.

Early health reforms also prompted rethinking the role performed by the institutional center: no longer running much of anything, but instead guiding and incentivizing novel practices inside nonprofit and for-profit firms that engage clients on the ground. High-cost diagnostic procedures and access to specialists have come to be centrally rationed, either by government or insurance companies. But the daily work of physicians and allied clinical staff remains largely decentralized—now aiming to motivate healthier lives by patients, to change their habits and normative behavior. How regulatory mechanisms or market incentives conspire to alter the social architecture of local clinics remains quite hazy in this overall theory of organizational reform. Although the new decentralists in the health-care field are connecting these dots, as we detail in chapter 3.

The initial steps taken by the Reagan administration certainly resonated with the ideals of first-wave decentralists: advancing price competition among HMOs, pressing accountability and performance benchmarks from the center, even awarding Medicare patients a portable voucher to encourage voting with one's feet. At the same time, federal health-care costs had doubled every five years since the 1960s. So price controls, centrally enforced by Washington's regulatory apparatus and its sizeable purchasing power, when negotiating drug prices for example, became Reagan's lasting legacy. Higher deductibles and patient copays, ratcheting-up private costs, would be centrally pressed as well.

Reagan's health-care advisors pushed for salary caps for hospital-based physicians and expensive specialists, from surgeons to oncologists. While politically tough to advance, these jousts with the medical guild proved consistent with the efforts of first-wave decentralists in other sectors: encourage organizational diversity and local competition, while constraining and disassembling big and cumbersome institutions, like hospitals, the once-modern bureaucratic form that had come to suffer from high costs and erratic performance.[26]

Another lesson from the Reagan era for students of organizations was that a sector's history matters. The path blazed for decentralizing authority, resources, and know-how on treatment options down to local practitioners would be conditioned by the field's institutional origins. Medical care had long been delivered by physicians who worked alone or in small private practices, not unlike the shoe repair shop or butcher shop down the street, although grounded in a bit more technical knowledge. This resulted in a strong occupational guild reinforced by the high status of physicians.

But it also constrained the ability of health-care companies to experiment with new job roles inside clinics, or to shift deep-seated arrangements of power and expertise. The widening use of nurse practitioners and medical case managers for patients with chronic disease offer encouraging cases of organizational reform. Still, the extent to which decentralizing reforms actually alter the everyday practices of physicians remains conditioned by the guild's historical norms and tacit expectations for how clinical work is carried out. Thawing out and shifting such tacit and deep-seated *institutional logics*, as Stanford University sociologist W. Richard Scott labeled them, requires a decisive surgical center and nudging change in social relations among local practitioners.[27]

How to Shift Local Norms and Everyday Behavior

Fast-forward to a generation later—as Barack Obama comes into office in 2009—health-care costs are still spiraling out of control and discernible gains in quality or patient outcomes remain difficult to detect. Chronic conditions have become more concentrated in poor populations, hardly an uplifting sign of progress. Spending on health care by government and families equaled 4 percent of GDP in 1950. By 2009 the health sector consumed 17 percent of the nation's annual economic output, compared with just 9 percent of GDP in west Europe.[28] While Americans spend two times more per capita on health care than does Germany, our rate of preventable deaths is 23 percent greater.[29]

Today, the bulk of health-care costs stems from a small share of chronically ill patients—whose conditions are preventable and could be eased, if their behavior proved malleable. Two-fifths of all Medicare spending goes to care for the most costly 5 percent of all patients. The most expensive one-quarter of Medicare beneficiaries account for 85 percent of all public spending. One-fifth of Medicare spending aids the elderly during the final two months of life.[30] Health scholars know that local hospice organizations could lower costs, even offer a more humane way to end one's life.

Centralized rules and cost controls will certainly persist as contemporary reforms sink in. One lesson from health care is that a strategic, less clumsy center can realign incentives and norms via reimbursement strategies, funding for organizational innovations, and knowledge development. The reform of reimbursements, for instance, could nudge health-care companies to ramp up prevention strategies and discourage high-cost procedures by surgeons and specialists, as pioneered during the Reagan era.

Still, regulatory tools and monetary incentives won't likely prod patients to adjust their diets or get off the couch and go for a vigorous walk. Nor can hierarchies simply mandate novel practices that would motivate physicians or meaningfully engage patients. So the social-organizational challenge becomes how the center and medical staff on the ground can devise efficacious practices or novel clinical roles that successfully move patient knowledge and behavior. When prevention fails, few would withhold expensive specialists or diagnostic technologies to prolong life. Triage through faceless regulation remains an ugly prospect. So we are back to how health-care firms can motivate shifts in patient behavior and how they can help to manage chronic disease through novel practices in local clinics. It's this frontier that second-wave decentralists now explore.

Negotiating these crosscurrents, President Obama and a Democratic Congress approved in 2010 the most ambitious set of organizational reforms ever attempted. Mr. Obama—building from Mr. Reagan's blend of central regulation and local market mechanisms—also pressed various forms of decentralized action, interwoven with engineered incentives, aiming to alter the behavior of doctors and patients alike. First, Mr. Obama did not award any specific right to adequate health care, the typical starting point in Europe, justifying state-run medical care. Instead, the Obama reforms took the market of health insurers as a given, and then guaranteed certain protections to patients. The new stricture essentially tells insurance companies that they cannot deny coverage for individuals based on a prior condition; poor families are guaranteed coverage if they cannot afford to pay. So-called Obamacare creates a set of "shared responsibilities," referring primarily to "the obligation of individuals and employers to pay for insurance," as Paul Starr emphasizes.[31] This policy veteran notes that Mr. Obama had to emphasize politically how his reforms would play within a field of market dynamics, and retain frontline flexibility for the guild of physicians, rather than advance a single-payer or government-run agency, in order to gain sufficient political traction.

Second, within America's mixed market of health-care providers, Obama's policy designers rekindled faith in monetary incentives to move the system away from treating disease to preventing illness. We take you inside one inventive health-care firm in chapter 3, detailing decentralizing innovations that mark the logic of second-wave decentralists. They encourage new ways—inside local health clinics as one case in point—to induce patients with chronic and preventable ailments to change daily routines and lead healthier lives. "Changing behavior from the ground up," is how *Washington Post* health writer Alec MacGillis put it.[32]

Centrally allocated incentives, viscerally felt by local practitioners, offer the policy lever of choice, according to the architects of the Affordable Care

Act. Insurance companies are now allowed to raise premiums on smokers by as much as 50 percent above average health care bills. Employers gain tax advantages by enrolling their staff in wellness and disease prevention programs. Insurance companies must reimburse—and some health-care firms award bonuses to doctors who thoroughly cover—a list of preventive actions taken by physician and patient, such as providing immunizations on schedule and ensuring that mammograms are taken at regular intervals. Information must regularly be provided on exercise, smoking cessation, and nutrition.

It's a question on which second-wave decentralists typically obsess: how to engage clients, scaffolding up from their daily scripts and routines, while bumping their behavior in positive directions. The Geisinger Health System, an inventive firm spread across the eastern half of Pennsylvania, presses a blend of incentives from above and intensive attention to patients below to motivate healthier lifestyles. Geisinger's organizational architects work at the confluence of two streams of decentralized action—incentives and human-scale engagement with clients—to improve health outcomes. Patients learn how to feasibly lower the risk of chronic disease or manage it with the help of kith and kin when prevention fails.

Medical research lags behind studies inside schools when it comes to gauging the benefits of decentralized innovations. Our in-depth look at one health-care company in chapter 3 will delineate these organizational mechanisms and describe how clinic-level reforms interact with selective rule setting at the firm's center. And we discuss encouraging empirical findings from this and similarly inventive health-care firms. More generally, we know that costs range lower and preventive practices have grown stronger within decentered HMOs, compared with the pre-1980s hospital-based system—at least among regional firms, like Kaiser and Geisinger, which offer primary care via local clinics and face competition for patients and downward price pressure from employers within mixed markets.

But much remains to be learned on how health-care firms distribute authority, resources, and expertise within local clinics (and between the center and local units). We don't yet know how progressive firms are shifting practices toward prevention and the effects on the healthier behavior of patients with chronic conditions. Nor do we know empirically whether new roles inside clinics—including nurse practitioners, case managers, or case review teams—discernibly lift patient outcomes or lower costs. Much of the policy reform discourse remains focused on central mechanisms, including how to regulate specialists or expensive procedures, and how to drive down the cost of drugs. Important as these issues remain, they distract from understanding the decentered life of local clinics and the extent to which normative practices and deep-seated patient behaviors persist, or whether they display inventive drifts in healthier directions.

Decentralizing High-Tech Firms? Mixed Results in the Private Sector

The private sector by the late 1970s was vigorously pursuing Decentralization 1.0. The oil crisis, triggered by OPEC's manipulation of supply, signaled new global uncertainties. America's corporate titans were no longer in charge. The rising Japanese economy offered sharp competition, along with rising manufacturing capacity across East Asia. Our nation's manufacturers faced the music on vast gaps in wage rates and began to move production facilities and jobs south to Mexico and far to the East. Hoping to spark innovation through greater competition, Washington would push to deregulate certain industries, such as breaking up the AT&T monopoly into "baby Bells," sparking technological innovation and robust growth of cell phone retailers. Less successful over time: the deregulation of housing finance and related pockets of Wall Street.[33]

Ideas matter in the private sector as well, especially when considering alternative ways to organize design or production activities, trade or distribution. A succession of management gurus, also born of the 1970s, began to raise tough questions about the sluggish, bureaucratic centers of major corporations. The first signs of moving manufacturing offshore paralleled the rise of high-technology firms onshore—burgeoning first in Silicon Valley (when fruit trees still dotted this South Bay region), then along Route 128 in Massachusetts. Postindustrial realities were quietly taking root across the nation's economy, sparking a hopeful focus on innovation, flatter ways of coordinating work, and new forms of labor and social relations inside firms. Sandal-clad software designers came to spend more time laboring in the hip cafés of Palo Alto and Mountain View, Google's suburban home, than in their official offices.

High-tech enterprise hosted the leading edge of organizational reform, including how decentralized flexibility and creativity might become interdependent with a lean, more inspiring and resourceful center. We detail in our case studies how this fundamental faith in local discretion—to spur inventive means of acing centrally set performance goals—took hold in the finance and service industries as well. The high-tech "industry" is but one sector that's designed ands fueled vast markets filled with postindustrial products and human services.

Yes, makers of cell phones and sleek tablets must coordinate industrial-like production in societies that retain low wages and often-miserable working conditions. But this was not the form of labor or "production" that was coming to characterize work in our stateside economy. So contemporary management scholars and popular writers began to talk of how to decentralize supply chains, as design and production firms spread around the globe, along with the decentering of authority spurred by information technologies.[34] Postindustrial corporate leaders now speak of managing interdependence with local units or motivating and interweaving widely dispersed work teams.[35]

Is Small Beautiful for Big Blue?

IBM brought its first personal computer to market in 1981. This massive and largely centralized firm had essentially created the field of computer science, after its pioneering technology was devised and used by the military during World War II. By 1964 IBM was marketing huge mainframe computers of unprecedented speed and capacity. This growing company was vertically integrated, once thought to eliminate all uncertainties. IBM's subunits produced all the core components of their System 360 computer, including its operating system, peripherals, software applications, and even the keyboards and decks of punch cards, rapidly fed through the machine, like a poker dealer on speed. IBM's annual sales rose to $11 billion in 1973. The antitrust division of the Department of Justice even filed suit, claiming that IBM had come to unfairly dominate the blossoming field of computing.

But excessive centralization and over confidence would come to haunt Big Blue.

At first IBM enjoyed the same robust success in the personal computer (PC) field, even though Apple had pioneered the earliest small computer, tethered to that cute mouse. Still, IBM overtook Apple in 1985, winning 41 percent of market share. Then, departing from a centrally coordinated history, IBM aimed to capture more customers by segmenting its organizational structure, outsourcing innovation and production of silicon chips, software, and hardware peripherals to hundreds of firms spread about the globe. IBM—unlike Apple—never considered operating its own retail stores, here too relying on a dispersed range of retailers to market its array of PC models.

Most telling for students of decentralization, the technological innovators on which IBM relied were free agents—small and inventive design or software start-ups who readily sold their rapidly evolving tools to IBM's competitors, to Dell, Compaq, and Hewlett Packard (HP). By 1995 IBM's market share had collapsed to just 7 percent of all PCs sold worldwide.[36]

Apple and Microsoft, in sharp contrast, were on the rise, driven by a flatter, more innovative organizational structure, energized by looser coordination of creative teams and disheveled programmers that would yield user-friendly tools. Similarly, UCLA management professor William Ouchi and others celebrated the inventive success of task groups at the grass roots, helping to explain the rise of the Japanese corporation. Reform advocates writing in *Business Week* and the *Harvard Business Review* were all aflutter over "Theory Z" and "tight-loose management"—urging managers to shape a leaner center that would set performance targets, then loosen the reins on local units to inventively and efficiently perform against the centrally monitored benchmarks.[37] This sleek organizational model would be imported into government by the 1990s, as policy activists set accountability and quality targets centrally, then deregulated how local schools or HMOs would accomplish these objectives. One article from the Sloan School of Management talked of "corporate disintegration" and the likelihood of "more markets and less hierarchy."[38]

First-generation decentralists—especially in high-tech and other innovative industries—remain popular yet controversial in the corporate world. They have spawned a bevy of case studies, like when Carly Fiorina grasped the helm of HP, soon pushing to sell out to Compaq. Remaining members of David Packard's family accused her of destroying the "HP way," a deep culture weaving strong cohesion without stiff centralization, which had long inspired loyalty to and innovation within the firm, a stone's throw from Stanford University.[39] Still, hard-core evidence remains thin in business literature on the extent to which decentralized organizing—often paired with rethinking how central managers orchestrate, not dictate—advances innovation, staff motivation, or profitability.

How Decentralized Organizing Works

We have returned to the pivotal question of *how* decentralization works, *how* locally centered forms of social organization motivate and engage. Thomas Malone, MIT management scholar and student of decentralization, argues that delegated control of design or production units can yield three benefits to "lumbering giants." This includes sparking stronger local motivation and creativity, allowing "many minds to work simultaneously on the same problem," and accommodating flexibility sought by local operations.[40] Malone also emphasizes contingencies: whether to decentralize authority and know-how depends on what your firm is producing and for what kinds of work activities is local innovation truly desirable? Professional services firms, such as code writers, architects, and lawyers, often operate in decentralized fashion—resembling public firms, like schools or health clinics, where specialists often tailor their work to the highly variable needs or preferences of their clients.

Even American manufacturers by the 1980s were rejecting bureaucratically enforced, command-and-control production. Some were moving semiskilled production lines overseas, seeking cheaper labor, while retaining control of design and capital centrally. Even cosmetically hip Apple Computer began to move its manufacturing wing to a vast network of contractors, largely based overseas. Apple employs about 43,000 managerial and retail workers inside the United States. But its various products—iPhones, iPads, and the rest—are engineered and assembled by over 700,000 workers employed mostly in Asia. When President Obama asked Steve Jobs in 2011, during a private session in Silicon Valley, why the iPhone can't be made in America, Jobs bluntly told the president, "Those jobs aren't coming back."[41]

Tangible corporate reform took on a new life of popular metaphor as well. The fused notions of leaner management, crisp "production goals," along with inventive and decoupled networks of local shops came to hold great political appeal among centrist reformers and government leaders who became more critical of a moribund state bureaucracy. I joined a delightful meeting in 1974, as a rookie legislative aide, between a long-haired youngster named Steve Jobs and a long-winded California governor, Jerry Brown, each pitching government support of innovative technologies (it turned out that high tech didn't really require public subsidies). Jobs would go on to fuse "the '70s-era West Coast cultures," in Janet Maslin's words, "of music, microchips, meditation and extreme physical bravado into an ethos of exquisite simplicity."[42] Brown, the perennial California politician, talked of how the decentering, offbeat computer designers could teach top-down managers of public bureaucracies a thing or two. It was time to reduce our expectations of central government.

Still, the far-flung outsourcing of manufacturing or globally dispersed makers of electronic components may not decenter design choices or the coordination of production. After his extensive study of outsourcing by Silicon Valley and Italian apparel manufactures, sociologist Bennett Harrison concluded that big corporations still harmonize production overseas and sustain low wages and uneven working conditions, what he dubbed, "concentration without centralization."[43] The Intel's and Apple's, the garment wholesalers in New York and Milan, each capitalize design innovations and efficient production via contractors around the globe. Their headquarters still coordinate manufacturing, not by tethering workers under one roof, but through time-sensitive output schedules that synchronize a web of production partners. And it's the corporate center that reaps impressive profits, the capital accumulation that first benefits stateside staff then gets plowed back into the firm. Decentralization may stir a growing middle class, as wages ratchet up around the globe, but concentration of capital persists otherwise, unabated.

Big Lessons from Organizing Small

What has been learned from initial and sizeable experiments in decentering institutions, deconstructing the industrial hierarchy? How does decentralized organizing adapt to the crafting of differing products or services? How does the new localism come to serve or undercut an organization's center—whether advancing profits or public aims, often laboring within the expansive territory that now lies in between? What lessons do second-generation decentralists take away from their first-wave ancestors?

First, the intertwined tenets of first-wave decentralization—liberation from hierarchy and liberalized consumer choice—have proven to be necessary but insufficient conditions for motivating practitioners and lifting clients inside local organizations. Witness the mixed student achievement results from charter schools, now in the movement's third decade; the erratic quality and performance of HMOs; the inventive, yet at times exploitive, global networks of contractors and subcontractors. Yes, hierarchies have been razed and diversifying populations of organizations abound, be they publicly funded or privately capitalized. But overall results are mixed, and knowledge remains thin on how decentralized organizing works, or not.

First-generation reformers seem bogged down in that modern duality—setting hierarchies against markets, inevitably in conflict. This sticky postulate slows local organizing, like those adhesive traps to which the dainty feet of pests become inescapably fused. We have returned to Rousseau's old bargain as introduced in chapter 1, where central actors, eager to advance legitimacy and capital accumulation, hope to strike a deal with the reified individual. For the state it's the pitch that individual civil and property rights will be assured if the citizen buys into a secular, rationalized society that's come to be dominated by life inside institutions. For private firms, a relationship with the individual is codified through a labor contract, now enforced through economic incentives, to lift student performance or lower patient mortality rates. So the hierarchy becomes useful in rewarding the lone individual.

But the research in education and health care reveals that it's the subtle, more textured social relations and forms of cooperative work that engage and lift clients inside decentralized organizations. Neither factory-like hierarchy nor atomized market relations necessarily spur such motivating forms of social organization. In a sense, the most effective decentralists move beyond what sociologist Robert Wuthnow calls the "humanist agenda of emancipation." It's not simply command and control of routinized tasks or market exchange that nurtures social bonds between local practitioner and client.

Yet the policy debate—inside government, reform circles, and corporate headquarters—still flips between tightening the hierarchy's capacity to regulate behavior or "liberating" the individual to shop for better products or services in unfettered markets. Left out is the supply response and how a widening variety of organizations host more engaging social relations on the ground, or often fail to do so. This is the second lesson from recent research. First-wave decentralists—naively accepting of neoclassical economics—assumed that liberalized customer choice would spark the creation of diverse *and* effective organizations. But the supply response, no matter how legitimated and incentivized, remains uneven across differing postindustrial sectors of society. We know that parents often operate on thin information about the relative quality of schools, just as patients enter a nearby clinic based on convenience or the ease of tapping into one's health insurance. Expressed demand is often a blunt instrument for nurturing effective organizations on the ground.

A third lesson, an elusive mystery of sorts, is how the organization's center can induce behavioral change or engage clients on the ground. Neoliberal faith in markets and the decline of hierarchy will continue to spur incentives engineered from above. Promarket reformers urge portable vouchers in education, health care, and housing. Incentives blended with creative regulation encourage the growth of charter schools and HMOs. The Obama administration gave voice to the idea that merit pay be awarded to the single teacher—independent of school context—who boosts his or her pupils' test scores.

But accountability advocates who hark back to hierarchy (think, the once intrusive No Child Left Behind Act) and those eager "to get incentives right" miss a huge lesson from first-wave decentralization. Practitioners are motivated by peers, normative action, and efficacious tools of their trade—the social and technical glue that offers cohesion in particular local contexts. Central regulation or atomistic incentives alone do little to strengthen cooperative relationships locally, to help practitioners learn about and scaffold up from clients' own interests. When "the work is external to the worker . . . it is not part of his nature, he does not fulfill himself in his work," one reformer, Karl Marx, wrote a century and a half ago.[44]

A corollary is that the center is not necessarily the enemy of the local practitioner. First-wave decentralists still obsess on that pitched battle to secede from a constraining hierarchy. Yet we will see how second-wave decentralists do not necessarily view the center as a suffocating regime. Instead, central managers might craft a surgical operation that advances a motivating ethical mission, assembles public or private capital, and helps to shape tools and know-how that deepen the efficacy of local staff. Charter management organizations (CMOs), for instance, take on administrivia that preoccupies school principals in traditional schools, awarding them more time to look after teachers and pedagogy. Resourceful centers may select new staff who quickly comprehend the firm's mission and share an eagerness to engage clients. In short, the most colorful garden, when a thousand flowers do blossom, requires a caring gardener. How to shape a lean and enabling central unit is a question that helps to motivate second-wave decentralists.

The fourth lesson of early decentralization is that urban tribalism—be it defined along lines of race, class, or language—does not have to result from the local confluence of disassembled hierarchies and mixed markets. Sharp and segregating forms of new organizations do at times serve to privilege and protect certain classes. The move by gated communities to create their own charter schools is a distressing use of taxpayer dollars. The spread of state tax credits for affluent parents who buy their way into pricey private schools (just like vouchers) corrupts government's ethical core. Or, when low reimbursement rates set by government yield low-quality health care in public hospitals—while the affluent benefit from private, high-quality care—we again see the troubling vicissitudes of some mixed markets.

Yet many contemporary decentralists voice a cosmopolitan set of social ideals—aiming to devise inventive fields of organizations that celebrate America's blossoming diversity and the civic integration of these variegated tribes. Progressive charter schools attract a diverse array of kids and families, or take New York City's small high schools that do the same. Regional competition among HMOs to attract all kinds of families from nearby communities now weaves together a cosmopolitan bazaar of patients and practitioners. Meanwhile, coherent institutional centers—inside government and lightly regulated markets—retain the credibility to tax all and redistribute health care to the poor.

"Buy local." "Think globally, act locally." These aren't simply vacuous mottos of first-wave decentralists. They are spreading realities that stem from the ideological currents and macroeconomic forces detailed in chapter 1. These early activists have delivered a bountiful farmer's market, if you will, a rainbow of goods and human services that central hierarchies could never have crafted, forms of labor that the lone individual could never have simply traded. A panoply of organizations—nonprofits, clinics and schools, libraries and skateboarding arenas—all hosting human-scale work or expressions that act to thicken civil society, to bring diverse peoples into public spaces.

"Cosmopolitans suppose that all cultures have enough overlap in their vocabulary to begin a conversation," Kwame Anthony Appiah writes.[45] We are learning when and how decentralized organizing can sustain, or rule out, this cosmopolitan discourse.

The contemporary challenge is to ensure that local organizations actually deliver on their hopeful promises. To inform this long-term question we must learn how decentralizing firms actually work, and how second-wave decentralists are taking up these early lessons to animate their local work, to craft fresh forms of social cooperation. So let's next visit four decentralizing organizations in public and private realms that experiment in robust ways to advance these bold yet human-scale aims.

3

Organizing Health Care from the Ground Up

WITH MARY BERG

> My business, aside from the mere physical diagnosis, is to make a different sort of diagnosis concerning them as individuals. This comes perhaps to be the occupation of the physician . . . a lifetime of careful listening.
> —DR. WILLIAM CARLOS WILLIAMS, *The Practice*, 1932

Janet Tomcavage's tireless push to transform health care—one client at a time—goes back to her first patient as a nursing student in 1978. "She was diabetic, a bilateral amputee. She had such painful gangrene in her stumps, all she did was scream." Tomcavage couldn't stand it anymore so she simply quit. "I struggled with the heartbreak, the agony." She fled back home to a small corner of the Pocono Mountains, telling her dad that she just couldn't go on.

Luckily Tomcavage's father urged her to tough it out. He challenged her to be courageous, accepting of the suffering that accompanies medicine. "You have abundant energy," she recalls her dad saying. Tomcavage did finish nursing school. Patients across Pennsylvania might thank her father, not to mention fellow activists who now push to recast the ethics and local organization of health care. Tomcavage would spend the next two decades—mostly at Geisinger Health System—caring for diabetics, studying how prevention and lifestyle lowers risk, and how patients' own networks can spark healthy behavior.

Tomcavage radiates the warmth of a Sicilian Aunt Sophie rather than the top company executive that she is. Her dark curls and earth-colored eyes frame a reassuring smile. She currently serves as a senior manager on the insurance side of Geisinger, although she spends much of each week overseeing medical practices, traveling out to local clinics. It's her deep knowledge of chronic diseases gleaned from years of nursing that informs her grassroots strategies for advancing health and healing.

Speaking on the urgency of reshaping the organization of health care just months before winning congressional approval of his landmark bill in 2010, President Barack Obama said, "We have to ask why places like Geisinger in rural Pennsylvania . . . can offer high quality care at costs well below average.

We need to identify best practices across the country, learn from success, and replicate that success elsewhere."[1]

Tomcavage and her mostly female deputies—a dynamic team she calls "the ladies"—are reshaping how local staff engage patients across Geisinger's network of thirty-seven local clinics and three hospitals, stretching from the middle of the Poconos to Pennsylvania's eastern border. They began decentralizing via a two-pronged ethic of caring and cost containment. Quality is advanced through "treatment bundles" that guide local physicians' care of chronic or expensive patient conditions that are empirically linked to stronger outcomes. And Tomcavage's team is unrelenting in learning about these patients from data delivered by the center, along with local knowledge gleaned by new case managers stationed in each clinic, microsociologists of sorts who learn much about spouses or friends who lend a hand.

An unexpected irony surfaced as we visited and probed the far-flung Geisinger firm over a two-year period. New decentralists like Tomcavage demonstrate how a versatile yet surgically focused center defines core ethics and coaches local practitioners to think anew about their work. A share of these sacred commitments deals with various ways of getting to know what makes each client tick and who supports each patient. The core task of these new decentralists is to equip doctors and nurses to inquire about the patient's own motivations, then to host a local conversation about effective remedies. But it's from the lean central office in Danville, replete with Ikea-inspired decor, that Tomcavage's nimble team has adjusted the role of physicians across the hamlets of central Pennsylvania and made primary care economically viable.

From Guild to Regulated Care

Feisty independent physicians have long characterized the medical guild in America. But stiff doses of centralization mark the past half century of health-care reform, even the rationalization of everyday medical practice. Stern oversight of costs and allowable procedures surfaced soon after the creation of Medicare in 1965. One keystone of the Great Society, Medicare secured a basic floor of affordable care for the poor, elderly, and disabled. But it didn't take long for cost containment to follow on the heels of equity.

A regulatory overhaul in 1972 tightened how the federal government reimbursed doctors, clinics, and hospitals. The state's priority on equitable access began to slow the escalating costs of health care by micromanaging the work of physicians. Allied medical professionals had been paid for each remedy or "product" they delivered. Hospital-based treatment of pneumonia, for example, was billed each day at a set cost. This was before the rise of magical yet expensive diagnostic technologies, such as computerized tomography (CT) scans or magnetic resonance imaging (MRIs). Doctors could once indiscriminately order tests that were not as expensive, nor regulated closely by federal monitors.

This changed markedly in 1982 when two Yale scholars, Robert Fetters and John Thompson, working for the federal Health Care Financing Administration, devised a list of 467 products or diagnoses for which doctors or hospitals could bill. Each was pegged at a standard price within each diagnosis related group (DRG), regardless of the complications that might be required to treat a real live patient. Now Medicare could more efficiently bill the nation's healthcare organizations independently of the time required to remedy the illness. If a pneumonia patient returned to good health in twenty-four hours, the hospital and the doctor would be paid the same as for a sicker patient who might stay in the intensive care unit on a ventilator for weeks. But standardization served the government's interest of efficient billing and reimbursement.

Washington's embrace of regulated DRGs fueled the bureaucratization of medicine down below. Layers of new jobs proliferated within hospitals to minimize patients' stays or the length of outpatient treatments. Social workers were hired to ask the doctor on a daily basis if a patient was ready to go home. Discharge planners were brought in to find places to transfer recovering surgical patients, hoping to quickly free up hospital beds. Nursing agencies followed patients home and put them on intravenous (IV) medications, saving more money for the hospital and insurance company.

A new generation of medical residents learned to make diagnoses using fewer blood tests. They were trained to phone clerks to beg permission for an MRI. Agents for the insurers doled out reimbursements. This costly and complicated machinery of securing revenue for Medicare patients (a rising share of the nation's caseload) boosted operating costs for hospitals, health maintenance organizations (HMOs), and small practices. This centralization of health care did not improve the quality of care or patient longevity overall. Variability in these vital signs simply grew wider across hospitals and medical centers nationwide.

Geisinger Health System thrives under this regulatory apparatus. Their strategy has been to shift medical care from treating to preventing disease, especially chronic health conditions that can be avoided or managed through healthier lifestyles. The firm is managed by a slim and data-rich center that nudges and cajoles local physicians to manage chronic disease, help patients lead healthier lives, aided by Geisinger's own empirically informed "protocols" for diagnosing and treating common medical problems.

Geisinger is located in the eastern half of Pennsylvania, serving countless rural hamlets and a few urban centers. The firm grew out from its three hospitals, founded in the graying blue-collar town of Danville, deep in the Pocono Mountains. Geisinger steadily built or acquired a largely decentralized network of thirty-seven clinics that spread across the region. Each patient enjoys a physician within driving distance of a clinic or field hospital who can provide simple surgeries or treat uncomplicated problems (like hernia repairs or appendectomies). Labs and testing stations operate in almost everyone's community. Nurses or innovative case managers frequently make house calls to check on medications or learn more about a patient's support network. Geisinger operates a state-of-the-art hospital in Danville, replete with a neonatal intensive-care nursery, fancy PET scanner, and even a helicopter pad to receive critically ill patients. But the vast majority of patients are served in the far-flung clinics by family doctors and agile nurses who blend technical knowledge with curiosity about each patient.

The revenue streams of hospitals and health-care firms have typically been fed by the steep prices charged by medical specialists who might pay little regard to prevention and healthy everyday behavior. In sharp contrast, Geisinger executives—led by Tomcavage and her team—invest heavily in local case managers. And initial results are very encouraging. These nurses are lowering mortality rates due to poor management of chronic disease and slowing the escalation of costs, as we detail below. Overall, Tomcavage exerts a leadership style more akin to a firm and caring mother bear than a hard-nosed insurance executive. It turns out she is both.

Rethinking the Center, Nudging Local Reform

Tomcavage—a new decentralist extraordinaire—knows that contemporary health care stems from a fragmented institutional history. Medical care, going back to the Renaissance, was long administered by individual doctors, typically working as sole practitioners, although this high-status guild socialized and trained in similar ways. The modern state, from the late nineteenth-century forward, has been building vast hospitals, organizations run via hierarchical management.

America's physicians then experienced the sharp jolt of centralized control, after the passage of Medicare and aggressive regulation of practices and prices from Washington, even central approval of many procedures requested by local physicians. The rise of "managed care" situated in HMOs offered economies of scale and one way to adapt to the increasingly complex regulatory structure. Yet HMOs also provided a localized countervailing force to federal centralization of medical decision making. HMOs stoked novel market competition, not present when care was tied to bureaucratic hospitals and the age-old discretion protected by the medical guild. The change did kill off many small practices, as doctors shifted to larger firms, like Kaiser Permanente, Geisinger, or the Mayo Clinic. Static reimbursement levels also drove physicians into organizations that could operate a business side more efficiently. The share of physicians working from independent practices has declined from 57 percent to less than a third in the past decade.[2] So creeping centralization has resulted in a declining count of small private clinics, while stoking market dynamics among locally situated HMOs and hospitals.

The proliferation of specialists, tied to miraculous, but costly, medical technologies, spurred skyrocketing salaries tied to hospital-based practice. Over the past half century the medical establishment, largely run as a regulated truce between headstrong doctors and cost-conscious bureaucrats, has become remarkably adept at treating disease instead of promoting wellness. This continues to spur astronomical costs for patients and taxpayers.[3] Government has long tolerated hefty reimbursements for specialists who attack illness, rather than encouraging primary care and prevention.

Despite creeping centralization, the incidence of preventable chronic disease continues to grow, along with accelerating health-care costs. The roots of chronic maladies—poor diet and scant exercise—can appear early in a child's life and last, for most of those afflicted, throughout a lifetime. Tomcavage cites a single statistic to capture the underlying problem: childhood obesity already besets two-fifths of all four-year-olds living in Geisinger's half of Pennsylvania. This leads to early-onset type-2 diabetes and congestive heart disease and obesity in early adulthood, often driven by a lack of exercise. The prevalence of such chronic conditions can only be remedied by changing behavior. If present trends continue, fully one in three adults will eat their way into type-2 diabetes by 2050, according to the Centers for Disease Control and Prevention.[4]

When illness caused by poor lifestyle goes unaddressed, long-term costs for treatment shoot through the roof. The most costly 5 percent of Medicare patients typically suffer from these preventable diseases, and they generate two-fifths of all health-care costs nationwide, as introduced in chapter 2. The most expensive quarter drive almost 80 percent of all medical costs.[5]

So Tomcavage and her team have begun to turn health-care reform upside down. Sure, Washington must rethink its centralized policies and reimbursement structures. But Tomcavage began at the grass roots by learning more about patients inside each local clinic, then planting case managers to raise the quality of care and lower costs. And it's Geisinger's insurance arm that's fronting this bold experiment in decentralization, not the clinical side of the company.

Tomcavage repeatedly points to recent studies detailing Geisinger's emphasis on prevention—shaped inside local clinics, informed by inquisitive case managers—which is yielding impressive results. And benefits are especially strong in the pockets of poverty tucked away between the scenic ridges of the Poconos.

Income disparities are visible throughout the fading manufacturing towns and abandoned steel plants that snake along the Lehigh River—not all that far from preppy Lewisburg, home to Bucknell College, where pricey dress shops and tea houses line the main street. One dying coal-mining town, Centralia, near Geisinger's original hospital, literally imploded into the caverns below and whole neighborhoods began to sink. Underground coal fires still smolder in the aquifers lying beneath spent mine pits.

"We serve a population that is poorer, older and sicker than the national average," said Dr. Glenn Steele Jr., CEO of Geisinger Health System. To counter this trend, "we've launched several innovative programs aimed at bringing quality and value to healthcare." By vigorously decentralizing health care—enriching information about patients and distributing authority horizontally inside clinics—unhealthy trends and rising costs are being reversed. Geisinger's diabetic patients are learning how to lead healthier lives. Among patients with chronic conditions, hospital admissions are down by one-fourth since 2006. The new case managers—compassionate and experienced RNs—have reengineered the transition of patients back home from the hospital and sliced readmission rates in half. And for patients who require acute care in a Geisinger-run hospital, the occurrence of infections or complications has been cut by a fifth.[6]

Three Cornerstones—Decentralizing from a Surgical Center

We unearthed durable cornerstones—social-organization contours of Geisinger's decentralizing reforms—during our two years of visiting and probing this inventive firm. These principles, advanced by Tomcavage and the ladies, define shifts in the organization's ethical mission, forge new tools for medical staff, and reorder authority and social relations inside local clinics. Taken together, Tomcavage offers a manifesto for new decentralists in other sectors, eager to better engage clients and create more fulfilling workplaces for practitioners, recast in large part by a lean, inspiring organizational center.

These cornerstones of local organizing, undergirding Geisinger's institutional architecture, include: a vigorous *curiosity* about what makes each client tick; *experimentation* with innovative professional roles that flatten traditional hierarchies and rearrange power within clinics; and a *strategic and resourceful center* that infuses the firm's culture with information and data that support prevention and patient-centered health care, so that people get better even when living in poor communities. These key features of decentralizing organizations will appear in neighboring sectors, from education to international banking, as we discover in subsequent chapters. (A fourth cornerstone will round out these institutional foundations in the next chapter.)

The survival of human-scale primary care depends on rethinking the character of medicine inside local clinics. The shift to competing HMOs over the past generation has not only led to consolidation of private practices, it has also driven many family doctors out of business in the poor enclaves that dot the Poconos. Rising operating costs for small medical practices have long outpaced federal and insurance reimbursements.

To make primary care economically viable Geisinger sees itself differently, operating as the "country doctor" across the eastern reaches of Pennsylvania, from cities close to the Atlantic seaboard to far-flung hamlets of the central mountains. Each of Geisinger's thirty-seven community clinics is staffed by at least two, but not more than eight, physicians and the newly installed case managers. Together, they operate as the eyes, ears, and strong hearts of what's largely a rural health-care system.

Clinics are tailored to patients' specific needs, located close to their homes in communities where each patient is well known, and staffed by caring nurses, some of whom have cared for these patients since birth. Tomcavage and central colleagues have crafted these organizational cornerstones, while clinical staff members accommodate these innovations within their local practices. It's a constantly negotiated collaboration between the firm's central architects, like Tomcavage and her earlier mentors, and medical practitioners out in local clinics. While Geisinger created several of their clinics, many have been acquired, purchased from independent groups of physicians.

Other health-care firms, of late, also experiment with centrally coaxed efforts for shifting the motivation and behavior of patients and doctors. Our analysis focuses on change within the local clinics, driven largely by the new case managers who now share authority with the MDs. They work as microsociologists of sorts, delving into the patient's own motivations and their surrounding network of kith and kin, potential allies in motivating healthier behavior. This decentralizing strategy assuages central regulation and reliance on the age-old status of the physician. Instead, case managers diplomatically move to flatten hierarchy inside clinics and spark open conversation about the medical and motivational dynamics of patients.

Geisinger's leadership is experimenting on a grand scale. One-third of the firm's 787,000 patients are enrolled in Geisinger's own health plan, the insurance wing through which Tomcavage gains capital and leverage to advance her reforms. Founded with a benevolent grant from the wealthy Abigail Geisinger in 1913, the firm now rivals the Mayo Clinic or Kaiser Permanente in its range of organizational innovations and gains in raising health outcomes at lower costs—at least for patients with chronic disease. Geisinger's executives—many physicians—tend be soft spoken and modest in style. But they oversee a company whose annual revenues now top $1 billion.

When placed on a small canvas and seen through the eyes of a sociologist, Geisinger's careful strategy to recast social relations inside clinics is reminiscent of Georg Simmel's insight a century ago: otherwise insular communities can thrive when their leaders nurture close ties among the villagers *and* welcome friendly strangers who arrive with fresh perspectives and innovative tools. In other words, local groups become more versatile and responsive to complex conditions (or clients) when they host smart outsiders who dig in and stick around.

Cornerstone 1—Knowing Each Client

Any touch really has an effect

Geisinger's decentered focus on engaging each client is best told by patients themselves, along with Tomcavage's skilled cadre of case managers who hitch onto what makes their patients tick. It's a symbiotic tale of how a spectrum of caring professionals inside local clinics work in concert to produce exceptional results by motivating trust and a sense of mutual obligation with each patient. As chronic conditions are tackled, the case managers enlist stronger support from nearby kith and kin, scaffolding from the patient's own context. The new decentralists advance keen curiosity about their clients. As Geisinger CEO Steele puts it, "We have to have an unrelenting interest in learning about the clients. This has to be the kind of medicine you would want for your own family."

Patient Peg Adami agrees. Still spry and a tad sarcastic at eighty-nine, she shuffled around her dark and stuffy apartment one brisk fall morning. Behind her trailed a forty-foot tube that delivered life-sustaining enriched oxygen to her failing lungs. She and her husband of sixty-five years—"he's only *half* Italian," Mrs. Adami chided—live upstairs in a cozy, well-worn unit off an alley, set back from the gritty main street of Milton, Pennsylvania. The busy road is lined with failed storefronts, just a twenty-minute drive from the meticulously trimmed lawns of Bucknell College.

"We were on a cruise, and all of a sudden I started to spit up blood," Adami said. She had suffered from recurring bouts with chronic bronchitis (bronchiectasis), which Adami calls "bronchie." This lung disease caused by bacterial deterioration of airways clogged with infected fluids is still present from long ago when no antibiotics were available to cure infections. Adami contracted the disease in the early 1960s; it has made breathing increasingly difficult. Still, she had felt just fine of late, and she had decided to call and tell her case manager, Kenda Danowsky, who often pops over from the nearby Geisinger clinic to see how Adami is doing: "I just wanted to make *her* feel good," Adami said with a sincere smile. "I wanted Kenda to know *I* was having a good day. My sister in Florida has nothing like this! I'm always bragging to her about this great support program."

Danowsky, an instantly warm and savvy case manager—what Geisinger executives like to call a "nurse navigator"—invites respect from the crustiest of doctors at their monthly patient reviews. She was the second of now forty-one case managers recruited by Tomcavage, beginning in 2006. They now spread across Geisinger's network of clinics, the shock troops for shifting medical care toward prevention and distributing knowledge of patients and their lives beyond the physicians.

Danowsky told us that many patients with chronic conditions simply "don't have the instinct of knowing their bodies yet." But "people always respond to touch," she said. One regional director of case managers, Diane Littlewood, told doctors and insurers visiting the Geisinger center in Danville, "Any touch really has an effect. There's nothing like getting down on the floor and doing a foot exam . . . building that trust. You are sitting there, looking eye to eye."

Danowsky, for patients like Adami, offers both moral support and forceful advocacy inside the medical institution, from clinic visits to transitions to and from hospital-based care. Says Adami of her care manager: "She cuts through the red tape. She gets in touch with my Dr. Mogiano. She asks me a lot of questions to make sure I'm doing all right." Because of her poorly functioning lungs, Adami's body gets clogged with fluids that can lead quickly to trouble breathing. But Danowsky coached Adami about "how to get rid of excess water . . . you lean over and scrunch," Adami says, with a subtle demonstration. "Thank god I didn't have to get that catheter."

Adami was the oldest of nine children, from a working-class Philadelphia family. "They were struggling like mad," she said; she dropped out of high school to attend secretarial school. After raising her own eight children, Adami went back to work, landing a job with Chef Boyardee, the food processing company. Her husband already worked there as a shop foreman, overlooking the assembly line. "They made meatballs," Adami proudly reported. Her years in the plant likely worsened her lung disease.

A Gradual Shift in Institutional Logic

"But we always want to be efficient too," Tomcavage is quick to point out. "You pay us to cut off the correct leg," she says with a reassuring grin. How have Tomcavage and her earlier mentors at Geisinger turned this vast firm upside down? How have they moved in less than a decade to widen the range of clinical job roles inside a growing count of clinics, spreading out who shares authority and expertise, while lowering costs and boosting the health of their patients? How does a large and cumbersome organization shift the logic of what its core work is all about?

Make no mistake: Geisinger Health System is a private company that's eager to grow its market share, constrain costs, and turn a steady profit, most of which is plowed back into its reform agenda. In turn, this bolsters the center's resources to incentivize physicians to shift toward prevention, try treatment protocols that are backed by empirical evidence, and work in tandem with case managers to blend knowledge that stems from medicine with a dash of local sociology. The payoff to such holistic care, spurred by progressive ethics and salary bonuses awarded to *all* staff at effective clinics, is becoming discernible when it comes to patient outcomes and the firm's bottom line.

So Tomcavage and Geisinger's fellow leaders—on the health-care and insurance sides of the firm—are betting on decentralized ways of engaging and motivating patients, especially high-cost clients and those with chronic conditions. These are the clients that drive up avoidable costs, which could be lowered if patients opted to take better care of themselves. And any patient kept out of an ER or hospital bed—when needlessly admitted—saves enormous costs at Geisinger, like any health-care organization. Once in the hospital patient outcomes typically dip, as infection rates rise and the quality of social support collapses.

Geisinger's internal economics nudge these shifts in core ethics and institutional logics. Tomcavage's insurance arm helps to design and capitalize on several organizational innovations, including the efforts led by local case managers. The insurance and health-delivery wings collaborate to track high-cost patients, many with preventable chronic conditions. Tomcavage's department incentivizes clinics to shift their own logic toward prevention, then to hit quality targets. This matches with what Stanford University sociologist W. Richard Scott calls a "shift in institutional logic," how a sector's goals and tacit notions of how work is done begin to shift over time, whether tied to the firm's formal goals or not. The deep culture of Geisinger has come to prioritize prevention and holistic ways of understanding patients, how they can take stronger responsibility for their behavior by drawing on their support network.

This holds implications for the everyday health of patients and the mounting costs of health care that government and taxpayers share. "Without being paid as one of the professionals, the patients have also gone to work as part of the team. It's an art and a science," Tomcavage says. "In chronic care, the patients have learned how to make things better for themselves and in the process they are becoming their own best managers. If we could change behavior, we'd be golden."

Geisinger's notions of how to redesign primary care—thinking anew about relationships between practitioners and patients to achieve better outcomes—have moved gradually across medical associations since the 1960s, sparked by ballooning costs and the rise of managed care.[7] After nearly three decades of experimentation and evaluation, core principles of redesigning primary care finally crystallized under the mouthful, *patient-centered medical home*. This legitimated logic, of late, has become woven into the nation's ongoing debate over health-care reform. The core organizational logic accents the importance of steady attention to prevention and healthy lifestyles, building trusting relations with health providers, and motivating patients to adjust diet or physical activity.

Tomcavage is reaching back in time and adapting an earlier social form. Innovators within the American Academy of Family Practice first coined the phrase *medical home* in 1967, referring to nurses who may be based inside clinics but would also take stock of the patient's home setting and support network.[8] It offered a new job role and social technology for the preventive-care movement, emerging in concert with nurse practitioners, HMOs, and public health initiatives to stamp out smoking and the press for healthy lifestyles. Suddenly, by the 1980s, health care did not only imply medical remedies, drugs, and surgery; the counterfocus became proper nutrition, exercise, and prevention. Overall, we see second-wave decentralists like Tomcavage building from earlier local efforts relying on rich support from the center to coach patients toward healthier behavior.

The focused management of patients with chronic conditions first emerged within Geisinger in the late 1990s, stemming in part from Tomcavage's deep history with preventive care and type-2 diabetes. In 1995 Geisinger began to intensively engage patients who had acquired diabetes. Then Tomcavage was asked in 2005 to manage a corps of about fifty nurses to call and check on discharged patients, to arrange whatever it took to keep them from being readmitted. These nurses, crafting a new role, also cajoled patients to quit smoking, adjust their diets, and exercise more. They taught patients how to manage their diabetes. The aim was to avoid visits to the ER or readmission to the hospital. The nurses were located centrally and worked mostly online or by phone, while making house calls when necessary.

Prompted by Dr. Rick Gilfillan, an influential mentor to Tomcavage, Geisinger launched in 2006 the Proven Health Navigator initiative, a wider experiment for which evidence of results is just now emerging. With a deceptively simple direction and a great deal of faith in "front line staff," Gilfillan turned over the reins to Tomcavage knowing she could make it happen across the firm's network of clinics. Gilfillan challenged her to devise a system that would answer the question, "What are we going to do differently to care for Medicare patients that's going to drive better quality outcomes, but show a business case?" She'd have to demonstrate an economic return in terms of reducing hospital admissions, fewer tests and reliance on specialists, and lowering mortality rates.

Once again, drawing on her quarter-century of clinical experience, Tomcavage went about identifying Geisinger's highest-risk patients with repeat hospitalizations, and imagined new roles for nurses, doctors, and patients, moving away from disease management to illness prevention. The case managers were to help shake up social relations inside clinics, getting more information on the table about the patient's own motivations and surrounding social ties. This slice of patients was often older and sicker than the rest of the population, often suffering from multiple chronic conditions. "With a lot of recurrent diseases, seventy-five percent of the work is not diagnostic. It's really working with patients to manage their chronic illnesses. So a lot of it is about lifestyle reinvention."

Tomcavage also bolstered the center's data capacity to track risk factors among patients with chronic or other high-cost conditions—providing early warning signs to local clinicians. She defined and enriched the principle of learning about each patient, drawing from headquarter's data and local knowledge of her growing corps of case managers. And Tomcavage began thinking about the innovative role of these savvy case managers, and how they could enhance the clinical conversation about medical *and* social contributions to chronic disease. She aimed to individualize care for high-cost patients—hoping to inspire their own "activation" to alter their lifestyles, draw on kin networks, and lower the odds of sliding back into smoking, gaining weight, or being rehospitalized. Tomcavage found no contradiction in improving the quality of care, while lowering costs for certain types of patients—those for whom motivational coaching and behavior changes could yield robust results.

Cornerstone 2—Local Roles That Redistribute Authority and Expertise

Tomcavage's analysis of life inside local clinics has led to her multipronged attack on medicine defined as treating the biological manifestations of disease. The shift toward prevention and behavior change—central to Geisinger's new institutional logic—would not occur as long as the old role of expert doctor on a pedestal, assisted by the technically adept nurse, persisted. This way of getting work done and underlying social relations would not motivate patients to "activate" self-interest in healthy lifestyles, or tap into kith and kin to help manage their condition—without undercutting the quality of care.

What Tomcavage aimed to craft was a clinical sociologist with the technical expertise of an insightful, specialized nurse. So she borrowed elements of the gradual shift toward *medical home*, an approach that was gaining credibility in the primary-care world. Tomcavage realized that she must invent this new role of case manager that would challenge the autonomy of doctors and better utilize the skills of traditional nurses inside all of Geisinger's local clinics.

Just seven months after receiving her charge, Tomcavage handpicked her premiere case manager, Sonia Hoffman. Like Danowsky, recruited soon after, Hoffman embodied the values and skills necessary for this unique new role. She was to engage patients in the topic of behavior and lifestyle change while pushing hospital staff and doctors to blend motivation and medicine in crafting more effective patient care. Rough transitions were boosting hospital readmission rates. Patients were often rushed back to the ER after having been discharged too soon. So Hoffman quickly focused on calling or meeting with patients within two days of being discharged from the hospital to make sure they received the care they needed to avoid readmission.

Hoffman also discovered that patients were leaving hospitals without discharge summaries, new medication lists, or any link back to a primary care doctor. So as Tomcavage would describe it, "[Hoffman] began beating up on the hospitals if they didn't dispense discharge summaries with patients being sent home and if she ran into problems . . . and if we found cases that we thought could have been managed differently on the out-patient side, we brought them up." Via the inventive role of case manager, Hoffman nudged along attendant role shifts in patients and doctors alike, flattening traditional hierarchies so that nurses and doctors could work together as a team.

Distributed Problem Solving to Motivate Clients

"It's part of a primary care doctor's ethic to find out as much as possible about each patient we take care of," Dr. Susie Kobylinski told us one afternoon before chairing a monthly case review session. She serves as regional medical director for a cluster of Geisinger clinics that includes the Milton location, nearby her own clinical practice. "Out here," she said, running her fingers through a thick blond ponytail, "to get something accomplished, to change a person's life, a doctor has to know what makes each patient tick. That's my job here on two levels, doctor and director. And I love it!"

Geisinger's computer jockeys, back at the Danville headquarters, now flag patients who suffer from recurrent diseases and high-cost conditions—where even slight behavior change or more knowledge could significantly lower costs associated with being rushed to the ER or readmitted to the hospital. These include obese patients becoming diabetic, elderly patients with heart disease, lacking sufficient family support. As the data wizards report to local clinics about patients who face troubling risk factors, the case manager's job is to learn about the motivations of these patients, including their support network, and how medications or procedures can be better managed at home.

With these data at hand—whether yielded by the central computer or case managers—an egalitarian conversation kicks in around a large elliptical table in a room, which in the Milton clinic doubles as the staff lunchroom. Around the table sat nurse Danowsky, two primary care doctors, and the clinic's senior nurse. Tomcavage had driven over from Danville, about forty-five minutes away, representing the firm's insurance arm to voice concern for the quality of care, its cost, and how alternative strategies might advance these tandem aims. Kobylinski chaired the review, steadily interjecting medical insights, a dose of irreverent jokes, and a ready laugh, despite having seen patients since sunup.

These monthly roundtables, clinic by clinic, lie at the heart of Tomcavage's effort to distribute authority when it comes to problem solving. With her case manager at the center of the discourse, the meeting becomes an opportunity for, what learning theorists call *distributed cognition*, where a range of actors probe dimensions of the problem and brainstorm their way to better remedies.

Danowsky led off with an update on a patient nicknamed The Colonel. He was known as a confident military man, quite accustomed to feeling in charge. As of late though, he was getting very grumpy, suffering from a deteriorating heart condition. The Colonel had just been discharged from the hospital after an episode of respiratory failure. He was sent home with a bulky oxygen tank featuring a long, clear, plastic tube that delivered air to his lungs. Unsightly though it was, the oxygen tubing was keeping him alive. Shaped like a shiny green torpedo, the tank weighed more than fifty pounds. The Colonel pushed it ahead of him, tottering on two wheels, gracelessly bumping into furniture, as he struggled through his cramped apartment.

The lead nurse in the Milton clinic told the meeting assembled that The Colonel at first was so excited to be at home he didn't notice he was tethered to his cumbersome green tank. After a few weeks alone, unable to shed the oxygen capsule to take a bath let alone drive to the store, The Colonel began to seriously resent it. He reported feeling like an animal on a leash. Those who earlier saluted him sitting on his front porch or stopped to chat now averted their eyes, to spare him their pity at seeing him tied down.

Nurse Danowsky, the ever-inquisitive case manager, knew that he lived alone. This worried the diagnostic team gathered around the table. The Colonel's labored breathing had been treated while hospitalized. Yet how would they keep him from getting worse, and possibly rehospitalized? He was already more frail, atypically powerless in controlling his failing health. They could imagine it would not be long before he'd take a spill, break a hip, and end up moving out of his home to a long-term care facility. The clinical team struggled with how to address his shortness of breath, along with his withering psychological condition. Was there a better way to treat him that would keep him at home for the rest of his life? How could they prevent a disaster, like rushing him back to a Geisinger hospital?

At an earlier review, Tomcavage had shifted to a motivational framing of the problem, setting aside his medical technicalities. "This is The Colonel you're talking about, right?" she recalled from the prior session. "He sounds pretty bad off." Danowsky confirmed, "Not well at all. I really need some help with him. At first he seemed happy. When I would call him on the phone, we would chat for 30 minutes," Danowsky said. "He has an educated understanding of when to use his inhalers, or rather if it was water pills for his congestive heart failure, then he needed to start those. But something has come over him. I haven't seen him like this before. He no longer cares about his condition," Danowsky said. "I can't even get him to pick up the phone. When I stop by the house I ring the bell again and again, and I can see him inside but he won't come to the door. As you know," Danowsky continued, "He's been diagnosed with a terminal lung disease. It's not a nice illness. He's smothering to death!"

But Tomcavage had pushed for a better remedy, slapping her hand on the table. "Kenda [Danowsky] we know he doesn't need our sympathy. I think he's humiliated by having to drag that oxygen tank around with him. He doesn't want you seeing him like this. He's a colonel for heaven's sake! He's used to giving the orders! And now he's chained to 30 feet of tubing. Can't go anywhere because of that darn thing. We've broken his spirit."

The team right then and there devised an innovative solution. Soon after the patient review session ended, the blue and white Planet oxygen truck stopped in front of The Colonel's tidy single-level house. A hundred-year-old bayberry tree shaded the trim front lawn. An oxygen compressor the size of a cereal box was fitted into a small backpack with a waistband and strapped to The Colonel's shoulders and waist. He looked in the hall mirror and smiled back at his reflection. "I look like I'm walking on the moon." For the first time in weeks, he was smiling. He had been issued an oxygen compressor. It turned room air into an oxygen-rich flow. Now The Colonel could go anywhere he wanted. He didn't have to wind the long thick tubing around his hands to get to the bathroom or trip over a metal canister just to go to the kitchen for a tuna sandwich.

Before moving to the next case, Tomcavage paused to praise her case manager. "Good for you," she said to Danowsky. "We had The Colonel chained to his oxygen tubing! We forgot. He's a proud man. Job well done! Now, let's move on!"

Shooting Oneself in the Foot

Next up was Buck Strozzi, known as a "frequent flier" patient. "Our big-rig jockey was in the hospital again over the weekend, out by Lancaster." Danowsky again had the most recent information.[9] Strozzi, introduced in chapter 1, drove huge trucks between Pennsylvania and Ohio each week, at times pulling into a hospital along his route to get his leg drained of dangerous accumulating fluids. Everyone around the table nodded knowingly, sharing a common understanding of this patient and group frustration over how his medical issues could be improved upon. The precipitating event was still talked about: Strozzi had literally shot himself just above the ankle in a hunting accident.

To make matters worse Strozzi was diabetic, thanks to the decades of burgers, fries, and soda sustenance from his favorite truck stops across the Midwest. Despite applying all elements of Geisinger's world-class "diabetes bundle" (including monitoring of blood sugars, frequent HbA1c blood tests, lowering elevated cholesterol, and controlling blood pressure), this patient's illness spun out of control. Even with the nurses calling to check on him at home, they couldn't keep him out of the hospital. Strozzi himself saw no way he could change his job, which required weekly treks across the interstate.

Danowsky's update brought more bad news. "This time it came on so fast we couldn't admit him to a Geisinger hospital. We had to authorize admission to the hospital closest to the patient, an out-of-plan hospital." Although everyone in the room understood that to "first do no harm" meant that Strozzi had to go to the nearest hospital, they also knew it would cost the company a lot to treat him outside of the Geisinger system. Even though it wasn't anyone's fault, it might mean less of a bonus at Christmastime, since clinical staff had all been urged to avoid this scenario.

"His temperature was over 104," Danowsky continued. "His sugars were really high (over 500). An insulin drip was started. His oxygen saturations were low, so very little oxygen was getting to his brain. They thought they might have to intubate him, or perhaps it was pneumonia. But it seems to be the same old thing," Danowsky said with resignation. Tomcavage looked distraught, "Oh, lordy," she said. "Was he septic?"

"That's what they're thinking. It certainly looks like an infection," Danowsky continued. "We're waiting for the blood culture results to confirm our suspicions. Though he is coughing pretty bad. He could have pneumonia too I suppose. He gets so swollen around the scar tissue from the hunting accident. Driving that truck day and night, he can't keep the leg elevated," Danowsky said, shifting from Strozzi's medical particulars to the behavioral roots of his problem.

"He can't get off the cigarettes or the salt," Danowsky continued to methodically detail the underlying causes. "[That's] not good for his sugar diabetes, getting infections all the time! I feel bad for him, I really do." Danowsky lowered her head, and her voice dropped to a whisper. Everyone around the table new the basics of Strozzi's tortured story. They shared Danowsky's frustration. She was losing the battle to keep him well. And costs were going through the roof. Everyone was losing on this one.

"The doctors over there want him transferred to the nearest Geisinger hospital tomorrow," Danowsky said. But Tomcavage resisted, "Well, we will see about that!" He's clearly not stable enough to be transferred! And yes, he's costing us a lot of money, being out-of-plan for their hospital, but he's not going anywhere until he's well enough!" Danowsky was clearly appreciative. "Thanks for the support, Janet. Of course, I've told them that! But they don't want him taking up their ICU space either," she said. Again, we see an innovative, largely lateral conversation—a delicate balancing act that weighs the patient's well-being against Geisinger's stiff incentive to contain preventable costs.

Not every patient receives such attention at the monthly clinic roundtables. Tomcavage or a deputy arrives with data on those with chronic conditions or who are running up huge bills in the ER or a hospital—and the medical team digs in. Case managers, like Danowsky, carry caseloads of up to 120 patients, about one-fifth of whom fall into the "frequent flier" category.

Careful assessments of four additional patients—their medical condition, viscerally felt motivations, and social contexts—were taken up that afternoon in Milton, the review of challenging and high-cost patients lasting almost three hours. This remarkable session brought to life the kind of shift in institutional logic that marks Geisinger's decentralizing focus on knowing patients and collaboratively working toward inventive remedies. The blend of tracking data coming from the center with the local particulars and anchoring of support for patients, are relayed by these microsociologists, the caring and inventive case managers.

"The case managers are respected as part of the team," Tomcavage later emphasized, after we asked how she aims to shift the distribution of authority inside clinics. Describing the respectful, horizontal social interaction so clearly seen in the monthly case reviews, Tomcavage explains, "Even though the health plan (insurance arm) pays, hires, trains, and is responsible for the case managers, you wouldn't know it in this room. We're going to talk about cases, we're going to see what went wrong, and we're not going to criticize anybody—we're just going to look for opportunities." Tomcavage stressed the collaborative nature of local problem solving. "If you went to Lewisburg the docs would say to you, 'the person who's making this happen is the case manager.' We've seen case managers who were formerly put in the back closet now being located in the center of the clinic," Tomcavage said.

Recasting the Doctor's Role

Tomcavage has placed the case manager at center stage. This appears to have shaken up the distribution of authority within local clinics, especially by thawing out the doctor's once sacred role. Under the Geisinger model, the MD still makes complex medical decisions. Physicians aren't expected to spend time with relationship building, patient education, or the follow-up required to motivate healthier behavior. The doctors simply don't have time, nor is it the best use of their expertise. The federal government, for Medicare patients, still won't reimburse physicians' time spent on prevention. Instead, the MDs are coming to depend on Tomcavage's case managers.

It's not only the patients who benefit from the case manager's interventions. Kobylinski, the regional medical director, raved about how Geisinger's local innovations serve to improve the physician's life. "It's making our job a lot easier," she said. "I like resolving the medical problems my patients bring, and I do have time now to know my patients better." It's the case manager who attends to "the minute details, like ordering a hospital-like bed," Kobylinski said. "And it's not my nurse doing all these things, it's the case manager."

The case-manager role also shifts how patients and doctors spend time together. "It's a change in the concept of a visit," physician and Geisinger researcher Fred Bloom told us. "The physician comes into the exam room at 15 minutes (after initial conversation with the case manager), not like before, at five minutes." And the patient is directly implicated in this shift in who holds responsibility for crafting remedies. Case managers may go into the room to push a bit of tough love, encouraging patients to take responsibility for their own behavior. "Can we be firm but gentle at the same time?" Diane Littlewood asked, another regional coordinator of case managers. "The emotional piece is huge" (for the client), medical chief Tom Graf said. "What's in the remedy for me?"

Novel revelations surface as the knowledge and sensitivities held by physicians, nurses, and the case manager converge at the monthly roundtables. Tomcavage and her clinical sociologists, for instance, learned that patients bedridden in nursing homes were being sent to the emergency room to medicate treatment of heart failure simply because the clinics had no access to the intravenous drug Lasix, one easily dispensed to patients by pill or IV. Geisinger patients were being discharged from hospitals without end of stay summaries and getting readmitted to the same hospital within days because the nursing home or family caretakers had no instructions on how to care for them. By learning this from her doctors, Tomcavage pushed for medication lists and resources to give IV meds at the nursing homes for treating outpatient heart failure. This was soon extended to aid transplant patients, clarifying which prescription drugs could be provided in the nursing home—minimizing the incessant movement of people in and out of hospitals.

Putting the patient at the center also challenges old system-wide routines that kept the patient on the periphery, a distant cog in a scripted technical system of an arcane medical guild. Medicine was centralized because of the medical-guild power that doctors controlled. A patient's role was to passively follow the doctor's wisdom, glorifying the healing craft of the master physician.

Geisinger's leaders have come to see how "patient centered care" requires revamping the patient's previously passive role of blithely being treated for disease—and shifting the logic to prevention, advanced by physicians, nurses, and case managers working in sync. Within this context of a local clinic, how do case managers themselves define their new role? What's the logic of the work they do? And how does this invigorate Geisinger's decentering of social relations inside local clinics?

Local Case Managers: Raising Quality and Containing Costs

Danowsky sees herself as the "eyes and ears, the go-between" for patients like Peg Adami, who we earlier met in Milton. Nurse Danowsky coordinates Adami's cardiac and pulmonology specialists with her primary care doctors and transitions Adami to and from hospitalizations and nursing home stays. Once a week, Danowsky calls Adami to find out how she's doing. She asks about specific symptoms. Is she coughing or producing more sputum than normal? Sometimes they chat about family life. Through these weekly conversations, Danowsky can determine whether her patient needs to make an appointment with a doctor or pursue other treatments or tests. Danowsky laughs and shares that Adami often tells her friends that she can call Danowsky to "figure out what to do without using the doctor!"

Danowsky's work makes good business sense as well. If Adami and her eighty-something husband couldn't handle her care at home, she'd be spending more time in the hospital, generating skyrocketing costs from an acute care setting. But Adami is not aware of Danowsky's business acumen, or how health-care dollars are being conserved for others. Adami simply sees Danowsky's steady attention as improving the quality of her everyday life.

When there's a problem Adami is immediately "activated," in Geisinger parlance. She never hesitates to call regarding a developing problem. She sees Danowsky as the ever-available fixer. Adami once tried to get a prescription for Tobramycin, an expensive inhaled antibiotic prescribed by her lung specialist to keep her from getting serious infections that might cause her to be hospitalized. The insurance company wouldn't pay for the $1,500 a month bill, so Adami decided not to buy it without telling Danowsky. When Danowsky discovered Adami was sick enough to be hospitalized and the reason was the cost of this expensive drug she couldn't afford, Danowsky quickly secured the prescription for the Tobramycin with a great deal of telephone and paperwork and relentless advocacy, at a cost of just $21 a month. Through these close interactions, Danowsky can get her patients "the right care, at the right time, at the right place, from the right doctor," while always keeping doctors "in the loop."

Juggling her caseload of 120 or so patients, Danowsky must perform a bit of triage—focusing the bulk of her day on twenty older or sicker patients while at the same time concentrating on the complex care and resources needed for about ten really ill individuals, what she calls the "hard hitters." Adami is one of those charges with multiple chronic conditions always one slip away from hospitalization. This is how the case managers, whose paychecks come straight from the business insurance side of Geisinger, maintain a broad and deep knowledge of Geisinger's far-flung rural population. Danowsky is just one of two-score case managers whose medical and social knowledge at each monthly case review provides essential diagnostic, treatment, and systems redesign information for the entire Geisinger community.

The Patient's Role Changes

The old medical guild typically expected patients to be passive, largely ignorant actors who followed the doctor's orders. Tomcavage, in contrast, set out to "activate" patients, realizing the time and cost savings, along with motivational benefits, that could result if even a portion of Geisinger subscribers would respond to a dash of tough love dispensed by caring case managers. What if patients with preventable chronic conditions would rethink their diet, sedentary lifestyle, a new array of healthier behaviors? Even more careful handling of one's medication or simple procedures at home could keep them out of the hospital.

For patients, medical care can't stop on the weekend. "If the doctor's office is closed when [the patient's] sputum changed color on Saturday," Tomcavage explains, case managers and nurses have arranged for patients to "have a rescue kit at home specific to their own medical emergencies, ready to go, [and the knowledge to] implement it, and call their case manager on Monday, and let her know you started it. If you're not feeling any better, you'll get a doctor's appointment."

Or take heart patients like Adami, who learn from their case manager how to regulate body fluids. If their "heart goes into failure," they learn to read the signs and then to either drink water or take a water pill. "We're working on the fluid. We're working on that constantly," Adami said. "We're trying to balance. You're supposed to drink water but then you're not supposed to drink water. So it's kinda hard to understand."

Tomcavage admits that activating patients requires more than a hopeful verb. Awarding report cards is one device now used to help patients know how they are progressing in attending to their chronic illness. Among the most successful programs, the patients themselves have taken on the role of doing the life-changing work, in turn reaping emotional rewards and support from loved ones.

Cornerstone 3—The Center Advances an Ethical Mission

Geisinger's top managers, going back two decades, realized that careful surgery was required for the insular guild of physicians. They began by shifting toward a fresh set of core ethics—sacred principles that took into account an evolving context. Primary care doctors were struggling economically. Entire medical practices were closing their doors. At the same time patients with chronic conditions were driving up Geisinger's costs and those of allied insurers—costs that individuals, employers, and government could no longer afford. But changing patient behavior required altering the priorities and everyday behavior of medical staff as well. Simply manipulating rules and mandates from above would not solve the problem.

By the late 1990s the firm's CEO, Glenn Steele Jr., was pushing several innovations, designed on the health-care side, attempting to coach and incentivize adjustments in the behaviors of patients. Yet the incentives through lower premiums came via Geisinger's insurance arm. As Steele began shifting Geisinger's ethical focus toward prevention and behavioral change, he decided to move Tomcavage over to the insurance side. Tomcavage was to bring case managers into clinics and provide incentives to help shift physicians toward a holistic approach bolstered by evidence-based protocols to guide, not rigidly control, their practice. Steele and his young and spirited team would come to define and press this novel ethical framing in which high-quality clinical work was to be rewarded. And shared attention to high-cost patients who might better manage their own care, aided by family and friends, was to lift quality and contain costs.

Blending Inspiring Ethics with Professional Rewards

Costly medical tests or surgical procedures, when requested by physicians across Geisinger's clinics or hospitals, move up various levels of the insurance branch. Big-ticket items are pushed upward, arriving onto Tomcavage's desk. She must approve or deny them. One startling case even shocked this seasoned veteran: A patient, suffering from chronic pain, now urgently needed a liver transplant after overdosing on Tylenol, which she had consumed in high doses, poisoning her liver. Tomcavage repeated her look of disbelief, "Tylenol! We're replacing her liver, but what are we doing about the pain? If that's not solved first, we'll lose her. Because she'll ruin her new liver!" Tomcavage queried the patient's local physician. "Do we have behavioral health (a hospital-based therapist) connected here?"

Tomcavage researched further—"I'm somewhat of a Type A," she said to no one's surprise—"I discovered that Geisinger's central data team had never thought of tracking the behavioral diagnoses of patients' conditions for whom liver transplants were being requested across the network. "It was smack in my face around transplants. We're taking one transplant at a time." But no one at the center was digging through data to understand incidence rates or hidden biological patterns across Geisinger's patients statewide. "What are you doing for the population?" Tomcavage was asking.

This notion that careful tracking of Geisinger's patient population to flag high-cost or questionable treatments, or to catch an individual at risk, is another instance of how the center organizes for greater cost effectiveness inside local clinics. And building stronger data sets is tied to Geisinger's first reform principle: family doctors or primary-care physicians should not go out of business. Family doctors are historically disadvantaged by costly regulation from above and reimbursement schemes that still reward specialized medical procedures and discourage preventive care. "The burden of chronic disease is growing," Geisinger's medical officer, Duane Davis, emphasized, "Thanks to unhealthy behaviors that lead to lung and heart disease, obesity, and skyrocketing rates of type-2 diabetes. But both government and private insurers preserve higher reimbursements—or perverse payments," as Davis called them—"to specialists who treat the eventual medical problems, rather than incentivizing clinical staff that work with patients to change behavior, to manage chronic conditions outside the hospital, and to prevent avoidable disease for local populations." Davis stressed that the health-care system must shift to supporting effective primary care physicians and allied clinical staff to motivate behavioral change, along with treating disease.

The organization's center—in this case, the insurance arm of Geisinger—began incentivizing doctors who relay advice about smoking cessation and who urge patients to eat healthfully to dodge the dangers of obesity and diabetes. The shift in ethics is accompanied by crisp gainful incentives for local practitioners. Augmented payments to MDs and clinical staff who support patients' healthy practices have become more common at Geisinger than among other progressive health-care firms or insurers, like the Mayo Clinic in Cleveland and Intermountain Healthcare spread across Colorado and Utah.

The shift in core ethics doesn't stop here. Shifting patient behavior requires decentering authority and distributing technical knowledge laterally within hospitals and local clinics. We earlier reported on how Geisinger innovators steadily experiment with new job roles while learning about what motivates clients most at risk—whether risk is defined as very sick, on the verge of hospitalization, or high cost. This leads actors in the Danville headquarters to reshape how power and expertise are defined and more evenly distributed across doctors, nurses, case managers, and even patients, in local clinics. We came to see this as *centrally coached* decentralization. The center also invests in careful reviews of evidence on what diagnostic or treatment steps are more likely to pay off in terms of healthier patients. Let's turn next to this coaching from headquarters to engage and improve the practices of frontline physicians.

Evidence Shifts Local Practice

The phrase *best practice* is voiced inside Geisinger headquarters with the same exuberance heard in neighboring fields, such as the education sector. And like the challenge of nurturing human learning, the desire to specify a universally scripted treatment routine inevitably confronts the difficult-to-forecast variability of individual clients. Tomcavage and her cadre are quite aware of these complications. Still, Geisinger believes that clinical *protocols* in medical parlance can be built from accumulating evidence that demonstrates better outcomes for patients.

The underlying tenet inside Geisinger is that ethical clarity is not enough; everyday activities of doctors, nurses, and case managers must be coached and informed as well. Indeed, we uncovered a first principle of second-wave decentralists across the sectors examined in our case studies: the center must coach local practitioners on technical tools and knowledge, on how to better manage a diverse population, and on how to devise social relations and key activities that better engage clients.

The design of treatment protocols was made possible by Geisinger's system of keeping electronic medical records. Since first introduced in 2001, this record-keeping tool aids patients who move between Geisinger medical facilities. These data yield rich information about conditions, costs, and outcomes tied to the firm's entire population of patients. This ethical commitment to understanding the client's motivation is further informed by each clinic's case manager. And centrally, electronic medical records allow those at the center to share data with the clinics about categories of patients, incidence of chronic disease, fidelity to treatment options, and client outcomes. A bevy of questions arise in the monthly case reviews, often informed by data runs back in Danville: What superior treatments are emerging for diabetes? How many patients had each provider seen over the past month? What were the latest hospitalization and readmission rates? Are prevention efforts keeping patients out of the hospital?

Geisinger managers use the phrase *rapid cycle innovation* to capture the sequential process of analyzing patient data, trying out alternative diagnostics or remedies, gauging implementation in the clinics, then tracking client outcomes.[10] The approach helps to ensure that promising innovations reach patients as soon as safely possible. Almost two decades had been required to test and disseminate medical breakthroughs into acceptable health-care practice. But CEO Steele felt that this was much too long.

One secret to turning around data faster takes us back to embedding the case managers in Geisinger clinics to provide steady evaluations to central managers, like Tomcavage, who study and adjust local practices while constantly devising ways of cutting costs. The managers then feed this information back to the practicing physicians so they can make better treatment decisions when meeting with patients. In this way, Steele and Tomcavage see how innovations are received by clinical staff through the eyes of case managers, not merely relying on electronic patient data.

A multidisciplinary team of Geisinger physicians and research staff began to cull through the medical literature in 2005, the labor-intensive process of creating diagnostic and treatment *bundles*. They initially focused on the costly chronic diseases that could be eased or prevented through behavioral change. The bundles and protocols offer a fairly standard routine for digging into a patient's condition. The monthly roundtables offer the opportunity to design adjustments, as the physicians, nurses, case managers, and insurance reps gather to address persisting, high-cost patients.

Bloom, the Geisinger researcher, recognized early on that patients were not getting good treatment for chronic diseases like diabetes and hypertension when these illnesses were being managed like episodic medical conditions. He was among the first clinical scholars to synthesize best remedies for chronic illnesses and then build treatment bundles for fellow Geisinger doctors. Such evidence-based guidelines were eventually developed for seven treatment areas at Geisinger, including bariatric surgery for the morbidly obese, cataract and hip replacement surgery, lower back pain, lung cancer, percutaneous coronary intervention, and prenatal care. Similarly, the Virginia Mason Medical Center in Seattle had devised bundled treatments in cancer care and orthopedic surgery. Kaiser Permanente has drafted an empirically rooted bundle and treatment protocols for primary care as well.[11]

Hospital admissions and readmissions dropped precipitously across the Geisinger network after these treatment bundles took root in local clinics. The amount spent on treating chronic disease has plummeted and remains lower than ever before, compared with health-care firms that serve similar populations but do not use treatment protocols.[12] How doctors implement treatment bundles through electronic medical records are periodically adjusted as new findings are published. "Best practice alerts" are beamed out to local clinics when the clinical evidence seems conclusive—appealing to the scientific or professional motivation of medical staff. In this way reliable data are released that inform treatment decisions for physicians caring for all kinds of medical problems. "Because we can't count on monetary incentives alone," Tomcavage said, accurate data to help guide treatments are as good as gold.

As physicians situated in hospitals employed treatment bundles, Geisinger realized another round of savings. Patients were discharged from hospitals more quickly, and care shifted to the lower-cost clinics. Patients are now rarely readmitted due to ineffective outpatient care. In this way, the adoption of basic protocols and bundling of procedures spurred financial rewards for everyone at all levels of the Geisinger firm. Clinics and individual MDs are incentivized monetarily, up over $20,000 in some instances, to abide by these protocols, and their empirical bases are steadily explained by the Danville headquarters. Physicians learn more about each disease and how alternative remedies can be weighed.

Incentives going out to clinics or hospital units are shared across the local staff, from senior physicians to the front-desk dispatcher. "There's peer pressure (in clinics) to meet the bundle target," Tom Graf said. "Doctors want bonus compensation for nurses. All can see each other's (protocol implementation) scores." Even receptionists and those who schedule patients share in the incentive scheme, along with phlebotomists, and physical therapists. The clerical staff "often gets a $750 incentive bonus at Christmas," Graf said.

Simple routines lend order and quality to how Geisinger hospitals work in concert with case managers and local clinics. Case managers can initiate appropriate care as soon as patients leave the hospital; they can stay with them at other vulnerable transition points like moving to a nursing home or hospice care at the end of life. These are times when extra support is required. Networking of kin members and friends goes so much easier when the data follow the patient with the treatment staff and family.

Geisinger is now developing support systems for nursing-home staff. Nursing homes are renowned for being understaffed, and the existing staff members are generally overworked and sometimes lack data and clinical training. And they get frightened easily—putting a patient into the ambulance and unnecessarily sending them to the ER, even when minor medical problems arise. With training and data from Geisinger, Tomcavage and colleagues hope that nursing home patients receive state-of-the-art care, rather that advancing physical strain and exposure to hospital pathogens, reducing the cost for nonurgent problems. "It's like blasting a mouse with an elephant gun," Tomcavage said.

Situating Geisinger among Local Organizations

Geisinger's leaders think much about social context in a broader way as well—how to better situate their clinics and hospitals in local fields of allied organizations. These include unaffiliated hospitals into which Geisinger members are admitted in emergencies; these members then are discharged into nursing homes and rehabilitation and hospice facilities. By spreading their core ethics and innovative practices throughout the community, Geisinger's patients report experiencing more seamless care, reduced costs, and kindness when it's needed most.

Overall, the focus on the health status of members of their communities offers yet another way in which Geisinger's center advances innovative health care. Each clinic and each physician in the network struggles to respond to everyday patient demand, often squeezing in twenty people in a given day. Tracking their patients discharged from a non-Geisinger hospital is a related concern, or working with nursing home companies to better train their staff at their disparate locations.

And we loop back to Tomcavage's indefatigable case managers who identify these interorganizational weaknesses, seeing breakdowns in transitions when patients are moved, or how to remedy poor and costly habits that depress the quality of care throughout Geisinger's expansive region. These allied health-care organizations must be brought into the fold if prevention and public health are to become more salient. As Tomcavage repeatedly reminds everyone, when two-fifths of Geisinger's four-year-olds are already obese, the dialogue should be about obesity prevention in eighteen-month-olds and improved family practices, because for medical remedies it's already too late.

Patients nearing the end of their lives drive huge chunks of health-care costs in America. Elderly patients fare better and live longer, on average, when cared for at home rather than in a hospital at the end of life.[13] Trained hospice nurses visit terminally ill patients at home, coaching and supporting their loved ones as well. So Geisinger works with local civic groups and nonprofits to support less costly, more humane alternatives for the dying. The old (once-seen-as-modern) hospital-based institution of care has been turned upside down, as Tomcavage and her Geisinger colleagues focus first on the patient's needs within the local context: how case managers embedded in community clinics now join if needed with allied organizations and the patient's family, using their own social ties to offer the warmest, most respectful, end-of-life care.

In all of these ways, Geisinger's leadership not only adapts to their environment, they also work to improve surrounding conditions across Pennsylvania's eastern half. Geisinger recently won a state grant—for which they and Blue Cross offer matching funds—to take innovative practices out to the state's northeast region, aiming to raise quality, improve linkages among providers, and lower costs statewide.

Constantly in motion, Tomcavage and her colleagues even display a competitive spirit when it comes to talking up and publishing empirical results that stem from their organizational innovations. One evening she complained with a sly smile about how "Johns Hopkins publishes, publishes, publishes. We don't have people that just sit around writing, we're not attached to a medical school."

Lessons Learned—Recasting the Center to Enrich Local Practice

Geisinger's inventive leaders and local practitioners offer key lessons and potent strategies for lifting their clients in compassionate and effective ways. But how much can we generalize from this dynamic company, and does this form of decentralization, blended with a dedicated center, depend upon a few creative individuals? As social scientists would say, what's the external validity of this intriguing case?

First, the Geisinger Health System is not alone in the macroeconomic and institutional pressures they now confront. The old institutional logic is no longer tenable—simply treating disease without backing up to the underlying causes of a patient's medical conditions, the necessity of behavior change over time, and the immediacy of a patient's support network. These combine to make for a huge shift in how medical practitioners are rethinking their everyday work. Hospital care has proven to be more risky for most patients, and certainly more costly, than managing health conditions in one's home or affordable settings, like assisted living settlements. And the cost of health care, skyrocketing over the past half century, is no longer sustainable for employers, patients, or taxpayers. All major firms—publicly or privately run, and in between—face these pressures within the highly stressed organizational field of healthcare.

Second, Geisinger is not alone in how they ingeniously adapt to these shared contextual pressures, investing in this variety of organizational experiments. The nation's renewed debate over health-care reform has helped to spotlight firms that yield strong patient outcomes and lower costs, including the Mayo Clinic, Intermountain Healthcare based in Salt Lake City, and Kaiser Permanente, which has flourished in the San Francisco Bay Area. A variety of research centers—based in health-care companies and universities—now detail highly variable quality indicators, patient outcomes, and costs across the nation's hospitals and medical groups. They also help spread the word on organizational innovations.[14] Washington began to seed institutional reforms under President Obama's 2010 health-care reforms. Rick Gilfillan was the founding director of the federal Center for Medicare and Medicaid Innovation (CMMI); he was a former mentor to Janet Tomcavage as Geisinger's medical director.

So while the combination of Tomcavage, "the ladies," and their previous mentors at Geisinger offers a remarkably dynamic cadre for innovation, they are responding to shared pressures drawn from earlier generations of organizational reform, including the "medical home" model. They are incentivizing preventive care, and distributing diagnostics and remedies across a flatter, more diverse array of medical staff inside local clinics. Tomcavage and her comrades bring to life these inventive social forms, but they are crafted and molded from earlier institutional clay.

These organizational designers now advance decentralizing reforms by installing firm cornerstones for a social architecture that motivates deeper engagement with patients, shapes lateral problem solving inside local clinics, and energizes a lean, yet data-rich center. And what goes unsaid: the steady growth of Geisinger and the savings generated from local restructuring goes back into the firm to fund salary incentives, the spread of local case managers, and to advance empirically informed treatment protocols. Unlike schools or NGOs dependent on public funding, Geisinger earns a healthy profit, which is then plowed back into these organizational innovations.

Like decentralists before them, Tomcavage and her reform team don't rely on hierarchical controls, nor attempt to prescribe and routinize the work of doctors and nurses. In fact, Geisinger's approach makes certain work more complex. The center now generates clinic-level scientific data on individual clients, and the monthly reviews inject a variety of medical and motivational data regarding challenges facing patients. Institutional history matters. So altering the role of doctor and patient and shaking up entrenched structures of authority and expertise inside clinics require collaborative coaxing from the center, not impersonal regulation from the top down.

Note that Geisinger's new decentralists don't simply cut loose from a bureaucratic hierarchy, the political focus of their first-wave ancestors. They work from the hypothesis that nurturing deeper knowledge of patients and openness to alternative remedies requires a new institutional logic inside clinics—one that neither protects the physician's traditional emphasis on treating disease (rather than prevention), nor ignores the patient's motivations and support network. Leaders at the center and local practitioners, nudged and incentivized to rethink old tacit logics regarding how work gets done, are collaborating to shift outdated everyday habits.

At the same time, Geisinger's leaders reject pure market, centerless renditions of decentralization. In contrast, Britain's conservative government, led by Prime Minister David Cameron, proposed in 2012 to simply award $125 billion yearly to primary care physicians who would contract directly with hospitals or clinics to host their services. The central bureaucracy would shrink, and along with it, regulations like caps on the maximum number of days patients would have to wait to be seen by a doctor. Or, take proposals by House Republicans in the United States to simply award citizens health-care vouchers; patients would somehow discern effective medical practices or HMOs and then vote with their feet. Geisinger's leaders do read and adapt to market competition in their Pennsylvania territory. But they clearly organize local practice to lift quality for all and contain costs, often for low-income patients, in ways that fleeting consumers would never have the data or expertise to accomplish.

Decentralizing as a Verb

The Geisinger case also teaches us that decentralization is a relational and negotiated process; it confronts deep-seated (highly institutionalized) practices, reproduced via the distribution of authority, expertise, and resources across the center and local clinics. Thinking vertically for the moment, Tomcavage and colleagues believe that it's the doctor inside each clinic who holds the required medical expertise and power to arrive at diagnoses and make treatment decisions. But historically, doctors working alone have encouraged expensive tests, more hospital admissions, and inadequate understanding about what motivates a patient to get better.

To shift these tacit scripts inside clinics, Tomcavage has pioneered many new tools. She uses the case managers to collect and distribute discoveries about the patient and to promote alternative courses of treatment. She wields centrally collected data and material incentives to nudge doctors toward prevention and become open to holistic assessments of patients. The mix of organizational strategies invoked by Geisinger leaders depends upon the preexisting distribution of authority and expertise at the center and the local level. In short, decentralizing action is initiated from a point of origin within the firm (perhaps at the center), and it's aimed at a destination that gains in authority, know-how, and resources. But the discourse that emerges is negotiated, contested at times, and requires consensus to thaw out old habits and experiment anew.

The starting point for this process depends upon the earlier, well-worn logics of how work is supposed to get done in an organization. The Geisinger case led to the discovery of three forms of organizing—what we came to call *cornerstones*—that characterize the work of the new decentralists. But their intense curiosity about clients, shaping new medical and social roles inside clinics, and rethinking managerial priorities at the center all remain as decentralizing works in progress.

Geisinger's reform team doesn't ship down to the clinics performance targets or a box of tools and then disappear. Tomcavage and her network of case managers are constantly working with local practitioners to better understand client populations and to mull over remedies for specific patients. She uses friendly foreigners—again, the case manager role, along with fresh evidence on effective protocols—to question routines and stimulate fresh thinking on local practice. And regional medical directors, like Susie Kobylinski, serve to bridge the Danville headquarters with staff out in the clinics. This legitimates and seeds the center's ethical commitment to prevention, patient data, and medical tools and protocols that come with the firm's new institutional logic.

Perpendicular Logics and Incentives

Health care in America has become a mixed market of public hospitals and for-profit firms—most dedicated to a shared civic purpose—that is variably regulated by government. The past generation of leaders at Geisinger talks quietly about expanding their market share, working with major employers to sign up members, and reducing costs in order to widen income margins.

The spread of mixed markets populated by a variety of organizational forms—hospitals, HMOs, independent medical groups, specialized labs—leads to what we came to call a *perpendicular* organizing strategy for large firms like Geisinger. Its keen ability to maneuver in a rough and tumble health-care field yields strong revenues. Its stellar reputation, quality outcomes, and enriched relations with many patients all contribute to the firm's market share. Robust revenues can then, in part, be directed back to local practitioners in the form of incentives and bonuses—rewarding the shift toward prevention, human-scale problem solving for costly patients, and enforcing attention to evidence-based treatments by historically autonomous doctors.

So the center comes to hold authority through its core ethics, data, and innovative medical tools—as well as economic power that's exercised through material incentives. Out in the clinics, doctors, nurses, and case managers certainly work from altruism and professional standards. At the same time, Tomcavage can deploy *vertically* allocated incentives to advance inventive practices and distributed problem solving by a *lateral* array of staff inside clinics. Everyday work may be guided by the Hippocratic oath. But the likes of Adam Smith—getting incentives right—help to move how clients are vigorously engaged and remedies are tailored to motivate each patient.

Next we turn to a quite different field—international banking—to see this same kind of perpendicular organizing at play in similar fashion. Then we show how shared decentralizing principles—resembling the same cornerstones—permeate localized reform in schools, NGOs, and public institutions that depend on taxpayer financing. Still, without profits and market share, the center of organizations in the purely public sector often lacks the economic clout to succeed with the ideals and buoying effects of decentralized reforms.

4

International Banking Goes Local—Swedish Organizing in New York

The strong currents that move big institutions to decenter power and resources at times arise from deep below the surface. Take the World Trade Center Hub—the new subterranean warren of shops and walkways, fanning out like elegant tentacles beneath Manhattan's southwest tip. After visiting this retail haven you might thank Handelsbanken—a mouthful and not exactly a household name—the decentralized finance powerhouse that underwrites one key builder of the massive hub.

Handelsbanken hails from Stockholm, yet the geographic center of this vast bank doesn't matter much to the finance wizards sitting in their nicely appointed office just north of Wall Street. "What we don't need is a large headquarters," Mark Cleary told me. He's the deputy general manager of North American operations. "Responsibility is pushed out to the branch network. Even a teller can make a small loan."

Cleary's Third Avenue branch relies not so much on empowered tellers or ATM's stuffed with cash. Instead, the branch looks after a bevy of account executives, traders, and credit experts who move sizeable chunks of capital and vouch for the credit worthiness of major firms—like Skanska USA, the construction giant that extracted the melted steel and powdery debris strewn beneath the imploded World Trade Center. Skanska's nimble capacity to win bids and execute massive projects, engineered from its weathered office in Queens, is greased by daily credit decisions made across the East River, back in Cleary's bank.

In fact, Handelsbanken's unfettered account managers typically make their own decisions about letters of credit, hefty loans, and interest rates paid on short-term deposits. "In New York, Handelsbanken can give us the answer in minutes or hours on legal advice or letters of credit," Monika Sandberg said, the treasury director of Skanska's US operations.

Handelsbanken has operated on the "church-tower principle" since radically decentralizing who allocates loans and grants credit to customers. Each retail branch is charged with burrowing into its own local community. Each branch manager back in Scandinavia once could only do business with firms or families seen from the local church tower. Each customer is assigned a "relationship manager," not unlike the clinical case managers we got to know in the Geisinger health-care case. "The branch is the bank," Handelsbanken's leaders are fond of saying. The Manhattan branch isn't quite so quaint, but its account managers carefully nurture relationships with their customers, including Ikea and General Electric in addition to Skanska.

Handelsbanken is a household name in Stockholm. Even that girl with the dragon tattoo in Stieg Larsson's premiere installment relies on secret revelations by a former Handelsbanken executive. In the nonfiction world, the bank gained international acclaim when annual earnings jumped by two-fifths, even as competitors rode out the treacherous wake of Wall Street's meltdown in 2008. Its competitors referred to Handelsbanken as "the Taliban" of their industry, as it relied on the fundamentals of good banking, even refusing government bailouts in the depths of the Great Recession.[1]

Firms like Skanska and individual customers across northern Europe took solace, even financial refuge, in Handelsbanken, a firm known in Europe for its care with capital and intense commitment to knowing its clients. Despite the Continent's ongoing economic frailties, Handelsbanken passes international stress tests with flying colors. *The Economist* attributes Handelsbanken's vitality to "an extremely decentralized management model. Branch managers are the bank's key decision-makers, no loans can be extended over the heads of branch managers."[2]

Handelsbanken goes against the grain of steady centralization in the field of finance banking. One KPMG International review argues that banks worldwide have pursued "economies of scale through centralization of services on a national, regional, or global scale" over the past generation.[3] This typically involves "fewer points of contact between customers and staff, translating to lower costs" and higher profits.

Vast American banks continue to centralize operations and everyday decisions, especially during uncertain times. They often require potential borrowers and local branches to submit voluminous data, then wait while various analysts in headquarters work toward a decision. Meanwhile, branch managers lose discretion and experience few incentives to learn more about current and potential customers. "We don't have a call center, instead we have individual account managers, a number to call, 24/7 access," Richard Johnson told me, a Handelsbanken veteran based in Stockholm. Indeed, this radically decentered institution builds on the same organizational cornerstones set in place by the leaders of Geisinger Health System, along with the work of new decentralists in education that you will meet in the next chapter.

Back in 1972, Handelsbanken's new leader—a former professor well versed in motivational psychology—began to decentralize and disperse pieces of the bank's Stockholm headquarters, which had steadily grown since the late nineteenth century. He built a culture of local responsibility where branch managers shape the size and personality of their staff, even take the hit on loans when they go south. The bank is committed to learning what makes each client tick and responding locally to their particular needs, from massive New York firms to rural farmers in the far north of Sweden. And we will see how top managers view *decentralizing* as a verb in motion, a constant negotiation over the distribution of authority and know-how between center and branch.

We begin this story in the town of Täby, a comfortable suburb twenty-five minutes north of Stockholm. Here we see how a modest branch office steadily attends to its customers—led by a branch manager who's under pressure to earn a strong return on capital but never told from above *how* to hit performance targets. Then we report on the organizing methods deployed by Handelsbanken's first champion of decentralization, Jan Wallander, who radically devolved power and vast chunks of capital to hundreds of local branches. We return to the brassy Manhattan branch to examine how the bank serves clients with agility, building upon the cornerstones of second-wave decentralists. Finally, we examine Stockholm's contemporary role, what has become a lean and strategic center that attends as much to ethics and the firm's culture as to loan terms and rates of return.

A Swedish Sociology of Local Organizing

"You have to be in Rotary, they know I'm a Täby citizen," Siv Nee said, pointing to her lapel pin, shiny against her midnight-blue suit. "And it's fun, I enjoy it." No ancient church tower was to be found in Täby, a partly forested suburb with nicely kept flats and apartment buildings, home to middle-class and professional families, many who commute to Stockholm each morning. Retirees stroll the expansive shopping mall, a graying community center of sorts, during frigid winters.

Yet Nee, the "almost 50" manager of this tidy Handelsbanken branch—up a flight of stairs, marked by a colorless sign at the mall's edge—attends carefully to her growing list of customers. She has lived in Täby over the past seventeen years. Each day she carves out time to call or visit several customers, ranging from managers of over 1,500 small- to medium-size firms, to some 11,000 individuals who seek home loans each year or simply need to replace a lost credit card. "People here like to have a local bank," she said. Täby is one of 462 Handelsbanken branches spread across Sweden. "If you know the customer, it's good for us, and we benefit from satisfied customers," Nee said. "If I know there's a birthday, I'll send along a card or text."

Nee—resembling a handsomely aging Swedish actress while emoting the candor of a good friend—told the story of a Täby couple who had gone to their summer home; the husband discovered late one afternoon that his wife had mistakenly returned to the city with his wallet. He called in a panic, okay with driving forty minutes to the closest rural branch. But he would not possess a proper ID. The Handelsbanken branch would be closed by the time he arrived. So Nee told him to knock on that office door; she would call her fellow branch manager to vouch for the customer, scoring the necessary cash. "It's not like Handelsbanken wants to earn the last crown right now," she said. "But in the long run we will earn more through these relationships."

"The way decentralization works, the branch is the bank," Nee said, neatly inverting the factory-like hierarchy where central managers gaze down on subordinates. "You can decide everything." Her regional director reports directly to the CEO. "It's a very flat organization," Nee said.

The bank has invested much in Nee as well, stemming from its culture of mentoring, steadily nurturing future leaders from within the firm. Beginning as a twenty-year-old intern working at her hometown branch in Hallstavik, ten kilometers north of Stockholm, Nee never attended university. After several years, she left Handelsbanken for Manufacturers Hanover Trust, where the "credit reviews had to be 20 pages long, and we had to call to New York for everything, to approve anything significant."

Nee lasted just two years under this American-style centralization, returning to Handelsbanken and rising steadily in this much flatter firm. "I think it's more interesting when I can and my team can make decisions on our own," she said with a tone of pride and exuberance. "We can be a staff of 20 or 15, it's up to me. And I can decide salaries. You know, this is a decentralized company," Nee repeated, to make sure that I got it.

Handelsbanken's ethical commitment to localism "mirrors the Swedish way of being," one corporate customer, Elisabeth Mellbin, told me. "I find them to be very service minded, a distinct identity, a tradition of being serious," she said. Mellbin is the chief financial officer for Nomu Kollager, a fifty-year-old company that imports and sells ball bearings of all shapes and sizes. "For me they are purely Swedish, unlike doing business in Denmark or

Finland," she said with a restrained frown. We talked much of the nuts and bolts of the Täby branch, along with details of the bearings industry. But for Mellbin it's the cultural mores and ready responsiveness displayed by Siv Nee and her staff—the trusting social ties—that matter most.

Mellbin's firm helps to design a variety of bearings manufactured in China where labor costs are low; the bearings are then sold to makers of European autos, golf carts, even automatic teller machines. Her firm depends heavily on Handelsbanken for lines of credit to pay the bills. Chinese firms will even invoice Nee's branch "once a week, or could be everyday," then receive a cash transfer. Mellbin doesn't hold on to large cash reserves to cover uncertain billing from the Chinese manufacturers. "All our transactions go through Handelsbanken," Mellbin said. "So, we rely on them, it's very personal."

Mellbin sits with Nee and her branch staff each year to discuss "how much money we will need to borrow." Mellbin then goes to her central board to settle on the terms for loans or letters of credit. "As we have been growing over the past five years, we need more money to make bigger purchases." The Nomu Kollager firm extends credit to its own customers for up to thirty days, again drawing on accounts housed at Handelsbanken. Nee pegs a level of capital that's doled out during the year. She doesn't ask anyone in Stockholm for approval. It's Nee who assesses the risk and potential earnings from this global rolling of ball bearings, greased by her lending decisions.

Mellbin, outgoing and articulate, returned to the sociology of it all when asked why she felt so comfortable with Handelsbanken. "It has to do with how you are treated. It's not overly enthusiastic, and it's not under enthusiastic," she said with an ironic grin. "[Martin] Luther is sitting on my right shoulder, I'm trying so hard to get rid of him." Then, shifting to a more serious tone, "I feel at home here."

The Ethical Priority—Decentering Authority and Responsibility

Leaders at Handelsbanken, going back to the early 1970s, did not simply decenter their expansive institution to shake off the shackles of central regulation and then declare victory. Instead, they steadily kindled a theory of *how* to localize authority, capital, and social tools—aiming to attract trustworthy customers and inculcate a culture of shared responsibility, branch by branch. One business analyst, puzzling through how Handelsbanken had weathered the global recession, post-2008, in flying colors, terms the firm's guiding principle "low risk, high touch local banking."[4]

Handelsbanken was not always so profitable or spread about the globe in such a horizontal and decentered manner. The bank coalesced in 1871, patched together by Stockholm's modest gaggle of merchants. By pooling savings they could provide a pool of capital to collectively aid expanding firms. The bank remained small, operating on the core tenet that its officers should know customers well in order to evaluate the risk associated with each potential borrower. Handelsbanken did not shy away from expanding operations in the early twentieth century, while remaining cautious in lending only to virtuous, well-known clients. By the 1920s it had become Sweden's largest bank with almost three hundred branches nationwide.

The firm became highly centralized during the postwar period, faced with novel demands from the market and tight control of credit by government. Dividing banks into functional segments had become hip among US management gurus, and Handelsbanken followed suit in the 1960s. This meant that its locally rooted retail operation—focusing on deposits and emerging retail services, especially the explosive growth of credit cards—was severed from commercial lending. Even medium-sized loan applications now had to be approved by headquarters, taking over two months on average to review each of about 2,400 corporate loan applications in 1968.[5]

Handelsbanken also felt stiff pressure from Sweden's central bank to become more conservative as growth and high-risk lending surged across Europe in the 1960s. Inflation eroded the value of the Swedish krona, and real estate prices climbed at unprecedented rates. "The Central Bank of Sweden was continually demanding that the banks should reduce their granting of credit," Jan Wallander observed, the former academic who would be asked to take over Handelsbanken in 1970. "Profitability was low and the bank was in conflict with the authorities."[6] Government leaders took the unusual step of publicly criticizing top management. The CEO and several board members soon exited the firm.

The Pragmatic Decentralist

Wallander was a curious choice as the new chief. A former economics professor at the University of Stockholm, he held just a bit of management experience, running a small bank with the consonant-packed name of Sundsvallsbanken, up in the rural north of Sweden. Wallander experimented with letting branch managers build their client base and then control chunks of capital allocated to borrowers, large and small. One contemporary leader at Handelsbanken, Magnus Uggla, told me that Wallander "by necessity had to have a decentralized model" when earlier running the smaller bank up north. "You didn't have computers out in the branches, and you had rural branches way out on the other side of the mountain."

Years later in a remarkable memoir, Wallander traced his theory of decentralization back to graduate school and his early research. "My own doctoral thesis was . . . interdisciplinary. I had the occasion to acquaint myself with American sociological studies of the problems of working life." He wrote of being moved by the Hawthorne Electric experiment, infamous in organizational studies, where management researchers brightly lit assembly lines, piped in fresh air, and signaled that they cared about the well-being of workers. Productivity spiked under these experimental conditions. Wallander also delved into Abraham Maslow's account of intrinsic motivation, accenting the motivational force of self-fulfillment and "the need for appreciation."[7]

Emerging as Sweden's new age banker by the late 1960s, Wallander advanced a universal conception of what sparks worker commitment on the ground. It now sounds a bit dated, but his account of how to motivate local managers and nurture a spirit of cooperation and trust across levels of the organization persists to this day. "All human beings have certain fundamental needs . . . apart from the material ones, are the need to feel a sense of belonging, to get encouragement, to be 'seen,'" Wallander argued. The logic is so reminiscent of Kenda Danowsky's unshakable attempt within the Geisinger firm to nurture patients with a sense of "we're in this together," an ethical message steadily expressed by new decentralists in the education field as well.

Trust in—and Nurturing—Local Capacity

Taking charge of Handelsbanken in 1970, Wallander worried about the creeping centralization of a firm that he believed drew its strength from strong relationships with clients out in the branches. Local managers—potentially drawing on this somehow Swedish or Lutheran tradition of trust—were hogtied by central rules and operational procedures back in Stockholm. "Behind the desire for centralization lies a basic doubt about the employees' ability and a strong feeling that if they are not kept under strict control and told what to do they can go off in the wrong direction," Wallander wrote.[8] He also believed that the arrival of computer technologies would invite stiffer controls from the center, rather than nurturing a culture of local autonomy, responsibility, and human connection in the branches.

Wallander was not simply a theorist of organizational change. He turned out to be a durable in-the-trenches strategist as well. He turned the structure of authority upside down. He believed that vertical layers would only intensify competition for authority and resources, so he shrunk headquarters staff and pruned middle management. He even did away with annual budgets for each branch, a practice he came to call "an unnecessary evil." Wallander said that "there is no reason to disturb the people in the organisation with filling out all the forms that you need to make the budget. The best you can do . . . is not disturb them and help them to solve the problems that they will meet in the course of their normal job."[9]

Wallander established eight regional directors who essentially share healthy dollops of loan capital with each branch manager, then set targets for expected returns on their equity. To this day, Nee and her fellow branch heads draw down equity from the regional office, which they carve into home loans, commercial lines of credit, and retail services. Branches then retain much of the income earned from various transactions with their customers. Branch heads like Nee are set loose to figure out how to lower costs and boost yields on their lending and credit activities.

Wallander scrapped the firm's organization chart, that tidy pyramid with a few managers and thinkers at the top and replaceable subordinates below. He preferred to see organizations "more like a spider web with hundreds of threads showing the interactions of varying strength and character that took place between people in the company." He eliminated the advertising department; he stressed how branch mangers should nurture close relationships with respectable customers, not push retail products designed from afar.

Wallander's social cornerstones are reminiscent of Janet Tomcavage's strategy at Geisinger—flattening the organization chart and inculcating a spirit of collective responsibility for learning about and serving the client. "Decentralisation is at the very heart of Handelsbanken's organizational model. The model means getting close to the customer and being able to suit local conditions and match decision and action to the customers' needs and wishes," Wallander said. "It is a long and difficult process."

He operationalized his theory of decentralization by focusing on the everyday activities and motivations of branch managers and local staff, sounding much like American pragmatists, such as William James or John Dewey. "Reality is shaped by all the small, daily decisions that are taken at various levels of the company," Wallander said. He awarded to about half the bank's staff the authority to make unilateral credit decisions. "Each unit is presumed to work towards developing its own activities and maximizing its profit." Wallander celebrated after leading Handelsbanken for three decades: "The organisation was thus radically decentralised."

One recent study of Handelsbanken found that Wallander's long-standing emphasis on local motivation and client engagement continues to yield benefits in terms of staff morale and longevity. "The overall impression one gets from Handelsbanken staff is that they quite enjoy what they are doing," one analyst wrote.[10] "Especially for those who had worked for other banks . . . it was a liberating feeling to be able to choose which clients to serve, whom to visit in person. Work is more personalized, and the bankers generally feel this enabled them to provide better service." As Handelsbanken rapidly expanded into Britain, it snagged branch managers from competitors, and they began to enjoy client relations and gain authority over how to best respond to customers' own priorities, according to Uggla, the Stockholm-based executive vice president.

Avoiding Individual Incentives

Wallander also believed that individual bonuses—proliferating across American and other European banks since the 1980s—would undermine a culture that should encourage collective responsibility for serving clients and working together inside the branches. Carrots allocated to individual staff would intensify competition among senior staff and branch managers, and discourage cooperation. The American-style practice of highlighting individual performance would undercut local teamwork, Wallander argued. This also resembles the health-care case, where Geisinger managers deploy cash incentives to entire clinics in concert with shifts toward preventive care and cooperative problem solving.

Staff cohesion inside Handelsbanken branches is spurred by competition among the branches and regions to attain higher yields on capital allocations. Performance data are published for each branch worldwide. One overhears in corridors and conference rooms talk of the virtues of trustworthy commercial customers, along with risks associated with individual home loans. About half the bank's profits come from retail operations offered in the branch offices: deposits by individuals, credit cards, and small mortgage loans, according to Stockholm officials. The other half stems from earnings on loans and letters of credit granted to companies, from Skanska in New York to a shoemaker in rural Sweden. This unit competition is similar to how mixed markets of schools compete along shared indicators of performance or "value added," as we examine in the next chapter.

In place of individual bonuses, Wallander created a profit-sharing mechanism called the Oktogonen (Octagon) Foundation in which every staff member has an equal stake, from the CEO to a branch clerk. It's a device that's capitalized by Handelsbanken in every year that the bank outperforms its peers in Sweden and across Europe. The Oktogonen was valued at just over $2 billion in 2011. "I thought that it would be good idea if the employees were to become part owners of the Bank," Wallander said. Each can receive their cash share at retirement, presently equaling over $1 million for even the lowest employee, provided they have worked in the firm for at least twenty years.

Part of the bank's high-touch, low-risk philosophy involves being picky about its customers. Handelsbanken avoids risks that fueled Wall Street's meltdown in 2008, such as mounds of bad home mortgages or imploding hedge funds. Branches are encouraged to nurture trustworthy clients, reminiscent of small-town banking in Sweden, or say the American Midwest. And "giving people responsibility, including for losses," helps to build "a very strong credit culture," Cleary, the Manhattan deputy chief, said. In 2001 Handelsbanken staff made just over 400,000 credit decisions, of which about 390,000 were made by branch staff, according to Wallander's own account. Just 800 cases—large or somehow dicey loan proposals—came to the central board.

Wallander realized that decentering this massive firm required a shrewd and surgical center—one that sets crisp performance goals, designs recognizable product lines, and offers the data and technology that inform local branches. The center reinforces core tenets as well: the ethical accent on local discretion, personal relationships, and shared responsibility for the firm's vitality. "Decentralization is like pulling a rubber band," Wallander writes. "You have to hold the ends firmly, otherwise it will snap back in your face and you will have to start over again."

Let's turn next to this rock-solid cornerstone of Handelsbanken's strategy for decentering authority and capital—recasting the organization's center to ensure responsive and trusting service out in the branches. It exemplifies how Handelsbanken pulls from the playbook of second-wave decentralists.

Nimble Service, Lasting Trust

When Monika Sandberg needs to corral a few million dollars or secure a letter of credit—like say within the next twenty-four hours—she often calls from an aging, four-story building in Queens to Handelsbanken's tasteful Manhattan branch. She runs American operations for "the internal bank" of the construction giant, Skanska. Perhaps a major payment is due to a subcontractor working on the Number 7 subway tunnel beneath Times Square, or refurbishing the next floor inside the majestic United Nations headquarters overlooking the East River. Sandberg is the one who must raise cash, and fast. One-third of Skanska's $23 billion in annual revenues stem from North American projects, financed from Sandberg's shop.

Her easy smile and calm manner are rather deceptive. Late into our relaxed yet frank two-hour conversation, a bit like chatting easily with a youthful aunt, I realized that Sandberg operates more like a mellow taxi dispatcher. But rather than frenetically matching drivers to riders, she is borrowing money, securing credit, or making deposits from an array of banks, under great time pressure, still with measured synchrony.

She's keenly aware that Skanska's engineers, demolition teams, and construction crews must keep pace with tight schedules. Financial penalties may follow a missed deadline. Construction partners will balk if Sandberg can't assemble the cash or credit in time. "We have many, many accounts and many, many clients. If we are expecting big payments . . . at a certain point in the day, they move into our cash pool," then they are quickly deposited or invested to maximize yields. At the same time, "project managers are forecasting what their cash needs are to pay a bevy of subcontractors. When I log in, my colleagues are standing by (in Stockholm) to overview the entire cash position." So Sandberg meticulously avoids borrowing too early or repaying (lent) capital too late. The margins on lending cash or buying a credit chit—which buoy the bank's earnings—represent steep costs for Skanska, given the vast sums that Sandberg is moving around. Timing is everything for this mild-mannered finance wizard.

Trusting that she will benefit from nimble service, Sandberg often turns to Handelsbanken for a letter of credit or what's known as a surety bond for publicly funded projects, like revamping Manhattan subway stations. Both financial tools—required for new bids and ongoing projects—guarantee that if Skanska failed to deliver on the project, Handelsbanken would pay the Port Authority or the developer who's contracted with Skanska. This means that Handelsbanken is widely exposed if their customer, Skanska in this case, fails to erect the skyscraper or promptly bore a massive tunnel under the terms of their contract. Yet letters of credit yield "quite high returns," according to one top Handelsbanken manager in Stockholm, charging handsomely for the sizeable risk they take on. And the bank's reputation is built from keen knowledge of Scandinavian firms that now thrive in the New York area.

This is where the local discretion and particular knowledge held by Handelsbanken's account managers prove invaluable for Sandberg, since time is indeed money. Describing one project that involved a long negotiation with all parties, Sandberg reported that "compared with a more centralized bank, we had more expertise at the table [with Handelsbanken]." Or when a Skanska client wants to tweak or "remove a paragraph in a letter of credit deal, Handelsbanken in New York can give us the answer in minutes or hours . . .

given their high level of expertise," Sandberg said. She waits much longer when she's forced to rely on an American bank. Instead, the decentralized authority that Mark Cleary and colleagues back at Handelsbanken hold allows for quick decisions and the building of thick trust over time. In turn, greater trust makes each decision a bit easier for Cleary's staff, lowering transaction costs on both sides.

Sandberg did recall one instance where "closer coordination with [headquarters in] Stockholm" would have advanced a project more effectively. "It could have been a swifter process," Sandberg said in her direct, yet even tone. "He was a good guy [in the Manhattan branch], but he was broader and not specialized with specific expertise." Yet overall Sandberg talked of how "other banks have to go back to headquarters or a private law firm, and this takes time. Handelsbanken has an edge here in New York. I feel more comfortable having an expert on the ground." Echoing Wallander's original account of local motivation, Sandberg emphasized how "they take on much more responsibility here in New York."

Handelsbanken's agile operation springs to life when firms need short-term loans, or want to park or invest large chunks of capital. "It may be overnight or for three months," Sandberg said. Account executives in Manhattan quickly price such services and promptly negotiate the deal. She cited the fact that Handelsbanken has a strong credit rating and that they even weathered the post-2008 recession in shipshape. Whether Handelsbanken gets this business depends on Skanska's cash flow at the moment, along with overall market conditions. And Sandberg aims "to get a good interest rate" from Cleary and colleagues. They know that she can always turn to another bank. But "they are nice and professional," enjoyable to work with, Sandberg said. She kept returning to this tacit blend of hardheaded pricing decisions, deep trust, and the ease of daily relationships, even negotiating deals in Swedish.

The utility of decentralized authority, this structural authority to make decisions on the spot, within the branch surfaced in other arenas. When there's a "market event," as Sandberg said in typically understated fashion, she's back on the phone with Handelsbanken and others on Wall Street. "When the market is misbehaving, they get in touch with us too. What kinds of statements have federal officials made? Why is the Fed's effective rate dropping? Time is a crucial part of this business," she stressed. "They are able to give us expertise and advice in a swift way."

I asked whether this ease between Skanska and Handelsbanken stemmed from shared cultural tenets, even when negotiating lower interest rates or price concessions on short-term deposits. "The Swedish banks, we understand each other better . . . we trust each other better," Sandberg said. "I deal with a lot of American banks. They are huge, more bureaucratic." Echoing why Siv Nee back in Täby could stomach working at Manufacturers Hanover for only a couple years, Sandberg said, "Swedes are not as bureaucratic, we don't have that many forms that need to be completed."

"We can't exactly see White Plains from here"
NURTURING LONG-TERM RELATIONSHIPS

Back in Manhattan—comfortably disposed in a wood-paneled conference room sitting amid, oddly, Danish-modern furniture—Mark Cleary eagerly detailed how they move with such agility, enabled by the bank's radically decentered structure, to serve large American or Scandinavian firms, like Time-Warner or Skanska. "What you don't need is a huge head office. You have strength out in the branches." Cleary and fellow managers kept returning to organizational principles voiced by fellow decentralists in the health-care and education fields—learning what makes clients tick, what motivates them to engage Handelsbanken. In turn, this nurtures trust and encourages more versatile job roles and a steady rethinking of what the organization's center can best provide.

Once a young graduate student of Scandinavian languages and literature at University College London, Cleary speaks with care and precision, ever reflective as if still a linguistics student. His pride over the branch's work and success often surfaced during our two-year-long conversation, not to mention patient candor in fielding even critical questions. "We can't exactly see White Plains from here," an ironic play on the bank's church-tower ditty, "but we are closest to the customer." Handelsbanken's localized decision making has "become folklore, it becomes a culture," Cleary said.

"The branch manager is responsible for everything that the customer needs," as he put it. "They have been entrusted (by headquarters)." Handelsbanken's center has accomplished what other decentralists aspire to do; the firm's ethical commitment to local authority and shared responsibility feels deeply lodged in the branches, be they small-scale and retail, or Manhattan super-sized and corporate. It's in the air. Forty years ago Jan Wallander was devising strategies from the center to devolve this sense of collective responsibility out to the branches. Today this decentered spirit and local authority over lending and staffing appears to run even deeper within the firm's tacit culture, as Cleary emphasized.

At the same time, the bank's center in Stockholm is quite present in retail branches that serve individual customers across Scandinavia and northern

Europe, designing the form of checking accounts, ATM cards, savings options, and home loans. Each product line is designed and adjusted centrally, each sporting the vivid Handelsbanken logo. But unlike American banks, these product lines are not pressed on the client; they are soft-sold options for customers as individual relationships are built over time. Executives at headquarters—ensconced in Handelsbanken's gracious eighteenth-century palace, reminiscent of the US treasury building in Washington—set performance targets and monitor the progress of each branch around the globe. Headquarters offers specialized expertise, as Skanska's Sandberg mentioned, from legal counsel to currency transactions, along with the constant signaling of shared norms and a shared allegiance to the commonweal.

"It all comes down to relationships"

Handelsbanken leans heavily on one cornerstone of second-wave decentralization: that steady curiosity over what motivates each client. Talking of the branch manager's local authority, Cleary highlights that "being in the community, they know the character of people." It sounded so quaint, so civil. Sure, account managers talk through deals that offer attractive terms for clients. The finance game is animated by the desire for wider margins, stronger yields on equity. But I kept hearing from various staffers that it's the trust and comfort that undergirds the steady dialogue with clients, whether nurturing ties with villagers in rural Sweden or with gargantuan firms in New York City.

"It's all about relationships," as Richard Johnson, the Manhattan manager of corporate banking, put it. "When I present to senior management, they ask, 'How often do you talk with the customer? How broad is the relationship? What levels of management are you talking with?' We talk 15 minutes about the relationship and five minutes on some graph regarding the trends."

Johnson is a twenty-six-year veteran at Handelsbanken; he first joined the firm at nineteen years of age. And, like Cleary, he emotes the same openness and enthusiasm for the underlying social relations that mark the bank's everyday climate. For Johnson, decentralizing authority to his account managers is built upon trust inside the firm—mirroring the same curiosity and respect that marks relations with clients. This stems from knowing most colleagues quite well and a shared ethos dedicated to nurturing long-term relationships. Drawing on the Skanska case, "If Monika agrees with Anders, who's the account manager, then senior management doesn't need to get involved. I've known Anders for many years," Johnson said. Speaking of his entire branch staff, "I need to feel very confident that they are making good decisions." And once again, the deeper cultural dynamic—collectively held social tenets—entered the equation. "Trust is huge among customers from Nordic countries," Johnson emphasized.

The agility of Handelsbanken staff—given their decentered, unbridled authority—helps to advance long-term relationships with clients. "It's more important that the relationship manager knows what's going on, [that] they are checking with the customer on a regular basis." Firms often need letters of credit or short-term loans quickly, as Sandberg discussed in Queens. Rapid yet careful turnaround is key. "Sometimes we need to make a quick decision," Johnson said. "We agree with the customer over the phone. It's now eleven o'clock, we will have the FedEx out by 3:00. Other banks say, 'okay, we'll check with the head office and be back to you in two weeks.'"

The discretion that branch staff holds contributes to their nimble responsiveness for clients and empowers branch managers to reward effective colleagues. Johnson, like Nee outside Stockholm, hires and fires branch staff and makes salary decisions each year in consultation with fellow managers. "When we sit and talk about 10 percent or 15 percent [for a certain account executive], you know that I have the power to make the decision," Johnson said. "It puts more pressure on you and me to get ready, to specify a development plan." Bonuses remain off the table in all but a few units of Handelsbanken, but staff members know that higher branch earnings will boost the Oktogonen retirement fund. Johnson at times has hired more senior and sage account executives, but this addition to his salary bill means he can hire fewer younger staffers.

Negotiating Decentralization

Johnson talks of decentralizing management as a verb—a contested treaty of sorts between the center and local branches. Decentralization is molded over time, like wet clay; it is not fixed bedrock or a static social structure. He's held accountable for sinking earnings or when a client defaults on a loan. "I take responsibility for the losses, they aren't passed anywhere," Johnson said. So he steadily gauges when and how to involve branch colleagues in key decisions. Constant deliberation gets more information on the table and minimizes risk for the branch. This may require calling Stockholm for specialized expertise, say, on currency exchange issues or advice on a highly technical industry. At the same time, clients like Sandberg require quick pricing decisions, balancing the bank's wish for bigger margins against the client's desire to pay less or earn a higher return on deposits and investments.

"The account manager is responsible for all kinds of pricing decisions. I'm here to discuss it. If they want to take a loss on a transaction, as long as the overall profitability is fine, then it's their decision." Account managers "are used to being involved in decisions," but cultural variability comes into play once again. "It's an overall consensus agreement," Johnson said. "In Sweden there's a norm that everyone is involved in the decisions." So vertically conceived decentering interacts with typically lateral social relations inside branches.

Johnson thinks constantly about the tools his staff have at their fingertips to offer clients—a portion of which emanate from the center. His staff in Manhattan "bridge over to other traders in other countries." And "information flows from the center on capital markets to New York customers, which draws on (the bank's) European expertise." The occasional softness of national economies, as in Greece or Spain, spurs demand for fiscal knowledge directly from the Continent. And currency transfers often require a quick response from bank colleagues who are spread around the globe. So the center ensures that tools remain at Johnson's fingertips, even as he makes the ultimate decision over a pending deal.

Johnson returned to his ability to design financial mechanisms that prove responsive to his clients' needs. This often turns on simplifying decision making, cutting out paperwork, and shortening turnaround time. We try to be "less bureaucratic. Sometimes things are complicated in this market, but a lot of times they don't need to be so complicated." For example, Johnson has pushed to simplify billing for specific services. "This way of transparent pricing isn't that common in the U.S. market," he said. For one major Swedish company Johnson helped to draft a simple, one-page agreement, "just one page of text," he proudly said. Another case Johnson cited arose when he was a branch manager in Stockholm. He wanted to shift the branch office to a better location. When he checked with his regional manager, "he said, 'you don't have to talk to me about it. If you want to move the branch that's your decision.'"

Johnson also candidly highlights facets of decentralization that seem overly dogmatic. "We have conversations [in the branch] over who should book travel," he said, with eyebrows raised. "Siv negotiates the power bill for her branch" in Täby, "even though the center could negotiate a better price . . . but it's against our model." Still, Johnson's perspective that decentralizing management is an ongoing process, not a fixed feature of immutable culture, is key—a perspective that I heard from within Handelsbanken's mother ship as well, back in Stockholm.

The Ethical Heart of Decentralized Banking

Rising stars in the bank must spend time in Stockholm, "to become a real Handelsbanker," as Cleary puts it. It's an identity that managers cleverly invoke to denote tribal membership. That's precisely what Magnus Uggla did in 1989, returning to headquarters after founding the Manhattan branch. He soon took charge of a new initiative, mounted by then-CEO Arne Martensson, "to export the bank's model" to other nations. Uggla is now the bank's longest-serving executive vice president, watching after international operations in nineteen countries outside Scandinavia. He views Handelsbanken from a revealing vantage point—deeply committed to its decentered culture, while trying to put the bank's magic in a bottle and export it to wildly diverse settings, from northern England to Singapore.

Asked why he, Cleary, and colleagues succeeded in creating the robust Manhattan branch, Uggla opened with that ever-salient element of Handelsbanken culture, the firm "is built on trust. Yes, we have very difficult negotiations. But if you have a long term relationship, there is trust." Contrasting his firm with "American-style banks," Uggla said, "we are a relationship bank. Some banks are transactional banks, where they are looking for the big deal and then move on."

Uggla's analysis also stressed how "Americans are much more legalistic. It's very much about this is my role, this is what I can do. I see there's a problem, but that's not my role." So branch managers are constantly looking upward for approvals, for home mortgages to large corporate loans. "I know a Swedish guy married to a British nurse. If she's responsible for a certain thing, and someone in the next room is dying, she can't turn on the oxygen," Uggla said with a smile, signaling exaggeration. In contrast, Stockholm delegates authority to branch managers, and they thrive on responsibility rather than cautiously hiding out within a circumscribed role, he said.

Uggla beamed with pride when asked about the bank's booming expansion in Britain, even in the fading wake of recession, a boom built largely on profits stemming from letters of credit and lending to small and medium-size firms. "In the U.K. we started our branch expansion in Nottingham, a very parochial city," Uggla said. "We figured that if we can make it here, we can make it anywhere in England." Not to mention home to Robin Hood and Maid Marian, a fact perhaps not lost on executives at Barclays and Lloyds, as they continue to lose market share to Handelsbanken. The count of branches in England has climbed from forty-four to 163 since 2008, spearheaded by Anders Bouvin. Capital allocations now move from Stockholm down through four regional banks situated in the United Kingdom.[11] "We attracted a seventh-generation lord, somebody with a big castle, and the family had banked at Barclays for generations," Uggla said proudly.

Handelsbanken quietly stormed into northern England and "hired experienced bankers who had been at their company for 20, 25 years," Uggla said. "British banks have been very centralized. They are usually very frustrated. They have to fill out a form for 60 different products each week. It drives your behavior whether that's what the customers want or not," he said. And "American managers had come in to run the retail operations. You call a branch . . . and you get a call center in Scotland or India." Suddenly, the British defectors, now managing Handelsbanken branches, "say, 'hey, we have more say,'" Uggla said. Savoring emblematic stories, Uggla detailed how "we one-upped them in East Anglia," winning the loan deal to finance the renovation of the Norwich cathedral, built in 1096. "It gives new meaning to the church-tower principle," he said.

Uggla accented how Stockholm has extended decentralization way beyond what even Wallander had envisaged, supporting Johnson's view back in New York—that the localizing of management remains a work in progress. "He wasn't brave enough to let the branch managers hire their own staff, we did that in the 1990s." By 2002 top management had negotiated a deal with labor unions to allow branch managers to set salary raises, rather than continuing negotiations at the center. (Bank staff, even branch managers, have long been union members, another wrinkle of Sweden's cooperative socialism.) Still, Uggla remains perplexed over how to transplant the Handelsbanken model, especially in American-like environments where short-term profits reign supreme, where "you just have two quarters to show results."

Pitching the same organizational tenets heard in Manhattan and suburban Täby, Uggla hammered on the principle that "if you are a branch manager, you are like a CEO of a small company. You decide where to locate the branch and what customers to approach." And be unrelenting in learning, he said, about what your clients desire. "In other big banks, they have credit cards this month and home loans next, without listening to what the customers really want."

Uggla emphasized how the engineering of local responsibility requires steady work, constant dialogue about distributed authority. He tells branch managers to ask, "Whenever you are in doubt, what would I want your bank to do with my money," as opposed to simply "playing with other people's money." And since local managers are gauged on progress in lowering the ratio of operating costs to income, they get inventive in slicing costs. "Some of the branches have their own vacuum, and you see them cleaning their own floors," Uggla reported.

He views Stockholm's role as twofold. First, headquarters must continue to define and reinforce the Handelsbanken culture, trumpeting local authority and norms of trust and collective responsibility out to far-flung regional offices and branch managers. Flipping back to his beachhead in Britain, Uggla said, "In a way, our corporate culture is stronger in the U.K. than in Sweden. When you open a new branch you have to do the talk all the time, we have a long process when we hire new people." It reminded me of how immigrant diaspora reproduce purer cultural forms of the past, as novel adaptations unfold back home.

Second, the center helps make sense of the surrounding, often uncertain market and regulatory environs, along with keeping tabs on big chunks of capital. Stockholm must approve giant loans to large corporations, like Skanska or Volvo. "We have very large exposures, probably upward of 80 percent of our loan volume," Uggla said. Headquarters also tracks ever-changing market rules, pressed from the US or Swedish governments, along with the European Union. Stockholm directs the firm's information system, allowing top executives to monitor the performance of regional offices, pegged to agreed-upon benchmarks. In turn, the directors stack up the earnings and operating costs of each regional bank. And Stockholm runs a global human resources shop, "looking ahead as to the kind of people we should be hiring," he said.

Uggla seized on the question of why Swedes would devise such a radically decentered way of doing business. He promptly clicked on a smartphone app that ranks societies along various attributes, from "respect for authority" to "feminine sensitivity." Was a deeper cultural dynamic at play, as clients suggested, from Täby to Queens? "We're Lutheran in Sweden, in a small country, so we know each other," Uggla said. "We criticize the boss . . . [and] being cautious with expenses is just fine."

Pushing more deeply, Uggla harked back to humanistic ideals of the Enlightenment. "It's a culture of trust," he said almost in passing. "We believe that human beings are basically good, can be trusted and given responsibility. We just put them in a context where this happens."

Nurturing Leaders from Within

Leaders of Handelsbanken don't readily experiment with novel job roles, as we learned from other second-wave decentralists. Yet from Wallander's day forward the firm has squished vertical hierarchy and pushed against role specialization. These classic Weberian conceptions of modern organization run counter to the flat, lateral way in which work is organized inside local branches. Everyone must get to know the clients, what makes them tick, how service can become more responsive.

At the same time, the Handelsbanken culture is sustained by mentoring emerging leaders from within. "A vital part of our philosophy [is] to use internal recruitment [when] appointing senior executives," Wallander writes. "A large number of these executives have imbibed our philosophy with their mother's milk . . . which is a clear advantage."[12] Or, as Uggla put it, "we must be sure that we have the competence in-house to grow." He helped to attract Mark Cleary to the new Manhattan branch in 1987, then moved him into a widening set of responsibilities.

Mentoring is deeply woven into the firm's social fabric. "The culture, the management style tends to be inclusive, it's not dogmatic, it tends to be more collaborative [than American banks]," Cleary said. "Each of the branch managers who have been here . . . have been valuable in terms of watching how they manage." The term *coaching* kept arising in my conversations in New York and Stockholm. "Where you are responsible for a division, you are responsible for coaching," Cleary said.

The firm distributes a cultural manifesto of sorts, called *Our Way*, to staff. Among other core norms it "tells you how to encourage respect for other people in the bank," Cleary said. The operating guideline maps how each staff member creates a development plan, and "the head overseeing that person is responsible for making sure this is followed up," Cleary said. And "since there's a pushing out of responsibility, you really are responsible for your own development . . . if you push, it is really answered."

What happens when a rookie staffer arrives at Handelsbanken, unaware of the firm's culture-rich backstory? "Yeah, we do have younger guys coming in from an American bank," Cleary said. "They are used to more rigid, micromanaged environments." Sharp dissonance flares up when new account managers join the corporate banking section. It's "where there is the most culture clash," according to Cleary. "We have a pretty conservative, a strong credit culture. We won't look at it [lending possibility] just because it's a profitable transaction. It's the relationship that matters in the long run," Cleary said.

The draw of Stockholm remains strong for rising executives like Cleary, who serve the bank far from Scandinavia. Four years in, Cleary needed to improve his Swedish and benefit from a stiff dose of the Handelsbanken spirit. So the bank sponsored three months in Stockholm for Cleary and his family. "All the Norwegian vocabulary I had," harking back to college days, "slowly became more like Swedish," he said. The time "was to understand the culture better, not just the language. You become a true Handelsbanker so to speak." This mentoring process acts to pull rising managers into the bank's cultural center, to strength tribal ties and practical skills. "When I go to Sweden, or when on the marketing side, it's more comfortable for the customer, I speak the language," Cleary said.

Decentralizing in Competitive Markets—Lessons from Handelsbanken

This vast yet deeply decentralized bank offers a provocative case of how a culture of local authority and shared responsibility acts to motivate practitioners and clients alike, not to mention spark healthy profits in a treacherous market. The four cornerstones of second-wave decentralization lay just beneath the firm's surface, as revealed in the health-care case, easy to unearth and dust off. "It's all about relationships" was a phrase often expressed, as Handelsbanken managers pushed unrelentingly to get to know their clients, to build long-term trust and confidence in working together. There's little verticality to Handelsbanken, just three layers: Stockholm headquarters, regional directors, and the global archipelago of branches. Most of the action occurs horizontally, building reciprocal ties with clients and working collaboratively inside branch offices.

The bank is ever curious about and attentive to its widening range of clients. Locally rooted branches can serve their particular finance needs, from sheepherders in the north of Sweden to huge firms like Skanska or Ikea in New York. Handelsbanken is picky about its customers, building long-term relationships with sound and credit-worthy businesses and individuals. This limits how far we can generalize from this private sector firm. Still, as we saw at Geisinger and will discover in decentralized firms in the education sector, Handelsbanken learns about its clients through human-scale contact and sophisticated data systems, aided by the center. The bank has fine-tuned a social technology for nurturing a reliable client base. Then it pays close attention to the services and instruments their clients desire and dodges products designed by faraway marketeers.

Another cornerstone embedded by the new decentralists involves rethinking the role and surgical tools of the center. Stockholm is unrelenting as it reinforces the firm's ethical principles, those that define its rich, coherent culture. It also forges the finance tools that make its global network of branches more attractive locally. Top managers, like Johnson and Uggla, emphasized how decentering authority and resources in a vast organization is not a done deal—it's a work in progress. During Uggla's era even greater authority has been devolved to branch managers: control over capital, staffing, and salaries. Johnson continues to think through how to best involve his account executives in local policy and pricing decisions, even in the minutiae of maintaining an elegant office just off Wall Street. As the bank spreads throughout the United Kingdom, its cultural tenets, local authority, and products are championed by British disciples, the newly empowered branch managers. Once again, we see this symbiotic cooperation between a bureaucratically thin, yet normatively thick center sharing responsibility with responsive managers at the grass roots.

Handelsbanken managers offer a wealth of Lutheran jokes, typically delivered in understated fashion with a barely detectable grin. But there is something about the historical scale of Sweden, about the modesty and thrift of Scandinavian Lutherans that explains the core ethics, familiarity, and even caution that characterize the bank's unifying culture. Ironically, it operates in opposition to the impersonal centralization of glitzy American banks, while it beats these shortsighted competitors at their own capitalist game.

Experimentation with job roles is the one cornerstone of decentralization *nouveau* that's not essential to the organizational architecture of Handelsbanken, as seen in our health-care and education cases. Once the bank radically decentralized out to branch managers and pared down middle management, little appetite for specialization has reappeared. Instead, the Handelsbanken culture encourages lateral deliberation over local decisions. This seems to advance shared ownership of key decisions, in turn reaping the benefits or taking the hit, together.

I came away seeing little ambiguity in everyone's role inside the bank. The work of regional chiefs and executives is clearly delineated, understood by most. They are to provide attractive products and credit devices for the branches, then dish out information and incentives for hitting performance targets. The game is a bit simpler than shifting patients with chronic illness, or motivating blue-collar teens to engage with high school. But the bank's laser-sharp focus on lowering the ratio of costs to income—whether the branch is near the Arctic Circle or Rockefeller Center—allows branches to nurture relationships with clients and cooperate more tightly to hit an unambiguous target. Then, branch managers exercise wide-ranging discretion in order to engage and respond to widely diverse clients.

Perhaps it's a bit forced to categorize thinkers inside Handelsbanken as second-wave decentralists. After all, Jan Wallander laid out the blueprint to decentralize almost four decades ago. He drew on American theories of intrinsic motivation and localism, blending them with Swedish socialist thought. Still, these cornerstones—knowing the client, rethinking the center's ethical core, empowering local managers, and experimenting with job roles—have proved prescient in shaping the social architecture that's sweeping into health care, education, and neighboring fields. And Handelsbanken shows how these organizing principles can energize a robust firm in a competitive market.

It's fair to ask, how much can be generalized from the Handelsbanken case. This firm has clearly devised social forms couched within the norms and expectations for trust and mutual obligation that arise within Scandinavian societies. And the firm's decentered architecture was designed in part by a charismatic manager, richly informed by his remarkable application of motivational theory. Still, this firm now reproduces its ethical commitments and rendition of local authority with intent, displaying openness to contention and renegotiation long after Jan Wallander left his imprint. And the fact that the basic organizational model is being transplanted to a variety of societies and markets is testimony to its external validity.

Handelsbanken's organization cornerstones resemble those uncovered within Geisinger Health System, along with the pillars of decentralized schools in the case to which we next turn. I am not arguing that these social-organization features look identical across these contrasting fields, or undergird the infrastructure of decentralization with equal strength. But the similarities in how the new decentralists organize for local control, at the very least, offer institutional features that are ripe for empirical replication across other firms.

I was hard pressed to find critical assessments of Handelsbanken, either in the business media or academic journals. This was likely colored by the bank's unusually strong performance during the post-2008 recession and the financial aftermath left behind across much of Europe. Future research on decentralized firms in markets should define collateral measures of success to dig deeper into how staff experience local control, or whether certain clients are less taken by Handelsbanken's customs.

Textured cases, of course, generate more hypotheses than empirical answers. Along the way, for instance, I noticed that my in-house guides rarely mentioned disgruntled or lost clients. My two years of conversations and visits to New York and Stockholm led me through a network of top managers and the branch chiefs for whom each held considerable respect for the other. Research in the future should certainly consider actors who deal less well with local control or the ambiguities inherent in serving a variety of clients, or taking the hit for decisions gone awry. New work could more precisely estimate how these organizational features motivate practitioners, enrich trust, and further the social benefits that stem from decentralization. That said, Handelsbanken has certainly devised a form of local cooperation that adapts to the demands of markets while fulfilling richer human aspirations at deeper levels.

5

The Four R's—A School Where Relationships Come First

WITH LYNETTE PARKER

Pablo Alba, a lanky sophomore with a jet-black ponytail, volunteered little beyond a cautious glance upward to meet my eyes. He had been called to the principal's office for no clear reason.[1] But Alba soon perked up—a slight grin easing across this somber, mahogany face—when I asked him to describe his first year at City Arts and Technology High School.

It's a young charter school, dubbed CAT, that first opened in a San Francisco storefront next to the Saint Emydius cathedral in 2004. Two years later they acquired a circa 1970s public school, a boxy, beige two-story building that sits adjacent to a sparkling green knoll, looking across the graying end of the city's Mission District.

"You make a lot of friends, it's small." Alba soon came alive. "It's not an assignment to learn everyone's name." And teachers quickly forgot anyway, at the faceless middle school he attended. Each "teacher had to grade 180 essays, they didn't have time to check in, they had to deal with the trouble makers." Some parents work this city's blossoming market of school options, including Alba's parents and other lower-income families that sort into CAT. A few numbers to get your bearings: three-fifths of all students qualify for federal lunch subsidies. Yet nine in every ten enter college after graduating. This, after about one-quarter leave CAT along the way.

Just one year under his belt at CAT when we first met, Alba readily described his favorite teachers with characteristic brevity and affection, especially Danielle Johnson, a thirty-four-year-old history teacher. "She's a great teacher, she doesn't babble that much, she explains things really well," Alba said.

I had first taken note of this understated kid, articulate yet somehow disaffected, in Johnson's "advisory period," where unsure teens vented about growing up, prepared for public exhibitions of their work, and scoped out how to apply for college. Alba mostly kept his head down in advisory. Then he would look up, appearing a bit startled, and insert a fresh idea with razor-sharp precision. Say, on the topic of legal challenges to government secrecy: "these judges instill their own values on these precedents . . . that they deem as moral in essence."

Alba proved to be a remarkable, maturing teenager during the two years we followed him around, from school to home. He still blends slight reticence with inadvertent charm. But he wasn't unique among the 360 restless, often inquisitive adolescents who attend CAT each year, one campus of the flat and highly decentralized firm Envision Charter Schools.

This chapter digs into a third case of how decentralizing organizations—detached from a bureaucratic apparatus and centrally set rules—endeavor to craft social relations that engage clients, unite practitioners, and nurture mutual obligation among the collective's members. Envision's own center, staffed by a small team of creative and rigorous coaches, is showing what the decentering of urban institutions can do. Unlike conventional city schools—tethered to a downtown bureaucracy, labor contracts, and a mile-high pile of state regulations—Envision is free to set its own course, provided it selects incoming pupils by lottery and administers state testing each spring.

While evidence on the comparative benefits of charter schools remains mixed, as detailed in chapter 2, this inventive school shines a bright analytic light on the social architecture of local organizing that helps to account for CAT's success in moving its poor and blue-collar kids into four-year colleges. These new decentralists are focused less on the political battle of breaking away from a bureaucratic center and more on devising the pedagogical and social tools that engage their antsy adolescents.

Envision's designers have set in place organizational cornerstones that resemble the core features we discovered with Geisinger and Handelsbanken, although their clients and the task at hand differ greatly. We quickly realized that the decentered discretion afforded CAT by a charter-governance arrangement doesn't necessarily lead to these shared organizational features. But the odds of planting these cornerstones seem much higher, after breaking away from the confining hierarchy of urban schooling and hog-tied by thick labor contracts. The wider Envision firm also illustrates how a surgical and well-tooled center can help to design core activities and everyday practices in local units on the ground.

We tell the story of how Alba, teacher Johnson, and fellow members of CAT wield the pedagogical tools and in-your-face social relations that characterize the work of the new decentralists within the education sector. Their labor and social forms swivel around the four cornerstones of decentralized organizing. Similar to the prior cases, we discovered a core creed, driving ethical principles that nudge teachers to focus on relationships and shared obligations to fellow members of the community, along with high standards for achievement and the broader social development of their clients.

First, interwoven with teachers' everyday work is an *unrelenting curiosity* over what motivates each pupil, then discrete methods for *scaffolding up from their interests and immediate contexts*. This leads to pedagogical tools and tailored opportunities that fit specific students. As candid teachers get to know each student, these cautious adolescents become more trusting, coming to feel that their teachers really do know them and care about their future. CAT teachers and ever-present coaches from the Envision firm steadily push to grasp what makes their charges tick.

Second, teachers at CAT experiment with *versatile job roles*, asking how they can better engage and motivate their students—the imagery of "warm demanders" that principal Allison Rowland often painted. We detail how teachers work together—coaching one another to improve pedagogy, working through behavioral problems, and constantly sharing intimate knowledge of their students. At the same time, innovative devices like the advisory period, imported from elite private schools, invite flexibility in the teacher's role; the teacher now takes responsibility for tracking each student's well-being. Few students fall through the cracks at CAT.

The elasticity of roles and the focus on the each teen's multidimensional growth leads to a third organizational cornerstone—a shift toward more *lateral forms of discourse* with students and fellow practitioners. This doesn't displace the teacher's authoritative role, but instead signals a steady caring about each student's future and cues a sense of mutual obligation, not simply conformity to impersonal rules set from above.

And fourth, Envision's leaders build out from a lean *organizational center that expresses clear ethical principles*. Managers and pedagogical coaches constantly signal respect and curiosity for their clients and forge the everyday activities and instructional strategies that advance learning. The center ensures that new teachers focus on building relationships, nurturing engagement, and preparing students with a wide range of social and intellectual skills. These are sacred tenets of Envision. The center collaborates with teachers to improve the pedagogical tools they deploy, creating templates for hands-on, multimedia projects and public exhibitions of students' accumulating portfolio of work. The aim—accented and illustrated day in and day out—is to get every student ready for and applying to a bevy of fine colleges. But this concrete goal is approached by building a thick culture of respect and responsibility for the broad growth of these working-class adolescents—a deeply ethical mission that inculcates trust in teachers and their ambitious agenda for these youths.

New Decentralists Rethink Schools

Bob Lenz, who hatched Envision in 2002, shared the restless feeling of his teenage students after working in Bay Area schools for many years. He helped to redesign Drake High School, a suburban campus set in the flatlands of Marin County, engulfed by age-old redwoods and aging ranch-style homes. Lenz toiled with several reform groups to build smaller "academies" within this comprehensive high school, focusing students on discrete fields, like health sciences, digital media, or the arts and theater. Each student built a portfolio of work from Dewey-esque, hands-on projects, which addressed a renewable energy problem or public health issues, like AIDS or teen pregnancy.

He set out to inculcate "leadership skills" in students, from arguing persuasively to working cooperatively, dynamic competencies that kids in well-off Marin County might embrace, but not necessarily hardened blue-collar kids in urban schools, critics would argue. So Lenz decided to prove the skeptics wrong—drawing on California's policy mechanism for chartering taxpayer-financed, yet freely run schools. It's a bit like how the Queen of England once chartered banks or shoemakers to operate, blessing their operation and then lightly tracking their reputability.

Lenz didn't just spout theory about how to motivate restless teens; he devised a new social technology, an ethical mission, and durable pedagogical tools for sparking greater engagement among low-income youths. As Lenz fine-tuned his decentralized model of managing schools and devising inventive classroom activities, he arrived at what he calls, "our four R's—rigor, relevance, relationships, and results. Every teacher who comes in understands this," he told me. Lenz notes that institutional liberation from regulatory strings—unplugging from the centralized bureaucracy and thick labor contracts—is a necessary first step, "but the charter itself isn't a big deal. It gives us autonomy, so we can persist with innovation."

What's pivotal is "to be able to attract teachers and principals that have a shared vision," Lenz said. And he thinks most about nurturing company-wide norms and crafting durable pedagogical tools—shaped largely by Envision's bullpen of think-big educators, sage teachers in their own right. Lenz is pushing for a shared culture that permeates an entire school—attending to kids' broad growth, pressing high standards, and moving them into good colleges, so "it doesn't depend on the great teacher, like Danielle Johnson," he said.

Let's delve into how the four cornerstones of decentralized organizing come to life inside City Arts and Technology High School. It begins with a keen curiosity over what motivates their clients, what preoccupies the hearts and minds of these budding students, from their awkward doubts to endearing bluntness so often displayed by healthy adolescents.

Each Student's Story—What Makes Pablo Alba Tick?

"I hardly spoke up or shared my own opinions," Alba said haltingly, as he reflected on his personal growth over his years at CAT. A panel of three teachers was peppering him with questions, a friendly yet penetrating cross-examination that followed his final "exhibition," just weeks before graduating. Alba had covered three areas in under ninety minutes, ranging from the British Petroleum oil spill in the Gulf of Mexico and the promise of biodiversity to his own social and intellectual development.

It's another method for developing "leadership skills" in the parlance of Envision Charter Schools: sharpening oral arguments that draw on evidence interwoven with the classical Greek-like aim of knowing oneself. "In the beginning of ninth grade I was a very shy person," Alba continued. "But by the time I was in twelfth grade I was able to make the most convincing arguments of my class. It now has become a tool for me."

Fellow students sat in the audience—along with Alba's mother, an understated and warm *boliviana*—just behind the panel of persistent inquisitors. This lively and rather intense ritual, to which each graduating senior is subjected, would be talked about and embroidered by Alba's peers over the next few weeks. He was characteristically stoic and measured in each response. "Man, he's like a smart machine," one student commented. It all served to bolster CAT's rich culture, the emphasis on careful argumentation, the Socratic interrogation in the public square among a "community of learners," as principal Rowland put it.

Alba offered three "artifacts" within his portfolio—blending a science inquiry and self-reflective art piece with his evolved stance on the aims of humanistic educational ideals. It reminded me of how elite private schools challenge students on multiple fronts, rather than settling for the bland, easily tested curriculum handed down by the state. But these blue-collar kids, many raised in non-English-speaking homes, aren't supposed to be able to handle this wide panorama of ideas and forms of inquiry.

Advancing his ideology of schooling, Alba argued, "education not only broadens our knowledge, education is a methodology of instilling moral values." To bring his philosophical claim to life he had delved into the actions of

Private Bradley Manning, the army intelligence officer who leaked thousands of classified documents to Wikileaks in 2010. Alba articulated the moral and constitutional arguments on both sides of the question, should Private Manning be prosecuted by the US military?

Pressed by a panelist "to give another example of (legal) precedent," how prior cases helped to evaluate the actions of Private Manning, Alba shifted to President Nixon's subterranean attack on the *New York Times* four decades earlier after editors helped to leak the Pentagon Papers. Another provocateur asked Alba to detail his research methods. How had he checked the validity of journalistic reporting on the disclosure of classified reports? Another asked whether Alba had "encountered information that Wikileaks put up on the Internet . . . where they walked over the line of being immoral." Alba parried that, yes, in portions of "various documents they released, the names of three or four informants (appeared), informants that became targets of Al Qaeda."

Alba tacked back to hit another "leadership skill" he claimed to have acquired: "communicating powerfully." His second topic, the BP oil spill, centered on the biological and chemical remedies that had been applied and their impact on the gulf's declining biodiversity. This inquiry drew from his own lab experiments, using "liquid-based detergent and cotton balls to clean oil" in contrast to BP's reliance on "a toxin, oil dispersant, which we know to be ten thousand times more lethal to bio-entities than oil itself," Alba claimed.

As the discussion ensued—pushing Alba to be more precise—a lively interplay arose between Alba's ideological stance and the empirical sufficiency of his work in the chemistry lab. Leadership skills, as defined at CAT, pertain both to empirically assessable facts and to moral quandaries and philosophical ideals. Knowing oneself and studying the views and evidence proffered by others are essential in contributing to civil society. "Thinking critically," as Alba put it, is important because, "otherwise you end up relying on your own experience and your own opinions."

Shifting ground again, he spoke self-consciously about his battle to be less shy, to work comfortably with others. It made for a riveting fusion of classical, humanistic topics—digging into "what is the good life, what is the life we all aspire to," as one of Alba's interrogators said.

How teachers respect each student's story, like Alba's, from their family worries to particular curiosities, appeared to serve two purposes, tacitly weaving a sense of mutual obligation between client and practitioner. It first motivates students as they come to see that sculpting one's growth can be tied to the academic topics, social justice questions, and hands-on projects they tackle during the year. And building from their own stories helps to nurture those leadership skills, making clear oral arguments, building from evidence, distinguishing heartfelt opinion from verifiable facts. After all, these working-class youths readily voiced angst and confusion over seemingly narrow odds in getting ahead.

"Wrote about my first love, even though I'm a boy"

CAT is a noisy place. The principal's office resembles badly staged dinner theater: Kids wander through, asking all kinds of questions, or bluff their way toward scoring a coveted hall pass. A few times each year, the staff reacts with horror after a fight breaks out, especially when police must come onto campus. More typically parents wander in, speaking a variety of languages. A cacophony of sounds often blasts from classrooms, as students engage in lively, even meteoric debates or teachers break students into feisty, usually focused work groups.

But one sound is missing. No penetrating bell rang out during our two years at CAT, marking the end of class periods, where hundreds of kids instantly spill into crowded hallways, as you may recall from your high school experience. This clanging, ritualized sign of institutional regularity, much like an asylum, feels so endemic to high school. But Envision's leaders had silenced this signal. It was indicative of how students are treated with respect, as engaged partners in a shared enterprise.

The social-organizational principle of *mutual obligation* is a two-way street—it demands *reciprocity*, a consensus that teachers and students will deliver for each other. Teachers can set high expectations and be clear about what must be learned, be it results on standardized tests or public sharing of one's complex project with the CAT community. But it's the adolescents themselves—often nimble in dodging an assignment or deadline—who must execute this human-scale social contract. So teachers are trained to be both warm and demanding, "pressing clear expectations," as Principal Rowland told me more than once, a tireless young woman with engaging eyes and a tentative smile.

Many a day, hanging in the back of Johnson's advisory class or history course, Bill Clinton's talk of "personal responsibility" flashed in my mind, which he applied to women on welfare, or when pushing to hold teachers accountable. It's operationalized at CAT as a more nuanced and caring rendition of tough love. "If they see us give in," Johnson said, "they won't meet that higher expectation, that challenge." As one early staffer at CAT, Kyle Hartung, put it, "We consciously build culture, rather than having culture build around us."

Most students rise to the occasion. "Teachers really care about whether you learn," Alba told me early one chilly morning. "They aren't just getting paid and don't care." During a leadership meeting—Rowland's inner circle of veteran thirty-somethings—one teacher kept returning to relationship building. "We know what's happening in our kids' lives. We keep track of each kid, you don't let (them) fail." Some do. CAT's senior class is one-fifth to one-quarter smaller than the entering first-year class.

So the client is expected to deliver, shouldering her share of the load. This relationship stems from knowing each other well, a bit like a respected colleague. And this requires the gentle yet steady probing of practitioners, eager to learn about the client. As students come to see that teachers truly care about their futures, they share more, they buy in. This, as the new decentralists realize, sets necessary conditions for learning. Students grasp the personal and shared returns that stem from cultivating one's own growth, and they see *why* this reading on health-care reform or solar panel design does matter.

Alba told me in his junior year that "classes are getting a little more difficult." But his teachers were elevating him to "really a different level of independence . . . and responsibility. It's just up to you to find the motivation, to do it," he said.

Respecting Each Student

One foggy San Francisco morning, Johnson stood at the classroom door, arms folded. A damp draft seeped through the windows, framing colorless mist outside. Johnson is a stately young woman with wavy black hair; her eyes are firm but also somehow welcoming. She was in the face of two students hoping to rush in unnoticed. "Hey, you guys are 30 seconds late," Johnson announced in pointed fashion. Most of the sixteen-odd students in her advisory period were lagging behind in drafting their "personal reflections," working with partners to articulate six personal attributes, sharing the character of their families, and articulating career hopes.

Johnson, not happy with their sluggish pace, admonished the class, absent any moralistic attribution. "Today is a day about getting stuff done." A few students milled about; they were a variety of ethnic shades, most were dressed in dark brown or black—some boys sagging and the girls wearing gauze-like layers or simply schlumpy—with nondescript sweatshirts that buffered the city's cold winter drizzle. A few students made their way to a plastic file box atop a shelf and pulled out their prior listing of personal information, ranging from the mundane to the revealing facets of their still fluid identities. "Pablo can you turn around?" Johnson asked with her blend of unflappable directness and dash of warmth, as Alba fooled around with first-year student Ron Morales.

The two boys—easily accepting my listening in—proceeded to teach me something about CAT's way of nurturing self-reflection, blended with hardcore skills pegged to writing, reasoning, and public presentation. The nominal leadership skill at hand was "personal reflection," and Johnson hammered on moving each pair to articulate elements of one's identify, from favorite activities at home, to dominant affiliation groups, be they marked by ethnicity, home language, perhaps genres of music, or that ever-pressing adolescent issue, what to wear (a black or gray hoodie?). Work on this purported "leadership skill" also allowed Johnson to learn a bit more about each of her charges, what made them tick.

Alba spoke of his Bolivian roots, starting with his maternal grandfather, "a strong union activist" back in the home country. Asked how life differed outside La Paz, where he was raised until eight years of age, Alba said, "I enjoy the kind of dual culture thing going on," accenting the case of how "Bolivians tend to be over-exaggerated—everything is exaggerated." The soft-spoken Alba also observed how, "Everyday at dinner time, no answering cell phones, you sit down and you talk."

Morales, more brash and cocky than Alba, talked of his love of drawing. He pulled out a notebook filled with ornate sketches of tagging designs, ranging from intricate gang and goth emblems to Beach Boy–era sports cars. "Graffiti is kind of my life," Morales said. "I like the Japanese style, the katana curve, thinner and [representing] tempered steel." Morales was born in Oakland, "but my dad didn't want me to be in that type of environment." His mother split when Morales was a young boy. "She's not the type of person that can take care of me," he said without any apparent feeling in his kid-like yet composed face. Morales was quick to clarify that he only tagged selectively, "I don't do it on buses or walls."

Another pair of nearby students debated how to best draft their sets of six personal reflections, each filling about a page. They knew that a portion would be worked over and folded into their "benchmark portfolio," presented to the lower-division tribes, called *lunar* and *solar*. One youngster looked up to tell me, "I wrote about my first love, even though I'm a boy."

Johnson made sure the advisory period didn't drift into self-aggrandizing chatter. Each written draft would be subjected to her sharp pencil, be revised, and then folded into their portfolio as one of several "artifacts." Fellow students were invited to comment on each other's work in supportive fashion. "You will be graded on collaboration today . . . on that leadership skill," Johnson told these first- and second-year students, as she carefully socialized her charges to CAT's norms for peer discussions, constructively critical dialogue.

Months later, following a trial benchmark-portfolio talk by one pupil, as quiet yet attentive classmates looked on, a flood of pointed comments ensued. "There was no enthusiasm, no hook," said one. Another student urged, "more details, there wasn't a lot of information." Johnson—always scanning for when a student is about to venture a comment or question—closely monitored the tone to ensure that suggestions were specific about how the student could improve her public pitches.

As Johnson learned more about her cantankerous clients—especially what interests they brought to CAT—a reciprocal and trusting understanding became apparent. Students, in turn, constantly pepper their teachers with personal questions, hoping to figure out the grown-ups as well. It's a steady process of shared socialization that kindles a warm sense that teachers really do care about the futures of these kids, about the weaving of tribal ties. During a break between class periods one morning, a teacher tilted his laptop toward four surrounding students and clicked through a sequence of wedding photos. "We all know the teachers," Alba remarked. "They joke, they laugh. We've torn them down to tears," he said with a guarded grin, as if someone might scold him, "us giving them shit."

Alba often talked of hanging out in Noel Benoza's technology lab where fellow pupils service and dispense laptops to teachers. "He's kind of relaxed," Alba said. Given in part what made Alba tick, he won a teaching assistantship with Benoza, helping to "dismantle hard drives," set up PowerPoint presentations, and "re-set [laptops] for the school's server." Alba could be seen zooming down hallways with his cart, delivering a computer newly loaded for a high-tech presentation. Visiting Alba one month after graduating, he still talked of Benoza, "the key guy in the last two years."

CAT's leaders and teachers often talk of how their own relationships, committed to a supportive tribe of young practitioners, modeling the notion of mutual obligation in the eyes of students. "We see the teachers are close and get down," one student told me. "They are role models and we learn from them. They always speak with each other with respect . . . and have fun together."

As one student speaker, Josefa Figueroa, said at CAT's emotional if not raucous 2010 graduation ceremony, "We learned to let loose with each other." Holding back tears, coming forth in heartfelt tones, "Our parents and others supported us for our benchmark portfolios . . . we have held each other when we were proud . . . I have a second family at CAT."

Stretching the Teacher's Role in a Culture of Mutual Obligation

These teachers didn't just talk the talk. They went about engaging students at every turn, asking about family, digging into kids' own take on classes or assignments, pressing them to work harder, think more deeply. CAT teachers, aided by coaches from the center, steadily experimented with inventive pedagogical tools; they weighed how much time to spend on the state's official curriculum or when to sit quietly with a student to get beneath surface symptoms. In short, these teachers flexed the boundaries of their role, pursuing that age-old quest of social authority while remaining open to whatever issue might arise with students or colleagues. Part curricular expert, part moral guide and clinical counselor.

As Lenz shaped his charter network, he understood that teenagers are constantly in motion, especially those coming from mediocre middle schools or families where literacy and the life of ideas remains anemic. As writer Zadie Smith once put it, the feisty life of teenagers is based on "a relation with verbs, not nouns."[2] From the outset Envision staff honed a variety of project-based lesson plans. Lenz and colleagues also delineated a range of analytic proficiencies and cooperative skills, from how to search out evidence to back a historical argument to fitting solar energy panels into the needs of densely packed urban residents. And there's the ever-present focus on public offerings or pitching oral arguments before an evaluative audience—much like a skilled lawyer before a jury—often with a social justice twist at CAT's community events.

These cooperative projects, students working alongside fellow students, may last a couple days or an entire semester, culminating in a public exhibition. Along the way, that sense of mutual obligation to fellow members of CAT takes hold. "Over time our relationships with teachers . . . with peers have grown," Isis Green, a compelling black senior, told me. "We're challenged to work together in so many ways, it's a project-based school."

The school-wide exhibitions required study and design discussions, often bridging across classes. The solar-panel project cut across math, science, and digital media courses. Building one's case for the "most influential leader" of the Mexican Revolution required historical biography, mixed with the study of photography and multimedia techniques. These cross-discipline projects then became part of a student's portfolio and eventually the capstone graduation portfolio, each presented before an audience of peers, parents, and teachers. "Ceremony matters in the world," principal Rowland stressed.

Mentor First, Expert Second

This focus on collaborative projects, applied problems, and public performance also means that teachers must thoroughly rethink their pedagogical role. Envision's leaders constantly question and stretch the teacher's role—what's emerged as part conventional pedagogue, part avuncular coach and mentor to students, part inquiring professional who lifts colleagues as well.

After watching and talking with Johnson over the two years at CAT, I came to see her as a demanding Jewish mother—but one who displayed constant curiosity about her clients, one who sought to understand the motivations of each.

Teachers at CAT talked much about striking a balance: pushing no-nonsense expectations and challenging these reticent teens while being curious about their lives—growing up in homes where parents may not have finished high school, or where daily instability can erode a teen's underlying well-being. The advisory period "defines a distinct role for the teacher," Johnson said. "We see ourselves as generalists first, my real job is to be an advisor . . . how we get our kids back to core values. If you can't get these relationships down, the teaching isn't going to happen."

Like other second-wave decentralists, many teachers at CAT didn't shy away from complications that bubbled up in students' lives, from an alcoholic parent to an unwanted pregnancy. In this advisory role, teachers see that getting beneath these complicated layers is part of their job, allowing teachers to build trust and mutual respect, scaffolding up from the student's own commitments. The blended roles of trusted advisor and "warm demander" often led to stronger engagement. "She's always there for me if I need help, she's my advisor," said Morales, the graffiti artist, speaking of Johnson. "She's like, 'yeah, come in, what do you need?'"

For Elena Huerta, one spring morning her own tough-love mentors were in her face. "I had a dream I was gonna fail," this petite Latina sophomore admitted to her audience of peers. The three-teacher panel—examiners for her forty-five-minute-long benchmark portfolio presentation—was outside deciding whether her performance met muster.

Johnson had earlier briefed her students, who now sat quietly, listening to Huerta's three-part presentation. "Good audience skills are imperative," Johnson had emphasized. "Make sure cell phones are off. It's really rude to be texting while someone is speaking," she said, hammering on CAT's behavioral norms. What remained implicit was how Johnson was modeling the ritual and intellectual meatiness of the portfolio presentation for her younger students.

Huerta had been shaky from the start—leading with the "personal memoir" section of her portfolio. "My father left the house when I was 8 years old," she said, a flat PowerPoint slide failing to capture the bolt of sadness that swept across Huerta's face. "Thinking back to my past I went through a lot of hard times." Barely holding back tears, "I'm not a great public speaker, as you can see."

The projector flashed a pensive photo of Huerta's mother at age eighteen onto the white board. "I decided to use the story of my mom getting to this country as an immigrant." She had never talked with her mother about the harrowing trek from Mexico, the fear and resolve still fresh in her mother's mind. After retelling the story, Huerta explained, "The leadership skill I used was to think critically," providing the dead-quiet audience a dash of relief from the fear and danger reported by her mother.

Huerta moved on to describe her "green home project" conducted with fellow students, a design for an energy efficient apartment, displayed in nifty 3-D fashion with the help of architectural software. "Some challenges we had were running out of time and goofing off."

The panel's steady probing also revealed the versatile roles played by CAT teachers. They asked about how her work group might have functioned better and what other leadership skills she advanced. "What did you do to make a story, not just a list of information?" one teacher asked. They also burrowed into Huerta's personal development. Another pushed on, "What do you think it is about yourself that makes you a good collaborator?" Huerta compared lessons from CAT against social relations inside her home. "Like when my mom has a party, everyone talks to each other (in) little groups. But then in the end they all come together."

Another teacher asked, "You talked about changing, not being so shy. Do you think being at CAT has helped?" Huerta responded, "In middle school we didn't have the connection with teachers, you hardly knew any of the teachers. At CAT you know you can ask any teacher for help," she continued. "That's why they are here." The interplay spread across the audience of peers, implicitly legitimating how teachers are both caring and demanding, serving to buoy students.

Still, the teacher panel concluded that Huerta's performance was not yet up to snuff. One teacher argued that each of her themes, tracking against the portfolio segments, remained vague, lacking in detail. "I wasn't sure what you'd bring to the table for the upper division (next year)," this teacher said bluntly. "You really started to open up toward the end," one teacher said. "So, Elena, we want you to re-present next Tuesday."

Constantly Collaborating, Reflecting on One's Practice

Teachers also take on technically complex roles with one another—with the aim of creating more riveting pedagogy and knitting a closer community of practitioners. This too is reminiscent of the lateral discourse and collaborative spirit we saw inside Geisinger and Handelsbanken. Lots of between-teacher coaching goes on at CAT, again requiring agility in one's role and range of professional skills. Coaching unfolds in wide-open and candid team meetings; each teacher is assigned a coach, dubbed a "critical friend." The role of coach has spread across other sectors beyond education; it is another specific tool taken up by second-wave decentralists. The Boston surgeon and writer Atul Gawande likes to cite the legendary Juilliard violin instructor Dorothy DeLay, who coached virtuoso Itzhak Perlman among others, imparting "discipline, a broad repertoire, and the exigencies of technique."[3]

Rowland weaves tight ties among her staff and students with clear intent, drawing on simple tools to hammer on this collective ethic. She draws on CAT's "framework of building community," a three-page guide that articulates Envision's philosophy and suggests pragmatic activities. "We are explicit that we hold community as a core value," the document begins. "A learning community does not just happen—it is created intentionally at every level of a school and organization." The guide details methods for modeling community building, "like one featuring a hula hoop contest" among teachers, and another sketching how school-wide or class-level groups should meet periodically, "each school [in the Envision network] has developed its own rituals and formats for their community meetings."

Each Tuesday afternoon all teachers convene to discuss how to improve on various fronts. In addition teachers in the lower- and upper-division families meet separately each week. And Rowland's leadership team meets weekly, bolstered by senior thinkers, like Johnson, to tackle problems like the complications of police coming onto campus to help settle a fight, parents not attending portfolio exhibits, or flagging test score results. Then teachers return to their own classrooms, perhaps observed by their own "critical friend," often collaborating on projects across subject divides. It's all part of "community building," Rowland said.

Another intriguing example of the versatility displayed by teachers (not to mention students) arises when a new job candidate visits the school. Each would-be CAT teacher must enact a lesson with a live class. After the candidate leaves, students and teachers alike candidly discuss their strengths and weaknesses. One applicant walked through the events of 9/11 step by step—accented by the usual sequence of vivid, still disturbing photos—then discussed competing theories of what motivated this attack on US soil. But he allowed little time for student discussion, even knocking down one student's working hypothesis. This sparked a flurry of post hoc criticism. "He prepared an interesting lesson, but I only learned his side," one student emphasized. "People here have strong feelings, he'd have to be okay with that," said another.

The teacher's role at CAT moves far beyond delivering known bits of knowledge, easily assessed by multiple-choice tests. Instead, Johnson and her colleagues nurture discerning analysts, inquisitive youths who come to recognize a clear argument, able to gather empirical evidence then arrange a persuasive pitch on paper or before a discerning audience.

Scaffolding Up from Students' Lives

CAT's teachers go to inventive lengths to build from what moves these restless adolescents. Evening exhibitions occur five times during the school year, ranging from displays of environmental design, artistic work, and oral presentations, blended with computer graphics or a photomontage. Attended by parents, siblings, and fellow students, these exhibitions take on ritualistic significance, offering meaty content and signaling serious work by obviously committed members of the CAT tribe. And these exhibitions inculcate a feeling of shared ownership, responsibility, and self-confidence, reminiscent of second-wave decentralists in other fields. Angst and anticipation precede each event.

"Welcome to the Mexican Revolution Exhibition," the banner read in huge block letters, one damp evening at CAT just two weeks before the December holidays. By 6:15 each of four classrooms filled up. Rows of chairs were for parents and family members. Students waited their turn or simply showed up to join this well-known event; presenters were constantly fidgeting and flipping through their scripted index cards.

A second-year student, ill at ease, moved to the front of the class. Pulling out a stack of cards from the back pocket of his sagging jeans, he assumed the role of Miguel Hidalgo, allegedly the greatest hero of the revolution, and sketched his argument in English, then Spanish. He also projected a video collection of still photos, panning out, moving across evocative images of peasant fighters and battle scenes—emulating Ken Burns in overdrawn yet endearing fashion.

A stream of students came forward, each making their pitch via words and images over a ten-minute period. One young man slung one leg up on the ledge of a white board, emphasizing that he, Antonio López de Santa Anna, had lost a leg during the war, which "makes me a hero"; somber chamber music came forth from his video clip. One girl role-played Francisco I. Madero, accenting how she "gave land back to the people" and how being "a pure blooded Mexican" lent authenticity to her claim of being the greatest hero. "Vote for me!" One by one, each student enacted a personal engagement with history—becoming the historic figure they believed to be the most heroic and practicing their oral persuasion skills.

The clumps of teens in the audience were equally compelling, packed into the back, standing along the narrow sides of the classroom, encircling two scores of parents for almost two hours. They swayed and shifted nervously, like kelp in a shallow tide pool. Three girls dressed up for the evening event, wearing a finer fabric in black and removing a few piercings; four Asian boys whispered to each other between each appearance of the vying revolutionary heroes. A lone girl sat at the teacher's desk, smiling slyly while strumming sparse tunes on a ukulele, filling the gaps when PowerPoint files hit technical difficulties.

All this motion filled the room, except when a student was presenting. Then each student was silent, respectful. That sense of mutual obligation had been internalized. Each student felt they must respect and support their peers when presenting their portfolio, at times in halting fashion. The content was typically rich. But it's the shared activity, the recognized performance in sociologist Erving Goffman's terms that thickens the culture at CAT.

Centralized Testing, Decentered Practice

Advancing hands-on projects with visceral meaning is tied to one of Bob Lenz's "Rs," the one that accents relevance. It comes into play as teachers plan ingeniously, even to make the state's curricular content relevant to the everyday lives of these blue-collar kids, getting them to see the utility of acing standardized tests. While CAT's graduation rate is stellar, it's average test scores are not. So debate flared over the two years as to the appropriate emphasis and class time dedicated to California's official proficiency standards.

Unaware of this divisive issue among teachers, Bernadette McCormick just wasn't into US history that morning. She sat with her head down on her slice of table. The several tables had been placed end to end to form a wide U-shape. The twenty-eight juniors in the room stared at the screen as Johnson flipped through a series of handwritten bullets on the Progressive Era.

"What's progressivism?" Johnson led off. "It means to advance, to move away from tenements," one alert student pipes up. "Anyone, what did Teddy Roosevelt want?" Johnson pushed deeper into this unit, a clump of factoids appearing on the state test. "Make sure you have all this written down," she implored. The morning's agenda, always posted at the front, promised a "timed essay" during the final hour of the period.

Johnson, without skipping a beat, took three steps from her overhead projector and poked McCormick softly on the shoulder. The seemingly detached girl lifted her head, nestled comfortably in her arms, revealing a mop of purple hair set off by raspberry colored pigtails. Thick eye shadow and ample mascara applied in elegant fashion somehow contradicted the drowsy, young face that flashed a sly smile at Johnson. "If we totally fail it, can we make it up?" McCormick asked. A neighboring boy, hands in pockets rather than taking notes, careful that his sweatshirt hood covered most of his face, started to giggle.

But the unflappable Johnson pretended not to notice, pushing on, knowing that adolescents must signal resistance even when paying attention, at some level. "You are closer to college than in your ninth-grade class," she insisted. "You will have a professor with a question, and I had a blue book (in college). You are gonna have to write in a coherent way in a fixed amount of time."

Anchoring this cold morning's discussion in discrete themes, Johnson flipped off the projector and moved to the white board. "Look up here. You can use the Gilded Age, Upton Sinclair, *The Jungle* . . . remember our fact sheets for the progressives," Johnson reminded the class. "What did the evidence and interpretive chart say?" Another student volunteered, "About meat packing, contaminated meat."

Debriefing after class, Johnson told me that teachers are forced to spend more time on the state's curriculum in the eleventh grade, along with practicing clear and grammatically correct writing. Otherwise CAT's graduates would do poorly on college entry tests and jeopardize their odds of being admitted. At the same time "curriculum standards are so euro-centric," Johnson argued. "We wanted to add material." So teachers at CAT created a unit on immigration, which includes cooperative inquiries into topics that hold meaning to their ethnically diverse kids, including the multimedia project on the Mexican Revolution. Even curricular standards are advanced by tying subjects and ideas to the everyday trials facing CAT students and their families.

Life on the Edge of CAT Culture

Into our second year of fieldwork, we began to worry about "going native," about being pulled into the compelling character and nonstop commitment of key teachers at CAT. So we asked if we could hang out with a dissident teacher, a staff member who wasn't sure about the taste of the Envision Kool-Aid. Did all the teachers at CAT share the school's core principles? Did they all buy into the versatile roles that founding teachers, like Johnson, had come to assume? Was everyone really pulling in the same direction?

This quest took us to Ted Morgan, a middle-aged English and social studies teacher, who reportedly wasn't so tight with the school's leadership. He was certainly welcoming, quite comfortable with my sitting in the back of his room during our second autumn at CAT. Morgan didn't turn out to be a pedagogical conservative or to even be recalcitrant when mulling over the school's philosophy and inventive practices. But he didn't display Johnson's curiosity about the students, nor did he stay long after class to advance the CAT community. And Morgan felt strongly that students were done a disservice when teachers downplayed the state's curricular topics and tested proficiencies. Some colleagues felt him likeable, but he often "did his own thing."

At first I felt that Morgan was too attached to his desk, not constantly in motion like Johnson, who steadily nudged and encouraged pupils. Nor was he into greeting class members at the classroom door as they shuffled in, trying to avoid looking too eager, backpacks slipping off shoulders as lanky bodies collapsed into chairs. Still, Morgan reminded them in his clear, strong voice, "this is prep time, read and respond."

Earlier in the week, the class had watched the Michael Moore film *Sicko*, an exposé of health insurance companies, which makes the case for serious reform. Morgan stands out from the Benetton-like diversity and youthful fashion CAT students enjoy. He's a large man with thinning red hair, and he speaks to the class in an understated manner. Morgan made a living from "pet sitting" and then went into "high tech marketing," before finding more meaning in teaching. He's direct, even sharp if someone has their head down or tries to peek at a cell phone hidden in a lap.

After reviewing their preparatory notes, Morgan signaled, "Okay, inner, outer culture circle," prompting students to move eight chairs into a tight circle, surrounded by a loose-knit concentric ring of eighteen or so seats surrounding the inner core. "I'm gonna take that away if I see it anymore," Morgan said to a tall kid, eyes barely visible beneath his baseball cap. He sheepishly stashed his iPod into one of several available pockets.

Morgan, from his own seat at his desk, quickly reviewed the constitutive rules of the exercise, which would pit those representing doctors and insurance companies against patient-rights advocates. "What are the guidelines in being in the inner circle?" Morgan asked the class. "No side conversations, no cussing. Don't attack the person." He sounded like a boxing referee at center ring barking into a microphone that dropped from the ceiling. Morgan also employed what he calls, "step up, step back," where a student asks for the floor, walks through an argument, and then yields to another.

A lively and detailed debate ensued as students deployed both emotion and evidence to propel their positions. They drew on family experiences with the health-care world. Together, bouncing back and forth, these adolescents covered the core issues that one might read on the op-ed page or view on *Meet the Press*. Their arguments drew on the Moore film, along with additional print materials and evidence. Coming largely from blue-collar families, these teens also reported firsthand on exigencies associated with uncertain health-care coverage.

"Medicine became really costly, so what government did is make health care into a business to make money," claimed one debater. Another got to the root causes of escalating costs. "Americans keep smoking, eating [more], compared with other countries." On possible remedies, a third student in the inner circle disagreed with another. "You said you want the doctors to control the system. But they are the ones that are blowing people off!"

Whenever a student held the floor for too long, Morgan's debating norms were invoked. "Remember about step up, step back, and remember about academic language," Morgan implored. Over the forty-five-minute-long debate, Morgan would occasionally insert a factual correction, for instance, clarifying the role insurance companies play in the system. And halfway through, Morgan named five inner-circle students who had said nothing, prompting them to step up. He coached the students gently while he sat at his desk, reminding students of the expectations and ground rules for the exercise. Otherwise, it was their show.

Returning to Morgan's class later that month I found students eagerly working in small groups, talking up aspects of the Mexican Revolution. "Remember the (killing) two birds thing," he emphasized. "We are learning about the Mexican Revolution and how to do better on standardized tests." This is where Morgan departed from CAT priorities. "When kids hear standardized tests, the kids flip off," he said. "They say it doesn't matter, [but] it does matter big." Rowland would come to agree with Morgan, although she worried over how. "Teachers that teach at CAT are not the kind of teachers that believe in standardized tests."

Morgan waves off drill-and-kill didactics. He points to all the "group work and project-based learning" that he employs. "I'm trying to make sure we have engaging stuff for them to work on" that is always pegged to "learning goals," which overlap with the state's curricular standards, he said. Indeed, most teachers at CAT would reluctantly come to embrace spending more class time on preparing for standardized tests. They even threw pizza parties for students who cleared the state-defined proficiency hurdle. Some teachers paid greater attention to vocabulary. "*Connotes* and *denotes* are words you will see on the STAR [state] exam," one teacher lectured in class.

Yet even as teachers shifted to lifting test scores, they relied heavily on literature or documentary materials that held relevance in the lives of their diverse students. This ranged from reading James Baldwin on race and identity to mounting political debates over immigration policy. Pieces of the curriculum helped to animate project work as well. And teachers began nudging students to flex their "meta-cognitive skills," urging them to reflect on whether their argument was logical, and asking them, where's the substantiation, how can I better cooperate with my group to strengthen our shared argument? Again, we saw the emphasis on students taking ownership of their own development.

If Morgan was on the edge of CAT's energizing culture, he didn't turn out to be much of a radical. "It's also about relationships," he emphasized in between classes one day. "It's a lot easier when you have kids saying, 'Mr. Morgan is cool.'" And his pitch for nurturing stronger writing skills has now been strengthened by the center, bolstered through curricular guides revised at Envision headquarters. Later we learned that burnout and exhaustion from wearing so many hats were the afflictions felt by a significant number of teachers. It was exuberant conformity to Envision's aspirations and daily demands that seemed to spur teacher turnover, not dissident teachers failing to buy in.

Leading from an Ethical Center

Envision's 4-R's mantra—rigor, relevance, relationships, and results—comes to life amid the daily work of City Arts and Technology. These attributes steadily characterize the classroom activities, team projects, and wider public presentations that cast the social architecture of daily life at CAT. And these social or pedagogical formats are co-constructed, constantly adjusted in dialogue between central designers and frontline practitioners. Rethinking the center is another cornerstone that surfaced as we came to know key staff at Envision's modest headquarters, former teachers and innovators who spend much time inside their small network of schools. It too was reminiscent of the culture-rich centers of Geisinger and Handelsbanken and how they provide sacred norms and practical tools of the trade.

Like any effective firm, centrally determined goals are key. "We take kids into college, those who are the first generation to attend," said Erika Neilsen Andrew, Envision's vice president of instruction and learning. That core aim is fused to the requisite skills that kids must acquire and how teachers on the ground assess progress, she emphasizes. And "schools that feel hopeful are the ones that are getting results." So the center's role at Envision is to equip its principals and teachers with the right tools to enliven classroom activities and longer-term group projects.

Neilsen Andrew has long labored with teachers to build a tool kit of sorts, an inventive curricular handbook. It includes "course maps" for core subject areas and a detailed guide to hands-on activities from the "project exchange," an online inventory of ideas for portfolio units, evening exhibitions, and videotaped model lessons. Envision contributes to *Better Lesson*, a Facebook-like tool through which teachers share inventive projects and classroom activities.

Staff members inside Envision contribute to the codification of these inventive practices, while given multiple road tests within their classrooms. These curricular guides and specific classroom activities can be adjusted. But they serve as institutional pillars of practice for teachers new to the organization. For instance, the rubric for assessing benchmark portfolio performances was crafted from Envision's center with aid from senior staff, and then fine-tuned by school-level staff, like Johnson and Rowland. This tool judges kids on their presentational skills (ranging from eye contact and structuring the "story" in an organized fashion, to drawing upon "digital and/or visual elements"), mastery of knowledge, metacognition ("student recognizes his or her growth . . . where further development is needed"), and the student's response to questions and comments. Alba's father once told me, "They place a lot of emphasis on meta-cognition, thinking about why they were motivated, which eventually drove Pablo up the wall!"

Headquarters also manages key logistical tasks—offering back-office support to maintain the organization, ranging from securing new facilities, handling payroll and staff benefits, arranging for subsidized lunches, and raising private foundation dollars to augment state dollars for charter schools. And the center recruits new teachers—young candidates who are in sync with the ethics and methods of Envision. "I think people come to us who have a different mindset," Neilsen Andrew said, "not like 'I want to go to work for Oakland Unified.' Some people see it as urban Peace Corps. We are not unionized either." Through centralized recruitment and hiring, Envision teachers tend to share particular ethical commitments. "The roots of what we do is giving kids voice. Because (our) teachers come from a strong social justice background," Neilsen Andrew explained, "if you asked them, they would say they are preparing kids to have power over their own life."

A deeper role Envision's center plays came into focus during our second year at CAT. Senior staffers like Neilsen Andrew steadily monitor and deepen the largely horizontal social relations found inside this culture-heavy, regulation-light organization. This goes beyond logistics, codified pedagogical tools, and hiring. Culture building—from this inventive center's vantage point—occurs largely through face-to-face interaction with principals and teachers in formal meetings as well as in accidental settings, like browsing classrooms or chatting in the hallway between classes.

Eventually, I felt two threads of this community-building work could be pulled apart, like complementary colors of yarn that wove a durable cultural fabric. First, there's the moral commitment to nurturing and challenging these youths, too often underestimated by educators, who come from poor or blue-collar homes. This organizational ethic translates into unwavering faith in the smarts, the curiosity, and search for meaning and belonging that teens so often display, even when disengaging from a formal institution like the school.

These youngsters require that teachers "come from a place of integrity," as Rowland puts it. They figure out whether the teacher cares about who they are, about their future success. Because of the homes from which many students come, "they are not necessarily motivated to come to school," Johnson said. So we must nurture "a vested interest to get into it."

Envision's ethical focus—nourished with a dash of research on adolescent development—is to recognize that urban teens love to formulate sharp opinions even though they are unsure of their own commitments, their identity amid the swirl of interpersonal and political currents that swamp their young lives. "You may not agree, but you have to take a perspective," Johnson tells her students. "Some kids leave because we haven't shifted their academic identity," Neilsen Andrew said. "If they don't get to reflect on their academic work, they don't get a chance to stop, to reboot. We're constantly getting student work on the table."

This task of tightening the cultural tenets of schools originates in Envision's central office: selecting teachers carefully and professional practice among its staff. The norms of community, teacher collaboration, the work of one's "critical friend"—these cultural tenets are kindled at the center, with the light and warmth sent out to the schools, stoked by Envision veterans.

The premium placed on improving teaching practices offers the second ethical thread, reinforced from central staff and the principals they hire and work to retain. "We are relentless in getting to a culture where teachers take hard feedback," Neilsen Andrew said. "To do our best work we have to push each other." Teacher training before and during the school year exposes staff to in-class project ideas and how portfolio efforts and capstone performances are being adjusted. I saw Neilsen Andrew visiting CAT at least once a week, observing teachers, coaching Rowland, and regularly contributing to the school's leadership meetings.

"It's pretty tricky, because I think what we are doing is pretty complicated," Neilsen Andrew said. And at least one-fifth of CAT's teaching staff was brand new at the start of each school year. One afternoon a week is dedicated to professional development work. And teacher-led sessions occur weekly for each lower- and upper-division "family" of teachers. Teachers tied to the lunar and solar families meet separately to review the steps that lead toward a portfolio exhibition, to talk up college options, perhaps to publicly mediate a dispute or a pupil's misbehavior. If a student steals a cell phone or disrespects a teacher or peer, "they have to give back," said Neilsen Andrew. "We are definitely trying to teach kids that they have to take responsibility for what they do." Through these interlocking and structured meeting times, ethical commitments are bolstered and shared.

The school's principal is key to strengthening these ethical threads, to ensure they are brightly woven in rich colors through the hearts and minds of teachers. A half century of research on what makes for an effective school has resulted in quick-fix menus: a principal who's a "strong academic leader," a school that enforces a discrete, easy to dissect curriculum. Or reform advocates often argue that building smaller schools is the silver bullet for raising achievement. Indeed, the Gates Foundation spent about $2 billion in the 1990s, spawning small high schools across the land, only to abandon a generation of activists, even in schools that showed promising results.[4]

What's notable is how CAT principals, like Rowland, mentored by Neilsen Andrew from the center, go way beyond the pithy reforms du jour. Rowland hammers on sacred, complementary norms. The first pertains to how to connect with and motivate these high-energy teens. "The students aren't going to achieve if they don't have a relationship with, trust in, their teachers, unless they feel connected," Rowland said. "They have had enough experiences in their lives where there's not trust."

And the emphasis on building an inspiring professional community rings through in Rowland's management style. Early one year, she circulated and discussed a listing of "staff norms" for building a tight and reflective social organization, such as, "We respect the contributions and differences of every team member." On listening and speaking, "We strive toward consensus as we solve problems with a positive attitude." On integrity, "We are clear and transparent with our intentions and remain open to critique, change, and new ideas." This artifact—that came to inform the constitutive rules of social relations with students as well—could easily contribute to a new testament for second-wave decentralists.

Major Lessons, Persisting Challenges

City Arts and Technology High School certainly alters the course of many young lives. Watching the growth of students like Alba, maturing and blossoming during our two years together, was a sight to behold. The caring and careful work of teachers like Johnson, and leaders inside the Envision firm, such as Rowland and Neilsen Andrew, engaged and often lifted these poor or blue-collar youths each day. These are teens with few advantages who otherwise would have attended faceless, vast high schools that route kids like Alba and Morales into dismal futures. While test scores still drift low to medium, the college-attending rate of CAT students works against all the odds.

Beyond these compelling individuals, what inferences can be drawn about the CAT organization? What does the wider Envision firm teach us about the promise and perhaps fragility of second-wave decentralization? Two major lessons emerge from this case, tempered by a postscript, a regrouping at CAT that unfolded in the months after we completed our two years of fieldwork.

First, the four social organizational cornerstones—unearthed in the Geisinger and Handelsbanken cases—surfaced again, easily dusted off and clearly recognizable inside CAT. Founder Bob Lenz made clear that independence from the regulatory state and bureaucratic school authorities offers the chance to "continually innovate." Organizational liberation is just the first step, a necessary but insufficient condition needed to build an organization that touches and lifts complicated clients. Envision then turns to the familiar cornerstones: eagerly getting to know the client, experimenting with new job roles and relationships (among practitioners and clients), shifting to plenty of lateral communication without losing a teacher's authoritative nature, and rethinking the firm's center.

Case studies are illuminating in seeing causal instances, but not in verifying their generalizability. We did see at CAT each day—as we sat in the back of classrooms, tailed teachers, or wandered though hallways—the small interactions that led to big results. When Johnson would gently needle Alba to be a bit more disclosing, building his confidence, or when teacher panels would publicly, yet gently grill a student for details on the causes of the Mexican Revolution or the sustainability of a rooftop garden. The classroom activities and longer-term projects—bridging topics, skills, and courses—were built atop the four social-organizational cornerstones. Engaging students, building deep trust with them, stemmed from ingenious pedagogical tools and inventive social relations.

Still, from a theory-building standpoint, we would like to learn which cornerstone or method lifted which students. Or what kinds of teachers are motivated to pursue the rigor and intensity of how CAT organizes instruction and social relationships? The intensity of daily life at CAT is not for everyone, whether a young teacher or young teen. The demanding press of teachers, to achieve and open up to the commonweal, drives out almost one-quarter of each entering class of students. And we discovered a fairly high turnover of teachers from year to year. But which organizational cornerstones are paying off for which clients? This remains a huge question for practitioners and researchers alike.

The second takeaway from CAT is that these human-scale organizations are fragile, even transient creatures at times. In a sense, the forces that make decentralization inevitable also constrain the efficacy of local organizations operating in rough-and-tumble mixed markets. The Envision firm once attracted sizeable chunks of private capital; it was the poster child for foundations that were eager to trumpet the promise of innovative charter schools. But as private funders shift to other reform fronts, small firms like Envision must draw back and survive on state apportionments, per pupil allocations that remain modest in California.

The organizational magic of CAT was originally performed by a founding set of teachers, including Rowland and Johnson, youthful veterans of huge, uninspiring public schools who aimed to craft a very different organization. But sustaining the energy and emotional verve to continue the work at CAT proved difficult. The scramble for dollars and fine teachers, which still challenge charter management firms, like Envision, contributes to the fragility. On the ground, inside CAT, it was the daily intensity—from dealing with family breakdown, to losing a prized teacher, to frequent meetings required to mesh cross-course student projects—that proved costly. Even these youthful, high-voltage idealists get tired. We suffer from "huge staff turnover," said Kristin Russo, one teacher who left for the East Coast. "We had three principals" in the first five years. Of CAT's eighteen to twenty full-time teachers, over one-fifth continue to leave at the end of each year.[5]

*

After Pablo Alba graduated, Lynette Parker and I wound down our fieldwork in San Francisco. That summer, though, I visited his family, in part to celebrate his admission to the University of California at Santa Cruz. But Alba fell victim to the uncertainties that swirl about working-class families. It was the beginning of a year-long postscript to the CAT story that would unfold, a final chapter in the uneven life of one grassroots organization, along with the exigencies that beset their worthy clients.

Alba was typical of the turned-on, steadily engaged youths who populated CAT, who also resonated so well to the school's intellectual demands. "What they told us is that this school gets us ready to go to college," Alba had told me in his second year. He even lent voice to the norms inside his school. "You learn the details about a learning community," Alba said. This bright youngster, emigrating from Bolivia at age seven, had entered CAT as a shy, yet bright and engaged kid. He graduated with effusive confidence, clothed in humility and quick curiosity to understand fresh ideas, to quietly read new situations. Even his nickname, Cusillo, meaning monkey in Quechua, reflects this youth's agility.

One evening he e-mailed me to describe his joy over a favorite video game, and he used a description from a questionable evidentiary source. "Whereas it is normally (Wikipedia) unreliable, this excerpt seems quite correct." CAT's metacognitive sage would have been proud. This maturing young man became more than an understated techie; he joined a Brazilian percussion group called Loco Bloco that performed in festivals throughout San Francisco. He was excited about moving to Santa Cruz, "they have a good computer science program," he said.

But outside realities took a swipe at Alba's future. He wandered into the kitchen. I was having tea with his parents in a compact space in which it was necessary to duck in spots to avoid the ceiling. They lived in the top unit of a refurbished Victorian, about eight blocks from Haight and Ashbury. When I asked Pablo how he felt about heading to Santa Cruz, his face looked uncertain. Not knowing what to say, he glanced at his parents, as if to say, "you didn't tell him?"

It turned out that Alba's father had to pull back on his financial commitment; his small business had fallen victim to a flat economy. "He was pretty much set to launch," father Chris Yerke said, "it left me in a position of not having much in reserve." Yerke renovates high-end homes in the Bay Area, and a couple of clients were slowing down work or canceling projects. And the university refused to close the new gap. "He was kinda mad at us. It was a big shock," Yerke said.

Alba entered City College that fall. He may go on to realize his dream of Santa Cruz. But his case illustrates one constraint facing the new decentralists in the education sector: the exigencies of uncertain family resources—even among parents who care deeply about education—may eclipse short-lived success so vividly observed in the most inspiring schools. Of the 115 first-year students, one-fifth to a quarter of the students has not finished at CAT over the years. Some shift to other less demanding high schools and eventually graduate. Still, this compelling school is not immune to the uncertainties facing blue-collar families, to the constant movement of kids and families who are unable to sink roots in one community and its neighborhood institutions.

We later sat with Johnson and Rowland, along with CAT's new principal, Daniel Allen, to review our draft chapter. Fact checking was in order, and we were curious about the school's evolution, now in its fifth year, as the founding cadre of teachers had moved on. Johnson and Rowland now worked at Envision headquarters, attempting to bottle and export the firm's magic to regular public schools throughout California. "Going to scale" was the hope, funded by a well-heeled foundation. Back at CAT, notable adjustments were being made.

Resource levels had continued to drop, leading to bigger classes, including more students packed into advisory periods. This was undercutting close relationships between teachers and youths, according to everyone around the table. The five or six "core teachers that were CAT" had now all left, Johnson verified. This weakened the historical spirit but also gave Allen a "clean slate" on which to make adjustments in the social organization of CAT.

First, "students weren't experiencing enough boundaries," according to Rowland. So a bell schedule had been instituted, and efforts were made to ensure that youths were "not cruising through the office" or wandering in late for class. And the school was under attack for being "the third most segregated school in the city," Allen reported. In the San Francisco context this meant that very few white students and almost no Asians were enrolling at CAT.

This shift toward tough love was blended with "bringing warm demanders to a school level," as Johnson put it, no longer simply lodged in a few founding teachers. "CAT has always had rock-star teachers," Allen said. But deeper structures were not in place to support all teachers. "We are trying to make CAT a place where teachers can have families," he said, rather than working twelve-hour days dealing with too many challenging students, and feeling burnout.

This update proved telling, as we had failed to see these tensions surface among the staff. The ethic of strong relationships with kids had not been as widely shared as we originally inferred, or had begun to dissolve in recent years. So the stability of such cultural elements—perhaps the crumbling integrity of the four cornerstones—erode a bit in decentralized organizations that rely on core staff rather than build a sustainable social order.

The time spent on projects, portfolios, and evening presentations had already been shaved back in the new school year. "We really focused on project-based activities, performance-based learning," Rowland recalled. "But that takes time, the resources weren't always there." So evening exhibitions were cut from five to just two times during the year. Now more time is spent in traditional didactics, getting ready for standardized tests, all aimed at boosting the school's performance.

The state budget did bounce back as California shook off the long hangover from the Great Recession. Charter school advocates keep securing bits of additional aid here and there. CAT advances with its adjusted culture and mix of learning activities. Decentralized authority affords the chance to make significant adjustments in the school's social organization in steady consultation with Envision's lean, supportive headquarters. And the ongoing story of CAT illustrates how decentralizing remains a verb—how the organizing of local authority and normative commitments continues to be probed and reshaped.

Can this inventive, decentralized organization—no matter how compelling in the short run—become truly sustainable? Can the human-scale ethics and teaching tools that still invigorate and engage antsy youths be captured and exported to large schools? Or perhaps it's the decentered Envision network that will become the norm in how "public" schools are organized—a colorful panoply of small, inventive organizations, run by largely private managers, still financed by taxpayers. Some reformers now call this "portfolio management," a corporate phrase, similar to investment portfolios, a metaphor that captures the diverse and variable deregulated schools operating in Los Angeles, Chicago, and New York.

City Arts and Technology High School still goes way beyond the menu-driven organizational changes prescribed by many reform activists and far-away policy makers. Lenz, Rowland, and Johnson—these are second-wave decentralists who are not satisfied with merely breaking away from the central state. They enjoy freedom from the downtown school bureaucracy and calcified labor contracts. But they journey far beyond simply seceding from the mass institution of public education—traveling into the hearts and minds of challenging adolescents while building a demanding professional culture that aims to enrich their own practices.

"Real relationships, true relationships is so what motivates the staff . . . to build your respect, your trust," Rowland told CAT's graduating class one June as hundreds of family members cheered, waving their hands in the air. "Seek relationships . . . they go both ways." The question going forward is whether the state or the market can spawn such an ethic, such a commitment, taking local organizing to a wider scale.

6

The Limits of Localism—Lifting Vets in Iowa

Kim Marovets served in Iraq, five miles from Baghdad. "We were shelled 306 times during one six-month period. I spent a lot of time on the floor."

She hadn't bargained for this. After leaving high school she joined the National Guard in Mason City, Iowa, blithely assuming that weekend drills would mark the end of her military service. Instead, this mother of four and ex-child-care manager was called to active duty in 2003. Seemingly overnight, leaving her family, Marovets found herself inside a logistics and supply base close to the Baghdad airport, arriving months after the American invasion toppled the regime of Saddam Hussein.

"I was such a caregiver before I went," Marovets told me. "I loved being a mother." Right up until Marovets packed her duffle bag, her already sizeable family was hosting three foster children. Her instincts would come in handy in Iraq while she endeavored to be a toughened den mother for her fellow comrades. "I remember being under this computer desk" during one rocket attack, "this kid is holding my hand." Marovets's comparative maturity and kindness were felt by many and were returned in kind. "My unit stood by me, everyone of them every day, from the captain to every private." She had never experienced such camaraderie and warm support.

Returning home, Marovets didn't enjoy such steady respect and affection. She had changed. "I found myself sitting in the car," wrought with anxiety, unable to find meaning in her new life back home. "I couldn't get out of the driveway," Marovets said. Her first Christmas was unbearable; her husband and kids were expecting the attentive, selfless mother she had been before. "My family was so angry that I'm not like I used to be." At one point she spent nights in the garage with a teddy bear and a blanket. "Each day I would think three hundred times about being in Iraq."

Her children so wanted to have their mother back. Marovets had e-mailed or called home daily, except when her base was under attack. But she just couldn't slip back into her familiar role of being mom. Her one daughter, Jessica, "got so mad one day she was throwing roller skates across the room," Marovets said. "She missed me the most."

But Marovets was no longer the same person, the automatic mom with no interests, no chutzpah of her own. Marovets soon went on antidepressants and would add alcohol to the mix. "As an E7 (Sargent 1st Class) and a woman, you're not supposed to show weakness." But "how come nobody could see how sick I was?" She mistakenly thought that counselors were only available in Des Moines, two hours away. In fact, two local clinics serve vets in Mason City.

"Since I was detached from this world, I did all the military jobs I could find," Marovets said, eager to remain embraced by her tribal ties. But as deployments of Iowa units began to wind down by 2007, along with military work, she moved to a civilian job, working part-time in a school cafeteria. "I do dishes, I bus really good," Marovets said with a hesitant, sardonic smile that lightened her otherwise weary face.

One afternoon Marovets was spotted in the kitchen, working at the National Guard Armory, looking detached and strung out. A counselor from Fort Dodge named D. J. Swoop had noticed her. Swoop had cared for many returning vets, who often suffered from trauma and unshakeable sadness—a feeling of coming home to what's now the foreign land. Swoop felt that Marovets, while at work, "was trying to hide." Right then and there Swoop reached out. "So, I said, 'did you try to kill yourself?' She was blown away that I was connecting the dots." Swoop looks back, "it's always mystified her how there were so many people around her, and no one knew what she was going through."

After sporadic counseling failed to buoy Marovets, she drove to Des Moines and showed up on Swoop's front stoop. "She had just grabbed pills," Swoop said. "She surrendered all her medicines, weight-loss drugs, Adderall for ADD." Marovets checked into the Veterans Affairs (VA) facility after two earlier suicide attempts. "The army chaplain sat in the hospital with us," Swoop reported. "I told her, you were a person in charge of troops. You ran a tight ship. You would expect more from your soldiers. Why don't you expect that for yourself?"

When Decentralization Fails

This isn't supposed to happen. Veterans like Marovets just don't slip through the seams of a tightly woven safety net, at least not according to VA officials in Des Moines at the center of this huge institution. But they do, and it can be an uncontrolled fall into a deep and dark crevasse.

This chapter delves into the limits of localism, how a small-town network of caring psychologists, job counselors, and benefits advisors—working under heavy caseloads and slight support from fragmented state and federal bureaucracies—do lose track of vets, many who live just blocks away. Remnants of those essential cornerstones of the new decentralists peek through the soil, like Roman ruins scattered across a forgotten province. But the loose network of local offices and caring souls I came to know in tiny Mason City yielded a rather frayed safety net—one driven by demand, by the assumption that veterans would surface from their emotional foxholes and knock on the doors of disparate service providers.

Like the other quarter-million women who have served in Iraq and Afghanistan, Marovets attended the obligatory two-hour debriefing on the difficulties of returning home. Then the modest array of Mason City agencies—a rural town that takes forty minutes to walk, end to end—largely lost track of Kim Marovets.

The three prior chapters described how lean centers bolstered each firm's ethical mission, animated by core designers who advance rich client data, coach their local practitioners to learn more about clients, then blend material and social tools to better engage them. But in northern Iowa—despite the heartfelt commitment of those who serve vets in Mason City—these organizational foundations remain brittle. Each practitioner is situated in a separate bureaucratic apparatus, which offers uneven and sporadic support to its local staff.

Stepping back, the VA has long struggled, across this vast institution, with the question of where to lodge authority and discretion over resources. President Lincoln established in 1866 the first bureau to serve military veterans. After two world wars and conflicts in Korea and Vietnam, just the VA's healthcare side had become an expansive, highly centralized organization. By 1994 it ran 172 hospitals with over 160,000 employees and a yearly budget of $16.3 billion. But the quality and cost of services came under heavy fire for being difficult to access by vets (months to see a doctor) and "for providing care of unpredictable and irregular quality."[1]

After such damning reviews of the VA's clumsy centralization—suffering from "command and control, military-style management" from its headquarters in Washington—the Clinton administration spearheaded a series of organizational reforms.[2] It provided a stage, beyond the education sector, on which Vice President Gore's team would try to "reinvent government." This involved setting clearer performance goals, focusing on lifting the quality of primary health-care services, and gathering data for each patient in order to track progress.

The VA's Washington headquarters began to decentralize management and give control to local units dubbed veterans integrated services networks (VISNs). This push to decentralize service delivery was advanced by contracting-out to a variety of local NGOs and for-profit health-care firms. Yet health-care delivery remains tied closely to the VA's far-flung network of hospitals. Meanwhile, client problems remain quite local, including when kin support and social ties are weak. Military vets make up fully one-third of the nation's homeless population.

Let's begin by first visiting the scattered local agencies that serve veterans in the northern reaches of Iowa. These visits revealed that the uneven capacity of virtuous service providers is no match for the severe problems veterans often face. We will then dig deeper into Marovets's case; she is one vet who struggled to admit her trauma and "weakness" and was pulled from the depths of depression by a caring VA counselor. Still, Marovets and her Iowa comrades remain unknowing of, or hesitant to negotiate, this loose-knit array of VA clinics, therapists, and go-betweens—even in this humble town of Mason City. Finally, lessons are drawn from this northern Iowa case: when do the cornerstones of second-wave decentralists fail to offer firm grounding for struggling clients?

A Locally Knit Safety Net

At the center of Mason City's central park, near the corner of First and Federal Streets, rest twin granite blocks; it is as if one boulder had been cracked in half. The granite blocks are surrounded by nine flat headstones that were sunk into the ground at irregular angles. The names of 3,441 veterans appeared carved into the tandem center stones the day of my visit. The count kept rising, as vets returned home to Mason City from Afghanistan or Iraq, dead or alive. What's less certain is whether the veterans' officials, job counselors, and medical staff—scattered across the town's local agencies—can sufficiently buoy veterans who remain upright but live in dark and unpredictable places.

At one level Mason City is a close-knit, supportive town. Most everyone you meet is friendly, quick to wave and offer a sincere hello. It's a graying, blue-collar town economically, population about 28,000. When travelers get off the interstate and snoop around, they hear of two claims to fame. Mason City was home to Meredith Willson, composer of *The Music Man*, and then became infamous for being a stone's throw from where Buddy Holly and

Richie Valens went down in a plane in 1959, after playing a festival in nearby Clear Lake.

Lending a hand comes easy in the northern reaches of Iowa. Residents are descendants of Scandinavian, German, and of late Latino immigrants and often mistrust faraway government. Going local is not a hip, avant-garde political movement in Mason City; it's long been a way of life. So there's plenty of talk about giving vets a leg up. Town parades regularly celebrated the return of National Guard units. The local media recently recognized the dwindling count of veterans coming home from Afghanistan.

But as I meandered through town, exploring the few agencies charged with lifting vets, the capacity of and coordination among these practitioners came into question. The count of the town's helping hands can be done on one hand. But are these local, often isolated agencies—even when loosely tethered to central bureaucracies in Des Moines—sufficiently robust to mend the deep wounds that vets like Kim Marovets bring back from overseas? Are welcoming intentions and decentralized organizing enough?

Deep Scars, Hesitantly Reaching Out

Let's step back from Mason City to gain a wider view of the problem and see why centralized remedies often characterize heartfelt responses. The National Center for PTSD (Posttraumatic Stress Disorder), housed within the Pentagon, distributes a tidy eleven-page guide titled "Returning from the War Zone."[3] "The days and weeks after a homecoming from war," it begins, "can be filled with excitement, relief, and many other feelings." A colorful chart lists other feelings associated with "combat stress reactions," like "loss of intimacy or feeling withdrawn, detached and disconnected." It warns that veterans might be "experiencing shock, being numb, unable to feel happy . . . getting into fights with family members," engaged in "too much drinking, smoking or drug use."

The prevalence rates are difficult to fathom. About one-sixth of all vets returning from Iraq or Afghanistan report suffering from depression or posttraumatic stress disorder. Just one-third of these seeks help.[4] Five years after the US invasion of Iraq, researchers at the RAND Corporation estimated that about one-third of a million vets suffered from PTSD or disabling brain injury.[5] And the symptoms surrounding PTSD can be even more severe for the some 260,000 women who have served in Iraq and Afghanistan over the past two decades. One-fifth have suffered from sexual aggression, over a third have experienced reproductive maladies.[6]

Still, these tallies and diagnostic language don't quite capture the pain, the emotional chaos that veterans experience when they return home; many of these vets survived the horrors of combat. Back in Mason City, Kim Marovets is far from unique in this regard.

Meet Roy Henagar, who was forty-five years of age when we first met. Like Marovets, he just couldn't reach out to others when he finally returned home after two deployments in Iraq. He never approached the VA edifice in Des Moines or the clinical outpost in Mason City. But he did connect with someone from his tribe, former marine Doug Waychus, whose wife, Rosetta, heads the cramped veterans office downtown. Henagar goes by the nickname Gunny, since he was a gunnery sergeant in Kuwait, then in Iraq. His e-mail address begins with oldtoolsniper.

Gunny remains an articulate, physically fit ex-marine. One frigid Iowa morning he detailed life in the baking, Persian Gulf desert. Henagar joined the military just out of high school. He first served as a young recruiter in Cedar Rapids and then was posted to Monterey, California. Henagar was told to grow his hair long, forget the buzz cut, and sport an unkempt beard. He served as a courier, "taking top secret documents around the world." Henagar would move on to gather intelligence in parts of East Asia. By then, the first Gulf War was on. Henagar was sent to a hazy military front, as George H. W. Bush aimed to rebuff Saddam Hussein's short-lived takeover of Kuwait.

"They took us out to the Kuwait border and dumped us there. We had no idea which direction the enemy was coming from. We had dug fortifications on the wrong side" from where they would eventually appear. Clear battle lines did emerge in the vast expanse of the desert, stretching into Iraq. At one point Henagar's unit was told to "assault all the way to the Kuwait International Airport," a ninety-mile line of attack. For three days "we were going through breaches, where everyone becomes a trigger puller," rooting out Iraqi soldiers hidden behind fortifications.

A row of bulldozers led the American advance, followed by ammunition and supply trucks, weaving gently through mine fields. Henagar had thirty-eight troops under his command, "only 20 percent of the guys had ever fired. They each advanced with a machine gun and five mortars and plastic explosives strapped to their backs, "to blow up enemy bunkers." Henagar is a decorated hero, in part because "I took over the rifles and shot these (Iraqi) guys off their tanks." Then, impassively, Henagar said, "After two or three fire fights you realize that some guys just aren't gonna pull the trigger."

"When we took the airport, the cease fire was declared, and there we sat," he said. "I lived in a hole in the ground next to a runway for a couple weeks. Seems like all's we did was dig holes and burn crap. Sometimes we shot at the enemy; sometimes we shot at each other. It's just the way it is."

Henagar felt angry and detached after returning home from battle for the first time, back in 1991, after fighting in the Gulf War. But it "wasn't right... to go tell anyone you're going to a counselor, that was taboo, it was a career ender," he said. Henagar realized that he had survived a terrifying experience, only to no longer understand normal life back in Iowa. He had sent to his parents several rifles taken after killing his Iraqi attackers. "Looking back, giving my mom those AK-47s was the craziest thing I could have done."

Redeployed to Iraq in 2002, Henagar was dumped once again at the Kuwait-Iraq border, this time to prepare American troops for desert combat. "I was that combat veteran who taught kids, too young to face [the perils], what to do." Yet Henagar was becoming a disaffected war hero. "What was hard was that I saw all the same mistakes, a mirror image of the first war." One day Henagar sat with a lieutenant discussing strategy, bluntly telling his senior officer, "We didn't learn anything in the first Gulf war." The senior officer turned to Henagar and said, "No, I didn't. I was in the eighth grade." This once-undaunted fighter would soon retire from the marines. "I had had enough."

A Warm Shoulder, a Fellow Marine

Henagar reported that he never sought out a counselor or joined a men's group at the American Legion, as fellow vets were doing. Soon after his second homecoming the VA opened a small clinic in Mason City, just blocks away from Henagar's spartan two-floor cottage. But he never stopped by. Seeking out therapy or a warm shoulder to lean on—no matter how local and discreet these agencies—would simply reveal his vulnerability. Only weak marines searched for help, as Marovets had told me.

"I felt, and still feel, like a spectator in a lot of ways. It all looks the same, but I don't fit in." At one point Henagar sent me a note; in it he was reflecting on his final days in Iraq, before pulling out. "Most of them were kids who grew up fast. War was something they watched on TV. It was simple, if they didn't like it, they just shut it off." His sign-off said, "Marines don't cry. Today I am not a good Marine."

Henagar—like many returning veterans—did eventually knock on Rosetta Waychus's basement door; she is the quiet yet charismatic head of the county's two-person office of Veterans Affairs. A handsome woman with straight, dyed blonde hair, Waychus somehow emotes acceptance and tranquility, chatting softly and with precision, as if she has little to accomplish that day. Few papers lay atop her desk. As details arise she'll politely ask her aide to find a phone number, dig out a form.

On my second visit, sinking into the chilly basement of the county office, a gracious stone building circa 1910, I began seeing how Waychus offered a warm island of serenity for clients, those like Henagar and Marovets who have seen terrible violence, who remain stuck in vast loneliness. Waychus somehow conserves her own emotional energy while deploying a wily ability to extract benefits for the almost four thousand surviving vets that live in and around Mason City. The state of Iowa requires each county to hire at least one person to help vets obtain disability or pension checks, sign them up for health care, and perhaps locate a psychologist or quality nursing home for elderly clients. Waychus is that one person for Cerro Gordo County, and she's juggling a growing caseload.

Waychus can push paper when she must. But her role runs much deeper. "I'm mom. Yep, I'm mom. I believe the number one support to veterans, such as Kim and Gunny, is to be here for them," she told me. "Whatever problem someone has, we're here to listen. We find a remedy." When Henagar first came by he was "feeling like a fish out of water," Waychus said.

So she arranged to have her husband, a retired marine, "accidentally be there" when Henagar was to return. "My husband helped Gunny find a job until the government funds came through." He introduced him to "the Marine Corps League and the VFW." This was a personal touch on top of Rosetta's official duties—to get the extra combat pay to which Henagar was entitled and plug into the VA's health plan. Waychus even helped him get a free hunting license, which Henagar much appreciated since he traps wild game for food.

Waychus extended that same helping hand and warm heart to Marovets. Her tiny county office is the first stop for many veterans after being discharged from the army or the Iowa-based National Guard. "Just being here to listen to her," was how Waychus underlined her role. "She knows she has only to call for anything, and we will be there for her, [that's] the most important support for Kim." Waychus made sure that Marovets's dependent children were added to her benefits when she was released by her guard unit, then she helped Marovets write a résumé and pursue jobs inside the Mason City schools.

At times Waychus's full-service approach includes gentle matchmaking between vets who shy away from new relationships. But Marovets waved me off the topic of possible romance. I asked whether she knew Henagar, since their stints in Iraq overlapped. "Oh, yeah, he's the one who turns the faucet off," Marovets said. "He's got too much intensity for me."

Still, Marovets did remain drawn to the men with whom she served. One day, talking over lunch, Marovets jumped up and sprinted to the bar, hugging a young sandy-haired man. Turned out that he had been in the same guard unit with Marovets in Iraq. "I think she's always gonna be with her comrades," Marovets's sister, Konnie, told me. "That's the worst thing for her, to give the unit up." This camaraderie among vets kept surfacing, deep ties among those who shared the experience of combat, then the heartbreak of not fitting in back home. How Waychus's spare office and rich spirit nurtured and widened these social ties proved crucial for Marovets and Henagar.

Distant Clients, Localized Health Care

Mason City remains a northern, rural outpost in the eyes of program managers down in Des Moines. These layers of earnest bureaucrats watch over the region's largest VA hospital and regulate the spigot of cash benefits, medications, and pensions allocated to Iowa's quarter-million veterans. It's the "mother ship" when it comes to health care, as Mason City psychologist Steve Holbrook puts it.

Veterans' benefits have grown sharply in the wake of wars in Afghanistan and Iraq, recently bringing Holbrook's outpatient clinic to Mason City. Des Moines officials report allocating $6.2 million in health-care services (excluding insurance benefits) for about 1,700 patients each year, two-fifths of all known vets in far-flung Cerro Gordo County.[7] It's a big region to serve with regularity; it stretches out by "a one hour drive in all directions," Holbrook said.

Mason City's outpatient clinic opened in 2008, just a mile from downtown, not long after Marovets and Henagar returned home from Iraq. The clinic sits right next to the state jobs office, framed by modest brick homes and the well-worn expressway that links Mason City to the interstate. Despite its proximity, neither Marovets nor Henagar had much to say about the VA clinic. Marovets was furious when a therapist reportedly told her to buck up, to get a grip on her life. "I was in a fucking war zone, and he's telling me to buck-up?" Marovets never returned to the local clinic. So by the time D. J. Swoop rescued her from a drug overdose and repeated suicide attempts, Marovets assumed that for serious help, she must get down to Des Moines. Instead, she may have benefited from care close to home, although that required reaching out, revealing her pain.

"One thing the VA is trying to do is to show that it's not a sign of weakness to ask for help," Lisa Niewoehner told me. She's a former therapist in Fort Dodge, more than an hour from Mason City. She's now the VA's traveling caseworker of sorts, trying to ensure that vets like Marovets are not falling through the treacherous cracks in the system. "We want our vets to have that warm hand-off, to find that go-to person out in the clinics." Niewoehner connects vets with the panoply of NGOs that provide local services, from contracting with private psychologists and delivering medications or servicing artificial limbs, to overseeing home health workers and dropping off medications for aging or house-bound vets.

Back in Mason City, Holbrook sees individual clients for therapy and facilitates groups. "They like the fact that it's just for them," he said. Vietnam-era vets still make up two-thirds of Holbrook's practice. The rest served in Iraq or Afghanistan. He stressed a point that helped me better understand Marovets's case and the challenges facing local organizations: many vets have suffered from stress or trauma inside their original families, long before they went into the military. A sizeable portion suffers from the childhood wounds of abuse or neglect; they had often witnessed intimidation or violence at young ages. They express "mixed feelings of betrayal" going way back, according to Holbrook. They constantly "scan their environment, they very much keep up their guard."

Holbrook certainly gets to know his clients—that cornerstone of new decentralists—at least the slice that comes forward. It's difficult to get on his calendar. Holbrook sees upwards of ten to twelve vets each day for individual therapy, then leads a "PTSD support clinic" two nights a week. His basic strategy is to "normalize their experience and reassure them that they're not crazy," as was plainly put by this former Southern California therapist. Many of his patients suffer from terrifying flashbacks, or often feel hyper, unable to calm down and confidently connect with others. They commonly report "blow-ups at dinner time" with family members. "It's hard to heal when you don't feel trust," Holbrook said. "No one moves to northern Iowa unless you have family here." But these relationships can be rife with history and hazards.

Heavy caseloads and the long-term nature of building that trust prove frustrating. "We're often just patching things up rather than uncovering the deeper causes," Holbrook said. "Do you really want to peel back the onion?" That's the question he gently presses on clients. Part of where vets get stuck, he says, is "are they willing to accept empathy from others." Trust building takes time, especially when seeing a shrink. Even a veteran psychologist like Holbrook finds it daunting, given the everyday constraints and the growing count of veterans that have returned to northern Iowa.

Other constraints stem from how the mother ship in Des Moines defines counseling and health services. "The VA has an emphasis on employment based treatment," Holbrook said. This is useful in terms of learning discrete "coping skills . . . becoming aware of what's gonna flip me out, or push me into a hyper-alert mode." But does getting a client to be "job ready" help to uncover root causes of distress?

Pat Wilson, a fellow therapist, sits just blocks away from Holbrook's clinic. She spearheads outreach to veterans from the Mercy Medical Center of North Iowa. Wilson has worked over time with the Iowa National Guard as well, organizing "enduring families support meetings," where vets come with adult family members and work through outbursts or subterranean tensions that are bubbling up at home. They share stories from the battlefield; they reveal deeply mixed feelings about being back home.

Wilson has mostly attended to the problems returning members of the National Guard face, many who never expected to go overseas, leaving spouses and young children behind. As the war in Iraq escalated, the military sorely needed more foot soldiers. The quickest available source was state-led guard units—typically weekend troopers who only saw real duty in the event of student protests or natural disasters. Returning to the states, "they do not go to a military base, they go home, they go back to their jobs," she said. "They drill again, of course, on weekends, but that may be the only time that they would see people who have had the same life experience." The state offices overseeing what has become the not-so-national guard have few links to the VA, no arrangement by which their war veterans could easily access health care. It's another gaping hole in the loose-knit support network: the lack of a coherent center—even coordination between federal and county efforts—results in fragmented practitioners and confused points of entry even in small towns like Mason City.

Wilson's strategy has relied heavily on NGOs and volunteers, spread across Iowa, even before the invasion of Iraq under George W. Bush in 2003. She helps to sustain seventeen crisis-intervention teams, each staffed by clinicians, police officers, vets, and volunteers, numbering four hundred statewide. They arrive at short notice when disaster strikes, ranging from floods or tornadoes to the return of a military unit. Group leaders, mostly therapists, have devised protocols that invite vets—most still in their twenties—to talk openly about their anxiety, guilt, and those ever-present nightmares.

"We've had soldiers report that their wives, trying to wake them up from a bad dream, [put] their hands around their wife's neck or reach for a gun," Wilson said. Ground rules are set for the small groups, like "no one has any rank," and "speak only for yourself." Military chaplains also attend "to discuss any personal spiritual issues," and "command cannot demand the revelation of these communications."

Wilson accents how "peers are always involved, because peers give credibility to the process." She works a lot with friends and spouses of vets to identify, "here's what to look for," and with vets themselves to reflect on "what changes have you noticed within yourself, your family members or your relationships?" Her discussions prompt horrific recollections, such as one vet who reported, "I had to run over the baby because they said she might be carrying a bomb." We don't "sit around and sing kumbaya, that freaks-out soldiers, let me tell you," Wilson said.

The Iowa spirit contributes to this reliance on local volunteers and ad hoc organizing in Mason City and statewide, according to Wilson. "It's Iowa. People say 'yeah, I want to help,'" she said. "Basically we're farmers, 'it's no problem, no shirt off my back.'" Still, organizational capacity remains weak, since neither the guard nor the VA supports much outreach to vets, beyond the single reentry briefing and a "warm handoff" to some kind of local provider. And if the vet feels uncomfortable in reaching out, there's no one there to make the first move, as we see with Marovets and Henagar. Wilson also pointed to a shortage of psychiatrists in northern Iowa, naming just two in this expansive region. And she had yet to meet the VA's Holbrook, even though his clinic is just a twenty-minute walk away.

This lack of coordination—even rudimentary networking in this human-scale town with these hard-working practitioners—kept surfacing in my conversations. The dozen vets I interviewed often knew Waychus and relied on her modest shop for a variety of benefits, but they rarely had heard of Wilson or Holbrook; at times they were paying for a private therapist. Equally telling, the practitioners had heard of each other, but made little contact, identifying with differing roles and funding streams. So, yes, the egalitarian benevolence of down-home Iowans is compelling. But it started to feel insufficient, as these disparate practitioners at the grass roots lacked the time, capacity, and wherewithal to knit a more durable safety net for their clients.

A related fact emerged from this local map of disjointed options for mental health services. No one in Mason City or in Des Moines knows how reticent veterans like Marovets or Henagar are faring at work or with everyday life. Services are demand driven, a loose and localized market if you will. So the vets that reach out to Holbrook or Wilson stand some chance of unlocking all those fears, all that angst and mistrust of employers or family members. But many simply don't reach out. They feel no touch points, no open arms across this patchwork of decentralized services. And "to do the kind of deep therapy these men and women need," Holbrook said, "they must have someone, something that's good in their life." For many, that's difficult to find.

Finding Jobs, a Place Back Home

I was first introduced to Holbrook by William Stuflick, a veterans specialist in the state employment office, next door to the VA health clinic. Unlike other connections between the VA and local practitioners, this linkage was reportedly strong, thanks both to proximity and Stuflick's can-do exuberance, his caring manner. I happened upon Stuflick through a local news story about Mason City's award-winning jobs office, which was recognized for its success in finding scarce jobs for vets in northern Iowa's tough economy. It's a local branch of the Iowa Workforce Development agency, not formally linked to the VA nor to Waychus's county-funded shop. But Stuflick proved to be a masterful networker, moved to find what his clients need, starting with a job.

Much of Stuflick's effectiveness stems from his curiosity over what makes his clients tick, knowing firsthand their angst over how to fit back into what's oddly become a foreign land. "The biggest problem is pride," Stuflick said. "When I came back I didn't ask for help or try to get benefits." First impressions are key for Stuflick. "They come in and look at me, and say 'who is this guy?' because I look young." Indeed, Stuflick looks like a craggy but youthful marine who just walked off the set of a patriotic war film; he has an ever-quick smile and eager spirit. "Then we share pictures . . . I wasn't an officer, I was an enlisted guy," Stuflick says. His clients quickly see that he's one of them.

"William actually called me and told me, 'I'm a veteran,'" Josh Douglas, a former Marine who did two tours of combat duty in Iraq, told me with a sly smile. He found Stuflick instantly helpful. He "found me a couple applications around Mason City . . . and contacted the hiring people," Douglas said. Stuflick also helped with getting Douglas set up with unemployment insurance. He landed a job painting Winnebago trailers up in Forestville, until the recession cost him that job. "He [Stuflick] helped out just about as much as he could, and he's helped out others that I've seen come through the door."

Stuflick is serious about the "one stop" promise of his shop. One homeless vet showed up with no place to stay, and he was running out of antidepressants. So Stuflick kicked into action; he found a shelter, called Waychus for emergency cash, and walked the vet over to the physician's office next door. The client had no car but ample skills in mechanics, so Stuflick secured possible jobs reachable by bus, at Walmart and a local truck repair shop.

Stuflick had enlisted in the army right out of high school, after growing up in Lone Rock, sixty-eight miles due west of Mason City and named after "a big rock found on someone's land," he clarified. Stuflick, with typical panache, claims to have "loved every minute" of his fourteen years in the service. He joined the Red Horse Squadron, stationed in an airbase north of Baghdad. Their job was to protect the runways, so that flights could come and go in relative safety. "You learn skills and advance on your own merits," Stuflick said. He was sent home after suffering an injury in an incident that he remained uncomfortable discussing with me, over my three years visiting Mason City.

"I've been through the system," Stuflick told me one snowy morning in his cramped, immaculately organized office. "If I hadn't met Rosetta [Waychus], I would still be floating out there, not knowing what was going on." Stuflick remains a huge fan. "We see people come from all over, even from outside the county, to see Rosetta." He reflected back on his return from Iraq: "I had a tough time. You were in uniform for 14 years. I didn't have slacks, just pants to go to church," he said. And "yes, I had some pride issues." Stuflick now works hard to thaw out his clients' hesitance to reach out as they timidly come through the door looking for work and someone who just listens.

Stuflick learns from the guard and army who's returning from war to Mason City, along with sketchy pieces of their stories. Then he makes about 350 calls a month, each meticulously logged in, to see how vets are doing in the job market. Stuflick is actually called a *navigator* within the jobs office (not unlike Geisinger's case managers), accenting the need to help clients maneuver through the VA's nettlesome bureaucracy in Des Moines or even Mason City. He insists that clients stop by, allowing him to gauge basic communication skills and whether they are ready psychologically to fit into a nine-to-five job. As therapeutic issues arise, Stuflick walks them over to the VA clinic. Thirty vets walk through the Stuflick's office door each month, seeking work, often revealing deeper barriers to holding down a job. A member of their tribe, Stuflick can quickly sense when a client still has one foot and much of his or her heart back in the military, still at war.

Stuflick also works to open up job slots for vets among a variety of employers in a tepid, largely rural economy. He sets up "lunch and learns" with about twenty local employers each month to pitch the employability of veterans. "Walmart, believe it or not, has been fabulous," he said. "I can call the managers and sit with their HR people as well." Another up-and-coming employer is Florida Power and Light, the firm that has put up hundreds of wind turbines across the flat expanse of northern Iowa. Humming like an old dishwasher, the turbines afflict the cattle according to some locals, but the firm employs a number of returning veterans.

While a formal organizational chart might not show it, Stuflick turns out to be a pivotal practitioner in Mason City's small network of organizations.

He has opened up access to jobs. He coordinates with Waychus to track when the next military division is returning home. And perhaps most important, he's a member of the tribe, with sensitivity to the emotional dynamics that beset shell-shocked vets. Stuflick proved to be a one-stop wunderkind.

Still, with a burgeoning caseload and the growing pressure to show successful job placements, at times Stuflick must revert to the logistical aspects of navigating clients through the maze of benefit options and possible employers. Even the warm and gracious Waychus can only buoy those vets who come through the door seeking myriad forms of aid. The question that kept returning to my mind was: who is there to engage troubled vets, to bring them into the light of new possibilities, first unlocking all the pain and confusion that lay just below the surface? And does the human-scale patchwork of practitioners found in Mason City offer this kind of sustained, necessary support?

Stuflick did talk about the ethical mission, the moral support he receives from his central office in Des Moines. Iowa has a "priority of service" policy, he emphasized, "vets are supposed to go to the front of the line." He believed that this came from the top of the state Workforce Development agency. "We have managers who are veterans, slowly we're taking over," Stuflick said with an understated grin. And "we have links with other services, it's just getting them into the door," he said. "You have the county," Stuflick said in an upbeat tone. "But at the VA level, it's such a big bureaucratic monster." Beyond basic data tools and this steady ethical push to lift vets, the agency's central office rarely came up in conversation.

Meanwhile, Down in Des Moines

I had a hunch that Mason City's archipelago of earnest yet segmented practitioners might be explained by fragmented bureaucracies in Des Moines. Our three prior case studies each pointed to a coherent organizational center that signaled clear ethical commitments and resourceful delegation of data about clients and tools for better practice. But could I find this principled approach to decentralization, to locally rooted services for clients, down south inside the massive mother ship?

What proved to be a daunting first step was simply gaining entrée to the regional headquarters of the US Department of Veterans Affairs. I spoke with friendly secretaries in the director's office, the planning unit, and mental health services. At one point I was transferred by phone to a budget shop that was located in Nebraska. "The Des Moines VA Regional Office provides compensation, pension, and vocational rehabilitation and counseling services for all military veterans in the State of Iowa," the official blurb reads, aid for about 270,000 vets in all.

Eventually I was directed to David Huffman, the "the back-up public affairs officer." He asked that I e-mail a blurb describing exactly what I was trying to learn. After mentioning my visits to Mason City, my inquiry was put into the rural health bailiwick, somehow pigeonholed by the public relations shop. This led to a helpful conversation about a new initiative created by Congress in 2006, of which Huffman and the operational staff were obviously proud. And this segment of the presumptive institutional center proved to be tied to Holbrook's clinic and allied health services in Mason City.

So one chilly, gray fall morning I drove out to Des Moines's 227-bed veterans hospital, a rambling low-rise structure, which emits a sterile, military-base feel. Entering through faux Roman pillars, a sign in large block letters reads, The Price of Freedom Is Visible Here. An eerie sense of tranquility enveloped these weathered buildings. I headed down the hill, dutifully following another helpful sign, Administration.

The hospital itself is set in dull green woods on the northwest edge of the city. It's a bustling place inside, white-robed medical staff and wheelchairs in constant motion, serving the weary and wounded. This facility hosts almost 300,000 outpatient visits each year, not counting vets admitted for more serious procedures; it is staffed by over fifty physicians. Nearby is the Office of Rural Health. It proved difficult getting into Building 3, home to the VA's rural health unit, as the main stairway was blocked off with yellow tape, as if a crime scene remained cordoned off.

At last, slipping into the mother ship, I joked meekly with Huffman about the VA's thick, almost impenetrable shell. "Well, we have to be careful," he responded. "Services for veterans have been such a political issue." The friendly yet cautious Huffman, along with a younger, clearly committed health specialist, Beth Muenchrath, detailed how their new initiative was being carried out across Iowa. It aims "to improve access and quality of health care for veterans in geographically isolated areas," one description read. The VA's goal is to ensure that "no veteran would be more than two hours away" from a health facility, Huffman said.

They emphasized how Washington wants to rely more on "collaborations with public and private entities for the delivery of health care, including mental health (services)." One set of PowerPoint presentations stressed how to unite local organizations. It was titled "Outside the box—leveraging local infrastructure is an important strategy for reaching rural veterans."[8] So this slice of the organizational center hoped to embolden NGOs locally, a favored strategy of the new decentralists.

The work of this enthusiastic segment of central bureaucracy included construction of Mason City's outpatient clinic, which houses psychologist Holbrook, along with a similar facility built at Fort Dodge. More broadly, this rural health initiative was building fiscal relationships with a variety of local practitioners and NGOs, eighty-three contracts with "community care agencies" statewide, including the companies or nonprofits that deliver the necessary home health workers and physical therapists, along "with doctors, clinics, ERs" for vets across Iowa's northern reaches, Muenchrath said. Their success depends in large part on a robust set of family physicians, so "we are in the VA becoming more pro-active, offering more education to inform primary care providers," she said.

A sizeable challenge for this office was how to manage their small army of nurses who work inside the homes of veterans. Staff turnover is high in these little firms. The staff consists typically of women who visit often cranky or volatile vets in the outback of Iowa. "The VA is looking at caregiver stress," Muenchrath said. "Most social workers are female." The array of health services offered "has been very male focused for years and years," she accented. This ignored the fact that many returning female veterans need "mammograms or pregnancy management services," Muenchrath said.

To address issues of access and cost, the rural health office in Building 3 was deploying inventive technologies to provide higher quality care. They were piloting a program to have vets phone in refills for medications, and were experimenting with high-tech devices that "send data on drug use," along with blood sugar and hypertension readings beamed from the veteran's home. The VA was even assessing "telephone care as a substitute for routine psychiatric medication management" (dubbed telehealth). Younger vets are "getting into Facebook and Twitter, they're using the social media," Huffman reported.

But how were these admirable initiatives actually reaching vets like Marovets or Henagar in towns like Mason City? Through "four or five caseworkers for central Iowa," was the answer. Huffman insisted that "most of our vets have caseworkers, individuals are followed." Muenchrath added that "any vet who's defined as high risk for suicide or flight receives extra attention from two or three people who focus on suicide prevention." The organizational architecture on paper for delivering services looked sound. But staff remained stretched thin, and data tracking the thousands of vets in Muenchrath's territory seemed equally sparse. Kim Marovets never mentioned enjoying this level of attention from Veterans Affairs.

I did manage to discover two pivotal facts inside the mother ship—after pursuing leads that stemmed from this guarded conversation and their gift of some eighty pages of budget tables, program sketches, and inspiring testimony before the Congress by the director of the VA's Office of Rural Health. First, all the rhetoric and good intentions hinged on the work of one energetic case manager, Lisa Niewoehner, at least for north-central Iowa, located in Fort Dodge and stretching over to Mason City.

Second, only one local player, Rosetta Waychus, had even heard of Niewoehner. The goal expressed in Des Moines was virtuous. "It's the VA moving closer to their (veterans' own) homes," Huffman, the PR voice, told me. But on the ground Niewoehner remained a largely unknown entity to her allied practitioners in Mason City.

A former therapist in her own right, Niewoehner turned out to be a forceful advocate for her clients. Her commitment and verve could be felt even during our initial conversation, a conference call that Huffman insisted on monitoring from his Des Moines office. With clients spread out across central Iowa, "up to two hours in all directions," the best she could do was offer "a warm handoff" to one of the new outpatient clinics ("their go-to person out in the community based clinic"), home aides, job counselors, or private psychologists. Niewoehner at times brokered a link to "a county VA rep," like Waychus, to untangle hassles with benefits. She also worked with Pat Wilson's network to set up the "enduring family events," where candid discussion of trauma, angst, and reentry was facilitated with partners and kin.

But Niewoehner reportedly couldn't build relationships with the county veterans shop, Mercy hospital, or even the VA's own satellite clinic in Mason City. "The VA is trying hard to reach all vets," Niewoehner said. "As long as they have someone they trust, whether a therapist, primary care physician, even a receptionist or intake technician, they have someone they're comfortable calling." With a current caseload of 283, Niewoehner admitted to "minimal contact with each vet yearly."

Mason City's key practitioners—especially Stuflick, Waychus, and Wilson—remain delighted that the VA recently opened the outpatient clinic, along with the center's organizational capacity to recruit primary care physicians and caring therapists, like Holbrook. Effectively weaving a somewhat tighter safety net, the VA has shifted to eager and efficacious case managers, as I saw in Niewoehner. But the challenges facing many vets, as we have seen, can be deep, hard to shake. Loose networks of practitioners do yield cash benefits, good dentistry, and job advice. But in the shuffle to be "warmly handed off" to another practitioner, how do vets tangibly benefit and does all that noise and angst besetting their heads and hearts begin to subside?

Marovets's case helps to inform this essential question, as she put her intensity and troubles to the test, in a sense challenging the capacity of these decentralized—if not disparate—offices in Mason City. Each practitioner—whether tied to the VA, county government, or regional hospital—tries to ensure that vets like Marovets don't fall through the cracks, or at least that they don't fall too far. But this loose collection of individual caregivers struggles to keep pace with heavy caseloads, with the disabling problems that surface daily among veterans who do come through the door. For vets like Marovets or Henagar, already down a dark hole or simply mistrustful of others, demand-driven, sporadically linked organizations proved insufficient.

As the VA's family-program specialist, D. J. Swoop, said one day, "They have such an attitude, they won't let us in to help them out." How well can any practitioner get underneath and thaw out such an emotional deep freeze? And does their "practice" really afford the necessary time, trust, and agility? So far, as I roamed about Mason City and Des Moines it struck me how each earnest practitioner labored in a modest, decentralized shop, loosely tied to weak institutional centers that sent down a growing list of cases, with perhaps a dash of ethical purpose or legitimacy on the side. But little else.

Organizing Lite Meets Heavy Struggles

Walking down the street in Waterloo one day, Kim Marovets was reflecting on "how my life was going nowhere. I looked up and there was the recruiter office." Two days later she was "in the army now." Marovets was twenty years old. At that time female recruits with only a GED were required to start in the reserves, which she did. She later shifted to the National Guard, and for the next two decades showed up for weekend stints of marching, becoming familiar with firearms, and occasionally appearing in local parades. Meanwhile, she had married, given birth four times, and set up a child-care business inside her home, while also taking in a string of foster children. Then in 2003 her unit was deployed to Iraq; overnight she experienced shock and awe.

Marovets never liked school; she hadn't done well. One day she talked of struggling with her required math class after returning from Iraq, doggedly making progress at the local junior college. "Why do you think I like college, when you grow up thinking that you're dumb?" she asked rhetorically. "When I went into the army my test scores were so low that I couldn't even be a cook." Her turbulent family background, blended with sturdy resilience, often seeped out through her shaky confidence.

Marovets had grown up in Waterloo, an hour and a half southeast of Mason City. Her mother was pregnant at fifteen with her first child. Her dad was a truck driver, "the kind of guy who would put a gun to your face, a boot up your ass," Marovets said. She attained the utmost respect from others and for herself during her time in Iraq. Returning home, she was different, not like the ever-selfless mom she had been. Speaking to the fundamentals of self-worth, D. J. Swoop told me one day, "She [Marovets] has this thing where her daughter wouldn't talk to her, and the marriage is crap. So, she must be crap."

This feeling of uncertain self-worth and panic over the inability of her husband and children to truly listen to her kept surfacing. Marovets had changed dramatically after fourteen months on the front lines of war. Now those closest to her—except her twin sister—didn't ask her what was running through her head and heart. Her family just wanted her to magically click back into being Mom.

"I had to wear a dress again, and it was very boring," Marovets told me. She was embarrassed to reach out for help, to approach the practitioners that help other vets get back on their feet. Marovets's struggles—likely rooted in her own childhood and now the trauma of war—ran deep into her psyche and soul. At the same time, three sets of social ties lent support or dumped salt in these open wounds. As her confidant, Swoop, put it, "She suffers from depression, but she's got some good networks in place."

Let's next examine these immediate social ties that Marovets did try to nurture in her sometimes desperate, sometimes angry way. These tenuous relationships offer clues for how these local practitioners—working in decentralized organizations—did occasionally backstop and slowly lift Marovets, how they scaffolded up from her own tribal ties.

"Someone Who's Been There"

Marovets relied on three social circles for support as she pursued elusive feelings of belonging, acceptance, and a sense of purpose. Two sets of ties are what sociologists might call informal: her immediate family members, who now lived with a shell-shocked woman in place of the wife and mother they once knew; and her former comrades from the National Guard, who survived after literally being in the trenches together. Marovets's third set of ties included the practitioners in formal organizations who have offered a helping hand. These linkages remain weak and uneven, although life sustaining at times: Waychus at the downtown vets office, Swoop at the VA in Des Moines, the school where she works, and, tenuously, her instructors at the local college where she seeks to achieve the education that will help her get ahead.

The challenge facing these practitioners—situated in human-scale organizations—resembles the core task of peers in our prior case studies: the crafting of cooperation between a teacher and restless teen, a doctor seeking to move a patient toward healthier behavior, or even a finance banker and client. The interests of tandem actors overlap in each setting, at least to varying degrees. But for Marovets or clients who share this feeling of disconnection, the lack of meaning in everyday life, we have much to learn from those social ties that provide emotional sustenance. This may aid the work of the practitioners who are eagerly trying their best to lend a hand. Indeed, the claim of new decentralists is that they can enjoy the unfettered ability to touch and lift such clients. And we earlier saw how their microstrategies often borrow from the character of informal ties and relationships that were once anathema to the roles and rules of formal organizations. So let's take stock of the social bonds that lend rich meaning for Marovets.

During respites between enemy shellings, members of her troop would rush outside, perhaps headed to the mess hall or latrines, or at times restacking sand bags and checking on the safety of trucks and their ammunition. One of her jobs was "to account for everybody," that is, to be sure that everyone made it back inside. A couple years later, one of the young soldiers that Marovets had kept track of came loping toward her, jogging across Mason City's town square. "Mom!" he shouted, followed by a warm and long embrace. He still remembers Marovets as the brave, decisive den mother of their cramped base outside Baghdad.

These deep tribal ties host and legitimate how Marovets has come to define her self, along with clarifying the old scripts that she can no longer enact. Three of her former comrades "went out of their way to hook up," Marovets told me. "They said they'd kick ass if I didn't call them." The closeness that comes from shared pain and resilience, in turn, holds implications for building trust with practitioners that don't share the same experience of being in that frightful crucible, surviving together. Even after seeking out D. J. Swoop and going cold turkey since overdosing, Marovets just wouldn't see a counselor. "It's better to talk with someone who's been there," she said. "There's no way, if you haven't been there, to comprehend" all that she had experienced.

Marovets does check in with Waychus. "She's been a god-send, she can navigate through [the bureaucracy] when you need it," Marovets told me. "She fixes things ASAP." At one point the National Guard was pushing Marovets to pay back $250 for not covering the cost of antidepressants. "The army is screwing something up," Waychus concluded, and "she took care of it," Marovets said.

Marovets would eventually see a private therapist for several months. Yet she found little solace or insight from this psychologist. He was neither tied to the Mason City VA clinic nor to Wilson at Mercy Hospital. Marovets also recalls seeing a vocational-education counselor in Cedar Rapids. But after entering the local junior college and finding the school cafeteria job, she reported having little time for counseling, a service that's yielded limited benefits in her opinion.

That was the extent of Marovets's contact with Mason City's network of community practitioners, at least over our three years together. This is not to say that Marovets did not benefit from the sporadic guidance and support she received from the likes of Swoop and Waychus. But what remains unclear is whether this is enough for veterans like Marovets and whether other vets like her fall through the gaps in this loose-knit safety net.

Key actors like Waychus and Stuflick in the jobs agency receive lists of returning military units and try hard to make their way through that list. But caseloads are heavy and if a vet is reluctant to seek help, as with Marovets, none of these warmhearted practitioners has the ability to track them down. A veteran has to have a glaring medical problem for Lisa Niewoehner to take notice and get him or her over to Holbrook's clinic. And regional caseworkers represent an untested experiment within a gangly institution that remains centered around the hospital in Des Moines.

So, it's Marovets's fellow comrades from Iraq who offer her that inner circle of trusted ties. Within her tribe, there's continuity with Marovets's pre-war role of selfless wife, supportive mother, custodian of foster kids, and paid child-care provider. Like the ex-soldier loping across the square to hug his former commander, other members of the guard saw Marovets as competent, caring, and courageous. She continues to "socialize at picnics, music clubs, over Facebook" with fellow vets. "We talk about our normal, everyday lives."

The military's macho culture is another story. It permeates Marovets's trusted ties, yet dampens her ability to share the trauma and horrific memories that she experienced after returning stateside. Soldiers at her rank are not supposed to show weakness. "I was supposed to be strong. I was a leader," Marovets said. "Because of her rank and being in charge, she is expected to not abuse drugs," Swoop said. So, it's been difficult, even humiliating for Marovets to come forward, to ask for ongoing help.

Just back from Iraq, she worried "they will kick me out" of the guard if any weakness surfaced. When she finally drove to Des Moines, suicidal and out of options, she broke down when with Swoop. "I started crying and stomping my feet, saying that my daughter didn't like me," Marovets said. "I had made my first two suicide attempts." So while her tribe of former comrades offers camaraderie and support, they also reproduce tight norms that dampen the impulse to seek help, failing to shine a light into the darkness in which Kim Marovets felt hopelessly lost.

She's Not My Mother—Frayed Family Ties

The National City Bank, built by Frank Lloyd Wright in 1910, offers an iconic symbol of early modern, small-town institutions. It's a two-story box, but covered in colorful tiles and topped by a perfectly flat roof that stretches out to wide overhanging eaves. It's at "The Hub" of the graying, sixteen square blocks of downtown Mason City. Across the street is a less gracious edifice, Lorados, a shabby western bar that plays reggae, displays a fine sketch of Elvis, and serves mediocre pizza. After a series of four text messages, Marovets decided that's where we should meet to continue our conversation.

She was thrilled that evening because her daughter, Jessica, had agreed to attend counseling with her. Now, three years back from Iraq, Jessica was showing a willingness to share her feelings and try and engage her mom. "Stop trying to change your mother," was one point that surfaced, according to Marovets. And her three "boys are talking to me," she said, as a sense of relief and hope inched hesitantly across her often worried face. "Bumpy roads can be fixed, it's not bad, it's just bumpy." But coming back together with her family was still proceeding at a glacial pace. She talked of how difficult it was, how the army had trained her to follow scripts and routines. "Tell me what to do, then I know exactly what's expected." No clear roadmap, no certain pathway had emerged from the emotional fog to narrow the distance she still felt from her family.

Marovets first met her husband, Bob, when she was twelve; they were two working-class kids growing up in Waterloo. They dated their last year of high school—although Kim wasn't attending school much—and they were married at twenty-four. She attended weekend army drills, ran her day-care program from their modest home, and raised her own three boys and one girl. She loved being a mother. "I was such a caregiver." Even though she "was just a peon then," in her life before Iraq. "I had connections, wow, weird, I had connections," she said. Her time outside Baghdad was jarring, dizzying as the months unfolded. But "I am [now] so different, so confident," she told me. She couldn't easily return to that earlier role as a self-denying mother.

Bob labored in a bakery for over a decade, and then he became a workman at Lehigh Cement Company in Mason City. One day Marovets checked his cell phone and found over two thousand text messages. "He takes a lot of breaks," she surmised. He certainly couldn't adjust to the new Marovets after her return from Iraq. She received little support from her husband. "You'd think he would have gone in [to see a therapist] after my second suicide attempt. He couldn't do it, he doesn't want to learn anything," she said.

Marovets's twin sister, Konnie Holman, told me "her family was like zero support. It was like falling out of an airplane without a parachute, not having any sense of security." Bob "called her selfish too," Holman said. "It's just infuriating, but that's what they saw. They come home to a whole new war."

Kim would soon leave the family house, separating from Bob, although moving into an apartment just across the street. She kept trying to connect with her husband, but he displayed no capacity to understand all that Kim had experienced, why she felt like a stranger in her own land. "I went over there and sprayed his weeds, he changed a spark plug in the lawnmower." After three years Marovets held onto some glimmer of hope. "My goal is to see a movie with him on a cold winter night."

Before Iraq, Marovets was the mom extraordinaire to her children. She was "loving, caring, compassionate, involved," Marovets's daughter, Jessica, recalled. She called her mom "twice a day all the way through school." When her mother went off to the guard for weekend drills Jessica would visit her. "She's always been in the army, I guess I thought that it was cool." Jessica was twenty-one when her mother left for Iraq. "I just felt that she's gonna die, it was pretty frightening," Jessica remembers. "It took them three weeks to get to Kuwait, and then after that she had a cell phone. She had e-mail everyday." Jessica even shipped a small Christmas tree to her mother in Iraq.

But "she wasn't my mom" when Marovets returned from Baghdad, forty-three years old and carrying a heavy load of trauma, a shaken sense of self. "My mom came back on a Saturday, and I had my second child on Tuesday," Jessica said. "She was actually in the delivery room, but then didn't have much to do with her [the grandchild] until she was 1." Marovets came back much thinner and seeming like an alien to her own family. "She can go days without talking with me," Jessica reported. "She's afraid to get attached. She thinks in some weird way that we're gonna leave her. She doesn't call and ask how my day is going, what my kids are doing." Jessica concluded that she had "to learn to love her as someone else."

Marovets's twin sister continues to watch and listen, then figure out how to be supportive. "She was trained and had this intense experience over in Iraq. The same person isn't coming back," Holman said. "I just listened and didn't judge her. I didn't give her a lot of advice, because I wasn't in Iraq, I wasn't in her shoes. I think she's always gonna be there with her comrades, she's still linked to the 1133rd." Holman worries that the military doesn't do enough for vets and their families.

A year after finishing fieldwork I checked in on Marovets, taking a day to drive out from Chicago. She had made discernible headway, drawing strength from her military comrades and continuing visits to Rosetta Waychus's basement office. Marovets graduated from the local college. Family relations had continued to ease. "The boys are talking to me," she said. "Kim's still independent, she has her own friends and her own little house," Holman said. Kim had won over over Jessica, at least enough to care for her three grandchildren, now ranging from four to eleven years of age. One grandchild had become extra special. "Callista and my mom are very, very close," Jessica told me. "They love her, and they know she's grandma."

But Kim and Jessica fell out again recently, this time over wedding preparations for Kim's oldest son, Jason. "She kept treating me like I'm a child," Marovets said, and a major blowup ensued. So Jessica told Marovets she could no longer care for the grandchildren. They had been estranged for a year, with no end in sight during my final visit. Marovets was devastated and hoped to work it through with her daughter. The former child-care provider told me, "That's why I like kids, they don't judge you. They take what you offer them—respect, love, and affection."

Marching to a Different Drummer—Is Decentralized Organizing Enough?

This case of veterans and practitioners struggling to reach out and connect offers a cautionary tale. Mason City provided a small canvas on which to explore this colorful story, one that pits vets suffering from angst and dislocation against a clump of decentralized offices. One might assume that returning members of the military would slide easily back into small town America, where community groups and that can-do spirit thrive.

Yet we uncovered how these local branches of the VA and Mason City practitioners are so loosely tied to uncertain organizational centers, distant headquarters of Veterans Affairs or the state employment office, which offer sporadic resources, sparse data and tools. This trickling spigot of dollars and weak coordination of local services conspire to limit the effectiveness of caring practitioners like Holbrook, Stuflick, and Waychus. They respond to those vets knocking on their doors. Yet others, like Marovets and Henagar, go unnoticed. The division of labor across their shops—helping with cash aid, jobs, health care—makes sense bureaucratically. But weak, fragmented centers and patchy information about clients—seen and unseen—means that segmented offices only address narrow slices of their clients' complexities.

The efforts of these warmhearted practitioners remain admirable. But no matter how locally they are situated, Mason City's small bevy of counselors and clinicians often remain distant from their potential clients. The daily demands from the vets who *do* express demands—looking to get off drugs, find a job, sort out a health insurance problem—already stretch Holbrook,

Stuflick, and Waychus to their limits. They find little time and no organizational incentives for cooperating with each other. The four organizational cornerstones of potent decentralization at best are fractured in Mason City.

Let's consider in this final section the lessons that can be drawn from this case. And as we continue to sketch a clearer theory of effective decentralization, what can we rightly generalize from these quite human struggles found in northern Iowa? Plenty of communities across the nation, populated by small clusters of decentralized organizations, aim to backstop and lift vulnerable clients. What are we learning about the core foundations of decentralized organizing? Where has local organizing—or the central agencies that try to support local units—gone wrong?

The Dilemma of Demand-Driven Organizing

Two major lessons emerge from this case that speak to how local organizations can do better by military veterans. The first pertains to individual practitioners, especially the welcoming and resourceful efforts of Waychus and Stuflick. They both held access to economic resources on which the survival of vets depends: cash benefits and the potential of finding a job. And both practitioners offered a warm shoulder on which to rest one's head: they are patient listeners who created tranquil and respectful settings in which to hear out their anxious clients. It's this blend of being inviting and trusting types, along with their position and access to economic essentials, that sustained their credibility with clients. In this way, the decentered autonomy and proximity of Mason City practitioners works, at least for those vets who reach out.

The dilemma for decentralists—at least in this Iowa town—is that the practitioners feel efficacious in dealing with the veterans who stopped by, who took some risk in revealing their vulnerability and setting aside the obsession with self-reliance. Yet these down-home organizations fell short in keeping track of clients who timidly expressed a need for help, or failed to show up at all. Stuflick and Waychus both tracked lists of returning members of army or National Guard divisions. But no one was responsible for connecting with vets who disappeared from view, from the civic space in which practitioners could legitimately reach out to them. Weak central bureaucracies and episodic coordination in Mason City meant that vets like Marovets went unnoticed for years. Strung out and suicidal, it took a random, momentary interaction with D. J. Swoop to finally pull Marovets back from the edge. Demand-driven approaches to decentralized organizing run these deep risks.

My Kafkaesque struggle to penetrate into the Veterans Affairs administration center in Des Moines, buffered by PR officers and showered with

PowerPoint presentations, was emblematic of a bureaucracy that displays shaky capacity to follow clients over time and equip local practitioners. This situation may be improving inside the VA. They did construct Holbrook's outpatient clinic in Mason City, and they now experiment with regional case managers, hiring energetic staffers like Lisa Niewoehner at Fort Dodge, who occasionally gives Waychus a call. Still, the fragmentation of cash benefits and direct human aid, including mental health support, kept arising at every turn.

Niewoehner's new caseworker role—drawn from the playbook of new decentralists—aims to link hundreds of veterans to local services, along with contracting with the panoply of private firms and NGOs that deliver services across the region, especially for elderly or homebound vets. Still, her rising caseload and stretched travel times require that she simply provide a "warm handoff" of clients to other practitioners. This more effective shuffling of clients is a plus, but it prompts worries of whether the deep psychological abyss that traps so many vets is really ever explored.

So Mason City's loose web of support for veterans remains a demand-driven mixed market of disparate offices. That is, vets who hold the knowledge and confidence to knock on the door are warmly received. Yet before they even knock on the door, these clients must shed the military's norm that squashes admission of weakness and realize that "they aren't crazy," as Holbrook put it. But many vets can't move through this psychological mine field, or admit that family, friends, and former comrades remain insufficient to heal them. And when these reticent vets remain detached, unable to seek help, they go unnoticed. They fail to set off warning lights on anyone's dashboard.

Decentralizing under a Weak Center

The Veterans Affairs administration in Des Moines was a defensive center that displayed shaky capacity to embolden local practitioners, even to follow its most vulnerable clients. I never doubted the ethical commitment of staff inside these offices, or the caring qualities of those working from Des Moines or Mason City. But I never found a strong, resourceful center that coordinates local services—linking federal benefits, state-run jobs brokering, and medical services for vets in this tiny town. These disparate bureaucracies provide sparse resources for their local practitioners and little steady data about the health and psychological state of their clients.

In the absence of a strong center and coherent data about the condition of veterans sprinkled across northern Iowa, many vets fall through the cracks. Skilled therapists and listeners, like Holbrook, Wilson, and Waychus, sit ready to serve. They are local—even within walking distance or a short drive—for the thousands of vets who live in and around Mason City. But remember that Marovets only knew about Waychus. And even the most earnest practitioners rarely join forces. Wilson, working from the regional hospital, had heard that the VA had opened a satellite clinic—eight blocks away—but these two skilled therapists had never met.

This radically decentered nature of Mason City's practitioners does host flexible, even experimental roles—at times doing whatever it takes to speak to a client's needs. Waychus offers a range of supports and effective advocacy to ensure that vets receive the benefits for which they are eligible. She even attempts a bit of subtle matchmaking between vets when the opportunity arises. Stuflick serves both veterans directly and talks up their skills with a range of employers. In this way, he artfully shapes labor demand. And Niewoehner provides the newest role, earnestly trying to understand what a few hundred veterans need. But will the VA's central office take this chance to mend the center's fractured bureaucracy, inability to track clients, and tenuous human ties to Mason City's practitioners?

When I tell the story of community action in Mason City, some listeners and early readers respond by asking whether any formal organization, no matter how local, how inviting, could unlock the pain and distance felt by clients like Marovets or Henagar? But the helping hands and open hearts of these small-town practitioners do buoy many veterans.

The progress of Kim Marovets, inch by inch, has been remarkable, aided by Waychus, D. J. Swoop, and others. Admiration and respect were just two feelings I experienced as I got to know her. Both her story and her durable soul proved remarkable, as she has moved from a loving mother to soldier and back again. "It wasn't just one person" who ensured survival for Marovets, or even happiness of late. "Each person provided a piece," she told during my final visit to Mason City. "It took a village to save my sorry ass."

Over the three years that we had talked or shared a meal, I often paused, unable to fathom what Marovets had experienced during those unrelenting rocket attacks in Iraq, or the years-long emotional bombardment that greeted her back home. But at our final lunch, siting in a Denny's knockoff on the edge of town, her turquoise eyes lit up, a smile came across her face. She had not only graduated from the community college, but was now starting her bachelor's degree program. With no apparent irony in her voice, she asked, "Do you think it will be more difficult?" When not studying she takes care of her son's young toddler, and she's seeking rapprochement with her daughter. Kim Marovets is very much alive.

7

Learning from the New Decentralists—Cornerstones of Local Organizing

> Secularist audiences in general have trouble with ... movies and literature in which
> a single meaning is somehow sought and wrested from the teeming universe.
> There are many searches, many meanings, most of them partial.
> —DAVID DENBY, movie critic, 2012

We have journeyed across a wide terrain, dotted by a variety of local organizations, many thriving, some falling short. Most deny hierarchy and express little faith in the fleeting ties incentivized by markets. I have made the case for why unrelenting forces—economic and institutional—will continue to subvert big bureaucratic organizations. We reviewed the uneven results of first-wave efforts to decentralize. Then we unearthed the key cornerstones on which the new decentralists shape the social organization of work. Institutional histories vary across sectors, but these inventive architects build from shared principles, the conceptual foundations on which they organize labor and human cooperation locally.

This final chapter takes stock of what's been learned from the prior literature, enhanced by our case studies, and how these empirical lessons advance social theory. The future success of formal organizations—be they situated in public or private fields, or the vast terrain that's come to lie in between—requires that we devise more compelling forms of labor and cooperation on the ground. Social theorists share this goal with the new generation of pragmatic decentralists. This project is informed by the tools for local organizing wielded by the likes of Danielle Johnson, Mark Cleary, and Janet Tomcavage. The chapter closes with a look forward, accenting the challenges these reformers now face, especially how they puzzle over the synchrony between a lean and informative center that coaches, rather than controls, and agile practitioners who learn from and motivate clients on the ground.

This book began with the perennial challenge of how we humans struggle mightily to cooperate with one another, to form and fund organizations, advancing interests that are shared among individuals, even across entire societies. We all would gain if the quality of public schools zoomed upward, or if excellent and affordable health-care firms magically appeared. We feel respected when gaining service from smiling and responsive clerks rather then hitting a surreal phone tree at the end of an 800 number. Yet we keep getting stuck on *how* to organize locally, how to reshape the sluggish bureaucracies or vast firms that deliver goods and public services. Most Americans live amid plenty, but many feel little soul, only thin camaraderie inside the organizations in which we labor each day. So how can policy makers and corporate managers devolve authority, resources, and know-how in ways that advance fulfilling ways of working together?

Modern reliance on centralized hierarchies or unfettered markets is no longer tenable, unless we are going into battle or battling to the drive-up window for a cheap burger. Hierarchies and markets no longer host the kind of work most of us do, or animate and lend meaning to our everyday lives. So this volume has delved into three core questions. Why has America's renewed interest in localism arisen with such force and vibrancy over the past half century? What lessons did first-wave experiments in decentering the powerful expertise of large institutions yield for reform activists, pragmatic managers, and scholars? And what social tools now appear to advance the efficacy of the new decentralists as they draw from these earlier lessons?

We have gleaned logics of action and evidence of discernible effects from differing sectors of society to inform this consequential debate over decentralization. It remains a politicized discourse that too often resembles chatter at an uninspired cocktail party. To paraphrase David Denby, there are many theoretical claims and local studies, often illuminating partial truths. It's yet another postmodern revelation: many social scientists still endeavor to color in universal portraits of an idealized social physics or inviolable economic laws. Our cases illustrate the complexity of local contexts and the firms that operate within. That said, we have observed how the new decentralists must adapt to the same macroforces that drive localism and then build from shared organizational principles for decentering how cooperative work is arranged to better engage clients.

These converging workings of decentralized organizations dodge the threat of a postmodern free-for-all, with firms flying apart into uncertain fragments. Nor is this movement simply animated by charismatic leaders. It's been set in motion by strong winds blowing across organizational fields over the past half century, which either swamp firms, too cumbersome to adapt, or send them on similar (decentralized) headings. Let's first review the key lessons from the expanding fields of education, health care, and finance, along with the nonprofits that try to buoy our most vulnerable citizens. Then let's sketch how a clearer causal account of decentralization, tying the organizational cornerstones to local cooperation, can inform activists and scholars alike.

Mapping the New Localism

INEVITABILITY

Chapter 1 led with the stiff winds that have powered America's rekindled commitment to decentralization, as industrial forms of organization have ebbed. I detailed these strong currents that continue to sweep across the economic and ideological environs to which public institutions and many private firms must adapt. Millions of manufacturing jobs will not return to America's factories as long as wages remain sharply lower in Asia and Latin America. When just one in six Americans grow or make anything, the old industrial habits of breaking down production into highly routinized tasks—engineered and manipulated from above—will further fade as well.

As growth in sectors like education and health care zooms past shrinking blue-collar jobs—services provided in mixed markets—new forms of work and human-scale practice continue to arise. Large private firms may consolidate capital and make basic design decisions centrally, yet then decenter production and distribution to a panoply of small firms, as witnessed in the electronics industry over the past generation. So from the crafting of inventive software in Bangalore to teaching kids or mending wounds in Boston, cooperative work can only be coordinated and cajoled locally.

On top of the shifting nature of postindustrial work, the demographic imperative further strains the central state, as a shrinking number of workers now supports a burgeoning count of retirees. And government overall now depends on an economy that requires fewer and fewer jobs stateside, further stretching the state's fiscal capacity.

The state also suffers from declining legitimacy and declining trust in the assumption that these behemoth institutions make a difference. Indeed, the implosion of central authority and once-familiar moral beacons stems not only from material transformation. The nascent critique of America's materialism in the 1950s would come to question drab lives spent in white-collar cubicles, seeming only to serve distant corporate gods. Demographic and cultural diversity would collude after the 1960s to spark a kaleidoscopic array of lifestyles and moral pluralism. The breakdown of meritocratic pathways—clear routes for doing well in school and getting a good job—would further erode central authorities, from universities to faltering employers who can no longer deliver on their promises. As middle-class incomes flattened, then declined over the past fifteen years, the American Dream now appears more like a fading historical illusion. Century-old signposts for getting ahead—moving upward in the job market or gleaning meaning from one's daily toil—grow faint and fall.

Sensing these seismic shifts, government began toying with how to disassemble vast institutions in the 1980s, even to privatize who manages schools, hospitals, and military security in faraway places. Just as postindustrial firms begin setting performance goals centrally, then delegating authority to spur inventive practices locally, so too would Washington aim to "reinvent government." Struggling to show signs of life, indications of being effective, the state came to mimic organizational forms adopted by hip high-tech firms. So government fostered charter schools as hothouses of innovation, moved patients from hospitals to competitive HMOs, even leveled vast housing projects and handed out chits for families to find their own shelter. Portable vouchers were legislated for college students and parents seeking child care or a parochial school. The state's earlier trust in all-knowing institutions shifted to faith in the idealized consumer. The shift from monolithic hierarchy to diverse and decentered organizations has been remarkable, along with the creation of lightly monitored mixed markets of firms.

But what have we learned from these first-wave efforts to decentralize? Let's consider the empirical work earlier reviewed, as well as the key cornerstones and causal mechanisms revealed in our case studies.

Early Lessons

One huge lesson from the first wave is that decentering vertical levels of control—over resources and everyday work—may have been a necessary step, but it proved to be insufficient in motivating practitioners or lifting clients at the grass roots. We reviewed the uneven effects found in the sectors of education, health care, and high technology. Feisty charter schools have slightly raised achievement for students in some metro areas, such as Los Angeles and New York City, at least among families who enter these novel markets. But too often, children simply follow the learning curves of peers who remain in conventional schools. In health care the past two generations of reform have herded many doctors into HMOs; fewer patients enter the hospital, and when they do they enjoy shorter stays. Still, the quality of health care remains mixed across locales and costs continue to climb.

The business literature remains thin on tracking the empirical effects of decentralized management, despite decades of upbeat claims. It turns out that publicly funded experiments to devolve authority and resources are more carefully studied than private sector efforts. Still, when IBM or Apple Computer moved to devolve production and innovation out to independent units, or of late a global network of smaller firms, the hard evidence of human-scale benefits remains thin, beyond bottom-line profitability for the center. One ironic lesson is that government continues to mimic an organizational model—a lean center that sets production goals and then decentralizes authority to local units—even as the private sector has yet to reveal clear evidence of social benefits inside the firm.

This extant research on first-wave forays does point to key lessons—teachings not lost on the new decentralists. Breaking free of the regulatory bureaucracy long preoccupied the early localists, such as advocates of charter schools, vouchers across sectors, or a competitive marketplace in the telecom industry. These battles to break away or instill market dynamics persist in many parts of the country. Health-care reforms now consolidate small medical practices into competitive HMOs. Several state governments advance tuition tax credits for well-off parents to send children to private schools, arguing for competitive dynamics (with a dash of regressive income redistribution).

But these bloody tussles to break free of central control or install sharp-edged market dynamics still stem from the dusty duality between hierarchy and markets, discussed in chapter 1. The first-wave decentralists remain obsessed with the first step: winning that seductive liberation from the state or top-down corporate bureaucracy. They assume, like tearing down the Berlin Wall, a nirvana of individual freedoms and colorful innovation will instantly blossom. Or injecting competitive pressure among schools, HMOs, or public housing will spark a massive family exit from lousy conditions and into high quality organizations.

But such allegedly universal mechanics are constrained in two ways. First, it turns out that parents, patients, even profit-driven clients of finance banks make decisions in the particular contexts in which they live and form social ties, acting within deep-seated norms. They don't hire an economist to calculate the relative value-added of their neighborhood school, or read up on behavioral economics to "get the incentives right." Nor do they enjoy unlimited budgets to drive across town to a better school or health clinic. Parents view options through the lens of surrounding social norms, with limited information and uneven financial resources. They tend to choose schools whose staff and students look like their own kids. In other words, their cognitive scripts and attention to enveloping norms are in forceful play—just like how white middle-class parents make "choices" in the comfortable muddle of their particular contexts.

I have not argued that decentralized organizations can or should conform neatly to this human variability across local villages. Each of the organizations that we explored in depth injected new ideas, created fresh pathways, and provided social or economic support for their clients. Formal organizations rarely exist to reproduce static endeavors in unchanging environments. And without redistribution of resources and cross-fertilization of ideas, opportunity in America will continue to be set by a family's class position or purchasing power. We see this in the unevenness in school quality across neighborhoods, rich and poor, along with who buys concierge medical plans and who can only afford bronze coverage.

Still, firms meet their clients in their local contexts. And the four cornerstones of second-wave decentralization—curiosity over and ample data on their clients, experimenting with local job roles, distributing authority and technical tools more laterally, and rethinking the firm's center—enable these organizations to tailor services to widely diverse clients. It's far more than granting local flexibility; this social architecture serves to respect and build from the social assets of clients. The new decentralists have arrived at these shared cornerstones from differing institutional origins.

A second lesson about institutional constraints is that the carrying capacity of organizational fields—spanning geographical spaces large and small—is bounded as well. Only so many activists can weather the demands of creating and sustaining a robust charter school. Many small medical practices can't survive as health-care firms learn how to raise quality and achieve economies of scale. And the liberalized ability to choose one's school, clinic, or mode of public transportation doesn't necessarily spur the creation of equally accessible, high-quality organizations. The *local supply response* is constrained by the capacity of local actors and the resources they can muster. I soon return to what sociologists call *field theory*, including the dynamics that determine the population of diverse (or homogenous) organizations, which spring up and survive over time under decentralized or market-friendly conditions.

The same broad forces that power the new localism, ironically, often act to constrain the efficacy of decentralized organizations. Local leaders of even the most innovative charter schools must find inspiring teachers and affordable facilities. Yet the state's capacity to attract and equip such teachers is limited. It's tough for union leaders to think outside the box when pensions or health coverage are being pared back. We saw how weakly coordinated nonprofits, with no strong center to provide coherence, let veterans fall through the cracks. These resource scarcities and weaknesses in local organizing may nudge practitioners to look *more* conventional, not less, within a competitive market. Faced with uncertain resources and fragile legitimacy, charter schools promise college prep, the Veterans Affairs administration claims that medical staff will advance robust well-being. Again, winning liberation from hierarchy or faith in market competition doesn't ensure that old ways of getting work done will change.

First-wave decentralists, as they stumbled locally, did reveal the persisting role and pivotal contribution of the organizational center. How government regulates and reimburses differing kinds of physicians and medical procedures will continue to shape the balance between prevention and surgical remedies for chronic disease. The varying capacity of central leaders to deepen their firm's ethical mission—from lifting vets in rural Iowa to building long-term relationships with finance clients at Handelsbanken—thickens the culture and social cohesion felt by local staff. Decentralized units often lack the time or tools to follow their clients or systematically assess what forms of practice yield benefits for clients. Many first-wave decentralists still define the center as the enemy. The later generation, instead, thinks carefully about how the center can help technically and motivate ethically.

Perhaps most instructive for the new decentralists, early forays to localize proved most effective when firms eagerly learned from their clients—what motivates them to grow or change, how to engage them in deeper ways. A portion of this evidence comes from the early education sector, where fine-grain research in a vastly decentered field is detailing how rich forms of teacher-child interaction advance youngsters' cognitive growth and social skills. Or take the early evidence on how the "medical home" model would inform Geisinger's experiment with case managers—rethinking the roles and power relations that characterize cooperative work inside local clinics. These kinds of social mechanisms enable the new decentralists to learn much about what makes clients tick and how everyday practices can build from their own motivations and networks of social support. These lessons help to organize and shape the architecture now crafted by second-wave localists.

Cornerstones of Local Organizing

The new decentralists firmly plant the shared cornerstones on which their local organizing is founded. Four key cornerstones emerged over the course of our fieldwork, plus one broader discovery. Each might be seen as a working hypothesis, each awaiting empirical replication across a wider set of organizations. The case studies revealed these core principles and how they animated work inside a diverse range of decentralized firms. And we could observe how each social-organizational feature framed and affected human-scale engagement and cooperation between client and practitioner.

The benefits of these foundational cornerstones vividly surfaced, say when patient reviews in Geisinger clinics, marked by lateral and distributed problem solving, yielded inventive remedies. Or when CAT's charter teachers deployed projects and portfolios for their students—devised and codified from a lean center—this organizational feature exercised stronger explanatory power. Still, our qualitative evidence, while suggestive of causal effects across diverse organizations, remains insufficient to generalize to a wider array of organizations. Much more empirical work remains. The appendix details the strengths and limits of our methodological approach, the advantages and limits of case studies.

To review, the four cornerstones begin with how practitioners in decentered firms express *steady curiosity over their clients*, drawing on various ways for learning about what animates these students, patients, or clients. Few fall through the cracks in these personalized and data-informed relationships. Danielle Johnson constantly queried her students at the San Francisco charter school. Teachers talked endlessly, when a listless student surfaced, about what was going down at home or with peers. Geisinger's case managers, like Kenda Danowsky, steadily called patients, visited them at home, interrogated their spouses and kin—aiming to understand how tribal ties might lift the quality of daily life. Mark Cleary kept his pulse on how the finance chief at Skanska USA feels about Handelsbanken traders, especially their levels of confidence and trust.

There's something so basic, so traditional about this focus on getting to know one's client, be they young or old. Indeed, fellow bankers now tag Handelsbanken as "The Taliban" of the finance industry, a play on the fundamentalist nature of their down-home practices. But the new decentralists also import more contemporary ideas and pragmatics: lateral forms of authority and discourse, a distributed understanding across staff members of their client's preferences, and rich data about client populations and subgroups, typically compiled by a lean and well-informed center. Then there is the distinctly unmodern realization that technical remedies or didactic delivery of novel information doesn't often change behavior. Instead, the client must be pulled into a community, into a trusting relationship with practitioners. Membership in the tribe is purposefully cultivated. And the client's own enveloping context must be understood as well if these friendly strangers are to gain the necessary credibility to thaw out a client's old habits and open them to fresh ideas, novel behavior.

We also discovered how second-wave decentralists experiment with *new or recast job roles*. These posts may be crafted by local practitioners or be introduced by a strategic center. We saw how Handelsbanken's culture has long nurtured a highly participatory form of management inside its local branches. These village-level chiefs can adjust any staff role, aiming to advance client relations and enrich the bottom line. Geisinger's central managers have been more directive of late—requiring their local clinics to house a case manager that oversees high-cost patients, including those where behavioral change could lessen the corrosive effects of chronic disease. This advance of novel roles typically requires ongoing negotiation over authority and resources between the center and local unit. It's another arena in which *decentralizing* is best captured as a verb, an ongoing conversation across organizational levels.

Geisinger and the San Francisco charter school pushed hard on the third, complementary cornerstone—*rethinking the distribution of authority and know-how* across laterally arranged work roles. It's not simply that novel roles are being introduced; the new decentralists also shift how authority and expertise is shared among practitioners, locally and at the center. This parallels how social scientists have come to see "distributed cognition" or cooperatively puzzling through remedies within clinical or schools settings, moving beyond fixed rules and hierarchical forms.

Geisinger's agile case managers—clinical sociologists of sorts—advise from their medical knowledge *and* contextual information about their patients' home settings. The Envision charter school company hired and equipped principals who saw the utility of distributing power and discretion across their teachers. At the same time, we discovered in northern Iowa that laterally arranged roles—no matter how local and human-scale—can make for a tattered safety net when central coordination and data remain weak. Overall, the infusion of new roles and tools can be disruptive in a positive sense, pushing colleagues to rethink how they work, how they engage and motivate clients.

And fourth, the new decentralists are *rethinking the center* in allied ways. I have referred to the pivotal importance of a crisp and trumpeted ethical mission—be it sending every blue-collar kid to college, raising health-care quality, deepening trust with finance clients, or backstopping veterans returning from war. Without a thick cultural fabric, practitioners tend to lapse back into their own isolated work, as we saw in the Iowa case of disparate nonprofits, rather than coming together to track their clients, pursue more effective practices, and nurture a spirit of common cause.

These are the four cornerstones on which the architecture of decentered organizations arises. Each, of course, varies in strength across particular firms or local institutions. The particular history of any given sector matters. Decentering authority, resources, and know-how in the education field involves differing downward shifts, compared with devolving power and dollars in IBM or a global financial institution. Looking across firms, how resources, labor pools, and technologies flow through any given organizational field will differ from these elements in a neighboring field. And decentering is a relational process. If a gargantuan urban school district devolves authority over the hiring and firing teachers to local principals, this requires an ongoing negotiation between actors across social-organizational levels. This social process will differ if Apple Computer considers delegating design work to an east Asia firm, or government decides to shift regulation and economic incentives for health-care companies to encourage preventive care. That said, our case studies—situated across contrasting sectors—suggest that contemporary efforts to decentralize do manifest shared organizational features, at least when they display vivid signs of success.

A fifth telling dynamic emerged as we reflected on differences across the four cases; this dynamic emanated from the respective organizational field in which each decentralizing firm operates. It's not a cornerstone planted by internal actors alone. Single organizations rarely shape field-level dynamics, the rules and norms by which firms must play. With the first and second pair of cases presented—the Pennsylvania health-care firm and New York finance bank, against the California charter school and the loose-knit nonprofits struggling to serve vets in northern Iowa—we realized that their surrounding landscapes differed in one crucial way. Both Geisinger and Handelsbanken operate in organizational fields where their technical efficiency yields robust economic rewards. This offers notoriety and revenues when social relationships and everyday practices succeed, and in turn attracts new clients. Each firm can advance a strong argument that decentralized elements of their work contribute to stronger client benefits and long-term revenue streams. This serves to legitimate material incentives for local staff members who get with the program, who adjust their practices and effectively lift their clients.

In contrast, neither the charter school nor the archipelago of local agencies aiding Iowa vets enjoys such vivid economic incentives to attract more clients or show stronger results. In fact, their model of decentralized action aims to deepen relationships with fewer clients, a rationed caseload so to speak, not encourage an overwhelming count of students or veterans. Nor does their respective organizational field reward gains in performance. Even when test scores rise at the CAT charter school, or a higher share of graduates enter college, this human-scale organization doesn't win more financing. The principal receives a pat on the back. Similarly, the gaggle of agencies serving vets in Mason City lack the capacity to track clients or to measure service quality and client gains. So little feedback is heard from a diffuse center that's unable to allocate clear incentives, material or moral.

I am not suggesting that organizational fields energized with stiffer volts of market competition motivate decentralized social action more effectively. The Envision charter school network, for instance, displays signs of remarkable success in some years, as pupil achievement inches upward, even in the absence of well-honed incentives. Yet it appears that decentralizing firms thrive when the surrounding organizational field steadily rewards—with streams of fresh revenues or popular legitimacy—those that demonstrate higher quality and success. This requires that local units *and* a capable center gather evidence of effectiveness, along with succeeding in a field that yields contingent rewards. This, of course, favors markets in fields with ample client demand, along with steady private or public investment. But the firm's internal capacity and attention to tracking discernible benefits for clients remain pivotal as well.

Novel Conceptual Tools to Build Theory

The case studies revealed how the new decentralists wield new conceptual tools—forged at two organizational levels—as they work to reshape authority, resources, and locally held know-how. This section advances how we might theorize their explicit or tacit notions for how to rethink local action and social cooperation. Their conceptual innovations borrow from recent advances in the social sciences, both from the sociology of organizations and contextually sensitive notions of individual learning and behavior embedded in sticky cultural milieu. The aim is to causally explain and empirically substantiate how decentralizing organizations arrange social cooperation in ways that engage clients and frontline practitioners.

At one level these organizational architects carefully delve into their client's motivations, embedded within thick and particular contexts. Moving up to the firm level, they no longer assume that hierarchy can usefully regulate practitioners or clients down below. These designers don't shy away from competitive dynamics inside markets. But it's the quality of social engagement on the ground that will advance their organization's position over time. What's pivotal is linking the structured process of decentralizing the coordination of work to how the craft of local practitioners is animated, which in turn aims to motivate clients. This conceptual linchpin promises to advance social cooperation in postindustrial societies, at work and within the public square, as faith in hierarchies and markets fades. Let's turn to this and allied conceptual tools, often tied to breakthroughs in social theory that have emerged over the past generation. This ferment in the circles of activists and academics now yields fresh varietals when it comes to how we organize cooperation locally.

Rethinking Two Organizational Levels

The new decentralists rethink human cooperation at two interwoven levels of social action. They consider how the firm is positioned in an organizational field, and then how the center enables more effective practice locally. The new social architects do not swerve between naive notions of hierarchy or market. Instead, they devise organizational forms that adapt to macroshifts in their field. These adaptations unfold at two levels, including how the firm acquires resources and legitimacy from an evolving environment and how local practice attracts and lifts clients.

We have seen how a sizeable part of this adaptive process involves recasting local relationships, now structured or coached more flexibly between practitioner and client, not prescribed and routinized from above. This new social technology stems from shifts in everyday culture and how a variety of disciplines have come to understand human learning and motivated action as being situated within one's tribal ties. And this recasting of local work draws on prior institutional forms, not from out-of-the-box innovations absent what came before. Remember how Geisinger's managers drew from the "medical home" model for their caseworkers, a social form with origins in the 1970s. Teacher Danielle Johnson draws from the democratic relations advanced by John Dewey in the 1930s. So the new logics of work exhibited by practitioners often pull from the wider organizational field and its social forms or economic dynamics that wax and wane.

One telling shift inherent in the work of new decentralists is that they are no longer well served by the vertical controls inherent in hierarchy, or by the notion of a lone individual making choices in a market, or enacting some autonomous form of practice. Pyramid-like representations may still capture the Vatican or military generals, or perhaps one's autocratic father. But once postindustrial societies gave up mass production and shifted their economies to human services or to coordinating the work of others, it's more valid to see centers and their local practitioners as *intertwined in lateral relations*, each adapting to evolving demands in their organizational field. This notion of decentering organizational action complements the past generation of work on social networks and how social ties within and outside the firm's official structure matter most.

Formal position in the organization still matters. Those residing at the center may hold greater resources or technical know-how. But it's the lateral quality and relational action that characterizes the constructed search for more efficacious practice on the ground. And in parallel fashion, the new decentralists see social relations with clients as more horizontal—a cooperative and mutually respectful tie—while moving the client to learn, to engage, to consider shifting one's patterns of behavior. To capture this shift in the social organization of local practice, I return to Simmel's insight from more than a century ago: these inventive practitioners are strangers who arrive from the outside, yet stick around to deliver fresh perspectives, new knowledge, and tools. Scaffolding from clients' own motivations and context, while moving them beyond the familiar.

Think Danielle Johnson, the inspiring charter school teacher, eagerly delving into what makes Pablo Alba tick, inquiring about his emerging passions. She doesn't go native, nor are they friends. Yet she proceeds to build out from his skills and interests. Or think about Janet Tomcavage's inventive case managers who gently upset the power dynamics once monopolized by the physicians. She has shaped a new role, deploying a savvy stranger into each Geisinger clinic. And this case manager provides fresh knowledge about the patient's own immediate context, tribal supports, and motivation for managing their own health. This lateral form of cooperation is also reminiscent of Graham Greene's literary use of the foreigner, who "brings in a whiff of a different world into the lives of the locals he meets," as writer Pico Iyer reviews. "From that point on, both are in the shadowland that lies between the existence we lead and the one we occasionally dream of."[1]

Recrafting Institutional Logics

These decentralizing reformers also play with—thawing out and reshaping—what sociologists call *institutional logics*. That is, the tacit or taken-for-granted ways in which work is supposed to occur inside firms. Sociologists, going back a generation, have described how work routines and conceptions of professional labor can be socially constructed and reinforced over time, especially when demands (emanating from the organizational field) to show results or efficiency remain weak.[2] So educators assume that classroom instruction must come in fifty-minute dollops. Medical organizations historically presumed that time spent on treating disease should eclipse any consideration of prevention. Many American banks believe that centralizing lending decisions reduces their financial risk, as we heard at Handelsbanken, whether hard evidence is at hand to verify this practice or not. These logics about how work gets done allow the firm to fit norms, expectations, even self-assured regulations that license who enters an occupation and how their labor is structured.

Early research on such tacit logics emphasized how they captured highly institutionalized activity in firms that survived on legitimacy or protective policies, whether they were productive and technically sound or not. Yet so-called neoinstitutional theorists have been unable to explain change in how work occurs inside firms, as they rethink job roles or practices, or as they adapt to evolving environments. Johnson and her fellow teachers, for instance, constantly debated how to build more effective relationships with their young clients. Or remember Richard Johnson at Handelsbanken, who emphasized how his firm's decentralizing experiment remained a work in progress—a verb not a noun, daily negotiated between actors at the center and those out in the branches. The new decentralists question old routines and think causally about how novel forms of social cooperation may yield stronger technical results—lifting learning, patient outcomes, even financial profitability.

Firms adapting to and hoping to thrive within their organizational field may abide by or actively challenge how to best organize work locally. We discovered how leaders with Envision, Geisinger, and Handelsbanken rose up above their firms to question and reshape the ethical mission and ways of doing work that once dominated their respective field. This is the second level of social organization in which the new decentralists challenge the old order.

They may draw on several strategies as they question weathered institutional logics. Actors and firms, for example, don't always agree on the goals or nature of the core project in their shared field, as sociologists Neil Fligstein and Doug McAdam argue. Health-care companies generally agree that their mission is to advance the health of patients. But this "does not imply that the division of spoils in the field is viewed as legitimate, only that the overall account of the terrain is shared by most field actors."[3] Geisinger's top managers constantly mentioned other companies that innovate to raise quality and lower costs, while focusing on prevention of chronic disease. They talk disparagingly of fellow firms who deny this shift in their field, including the ideological and technical changes advanced by President Obama's health-care reforms. So we see contestation over the ultimate aims or accepted means in organizational fields, and this likely defines the utility or ethical virtues of differing institutional logics.

Fields also vary in the kinds of organizations that populate them and technical demands and institutional norms that drive work inside firms. So we discovered stronger material incentives for enriching relationships with clients within Geisinger and Handelsbanken, given richer resources flowing in the field and economic returns that result from stronger ties between clients and staff. Still, the causal account invites additional research on what field-level forces result in the perception or experience of these more compelling incentives. Fields should not be reified constructs but rather should be unpacked to observe field-wide dynamics that touch such practices inside firms, as sociologist John Levi Martin emphasizes.[4]

We delved into how the impulse to decentralize the organization, shared across diverse sectors, stems from even broader economic and institutional forces in which fields are embedded. Here too, more work is required to understand these antecedent factors that span fields, so as not to infer their existence solely from their observed effects. If moral pluralism or the structure of postindustrial labor is hypothesized to drive decentralizing action inside firms, we must be able to see these root causes and observe their consequences. And these dynamics across levels of social organization are likely reciprocal, as Martin emphasizes. How health-care firms attend to the decentered work of clinicians differs, based on institutional history, from how schools or hightech firms respond to the same macropressures.

Contestation arises in fields for another reason. Firms and individual players vary in the power or control over resources they hold within what Fligstein and McAdam call *strategic action fields*. Rather than postulating widespread agreement regarding institutional logics and static terrain, these theorists accent how firms and actors often challenge established scripts and forms of work and vie for a stronger position within a fluid organizational field. So the Envision charter school company devises cooperative projects and portfolio-building strategies, which move its teachers away from didactic classroom lectures. And the firm now markets their curricular strategy and materials to conventional school districts. Or Geisinger seeks to shape federal health-care policy, even sending a former medical executive to head the first office of organizational innovation in Washington—spreading their good word and strengthening Geisinger's position in their field. These firms aim to nudge the wider field of play to accept their technical strategies or framing of problems and remedies.

Organized actors in fields don't always agree on the basic rules of the game, ranging from debates over conventional job roles or the right technology for getting the job done, to the regulatory structure that attempts to specify appropriate practices. Multiple logics often operate simultaneously within a field. Inside the San Francisco charter school we saw how teachers struggle to nurture students' analytic and research skills, while adapting to government's unrelenting push to raise test scores. Even the radically decentralized Handelsbanken strategically advances its own position in the finance field, expanding rapidly in Britain, by trumpeting its differences relative to centralized American banks. Settling into a niche and thriving often requires distinguishing one's organization from others.

Finally, individuals or groups within or across firms see everyday work through differing interpretive lenses. Iowa's local NGOs and the centralized Veterans Affairs administration differed in the kinds of treatments or supports that each believed were most urgently required for their clients. What's the relative priority placed on physical health, PTSD and mental health or employment assistance? Even when firms decentralize resources and discretion, these differing interpretations may not recede. So players within and across firms don't necessarily converge on a single logic for how to organize work locally. Instead, they interpret multiple strategies as they watch peers or competitors and then adjust their own craft. When Envision reinstated bells to mark when students are late to class, or Geisinger nudged physicians to grasp the social milieu of patients and not only their physiological condition, we saw differing views of what local work entails. This dissonance reflects a contest over normative (not necessarily empirically informed) notions of how to effectively get work done, the institutional logics that allegedly lift clients.

Overall, the new decentralists advance fresh ethics, work roles, and inventive ways to engage clients inside their own firms. They also act both locally and globally to challenge the aging institutional logics of their fields.

Mind in Organizational Culture—Rethinking the Logic of Everyday Work

Our case studies suggest one adjustment to how Fligstein and McAdam place a firm in the company of fellow organizations (the field of relational play, as the late Pierre Bourdieu would have it)—as they jostle each other over the aims, tools, and social forms by which labor is arranged and meaning-filled cooperation is pursued.[5] I agree that the constitutive rules of the game are set at the field level. And fields must adapt to the wider economic and institutional conditions, which are either nourished or challenged by the macrocontext. Indeed, the logics by which firms organize jobs and everyday work must first adapt to the conditions that characterize the surrounding field.

So the population of hospitals, HMOs, and regulatory agencies that make up the health-care field arrive at culturally embedded rules of the game that "construct the opportunity [for] people to engage in collective action," as

Fligstein and McAdam put it, that is, to cooperate on the ground to advance shared goals. As the federal government closes the gap in reimbursements between primary care physicians and surgeons, health-care firms will find it more cost effective to focus on prevention. Or if regular public schools fail to elevate the learning curves of working-class kids and government liberalizes parental choice, then charter school activists face a more favorable field in which to take root. Multiple players in the field contest what kinds of organizations gain sufficient legitimacy and material resources to survive and thrive. Alliances among like-minded organizations may gain the authority to alter the constitutive rules of the game across their field.

Yet precisely where and how work gets done—engaging clients and practitioners on the front lines—may draw on social forms that do not necessarily correspond to how the firm is adapting to its field. The unraveling of central regulation necessarily results in loose coupling between the organizational field, individual firm, and local practitioner. Our case studies revealed how micrologics of practice might travel independently of how the firm's center seeks to adapt to environmental demands. Some charter schools use their decentralized freedom to pursue highly conventional forms of pedagogy. They pull forward established social forms that differ radically from the progressive, relationship-intensive forms of "teaching" that Johnson and her colleagues displayed. Or take how Tomcavage at Geisinger equips clinical staff to learn more about their patients via resident case managers and electronic data built out from headquarters. This innovation allows her firm to track patients with chronic conditions that could be remedied in part by changing the patient's behavior. But note, health-care firms could shift toward prevention in a variety of *other* ways: incentivizing doctors to advise patients, e-mail messaging, or public health activities in the community.

The point is that the logic of daily work may evolve and settle along lines that are somewhat independent of how the firm is adapting to field-level demands. What distinguishes the decentralizing of who gets to craft facets of local work is that practitioners are spurred to devise practices that may prove more effective. Technical innovations and stronger social cohesion may bubble up from below rather than being coaxed from the center.

So if conforming to the field's dominant or fluid ways doesn't drive the micrologic of everyday work—including how practitioners engage clients— what social process do stimulate innovative (or retrieval of old) social forms? We watched how a diverse array of practicing strangers built the trust and common cause so necessary in raising the achievement of reticent teens, or moving patients to cut back on diabetes-inducing sodas. Yet what are the conceptual origins of the practitioner's social tools? And how does decentering away from hierarchical controls advance the odds of crafting more effective means of social cooperation?

Decentralizing to Rethink Cooperation

Two movements within psychology and the sociology of culture help to cast local forms of cooperation devised by the new decentralists. First, the scholarly descendants of George Herbert Mead and Soviet psychologist Lev Vygotsky continue to illuminate how the individual, from a young age, learns how to behave (and think) as a member of her immediate tribes, whether it's becoming efficacious inside the family, peer groups, or eventually work settings. We acquire behavioral scripts and routines that ensure a steady stream of acceptance, along with signals of competence and simple enjoyment. We may make calculations for how to maximize our own interests in neoclassical fashion. Yet the costs of diverging from normative expectations for how to behave are high, risking a loss of membership or status in the eyes of peers. Thus our social-psychological interests become intertwined with the rituals of social interaction that provide order and predictability for the small-scale collectives to which we belong.

The individual's mind also comes to reflect the social expectations and culturally situated meanings of various behaviors. Being "overweight" may be highly undesirable in one particular social class or cultural context, but not even noticed in another. How military vets listen and treat each other, observed Kim Marovets, radically differed from the lack of understanding that marked her interactions even with close kin. Firms like Envision or Handelsbanken consciously invite in new staff members that already hold conforming commitments, from an eagerness to connect with adolescents to enjoying work in local teams, responsible for plotting their own course and practice.

It's not simply that the individual grasps discrete values or tangible skills, like picking apples from a tree. "Many of our most common and paramount goals are incorporated into cultural understandings and learned as part of that heritage," as anthropologists Dorothy Holland and Naomi Quinn put it.[6] Cultural scholars of the last generation also emphasize that tacit expressions of membership, colloquial language, interaction rituals, even expected renditions of affection become representations *in the mind*, as anthropologist Brad Shore emphasizes.[7] The individual's immediate context matters as the source of these social and material artifacts, and one's mind comes to mirror how to behave and believe, embedded in that context. A key tenet of cognitive sociology is to focus on "the link between interpersonal structures, including social networks and institutions, and internal mental representations," according to Berkeley sociologist Margaret Frye.[8]

The interpretive lens and cognitive schema that result from this tacit acculturation into our local tribes also come to "bias" how information or perhaps behavioral interventions are understood by the client. We come to see our teachers, physicians, or business associates within the cognitive categories that map our particular social world, along with our position and status within it. So Pablo Alba came to understand his teachers as caring practitioners that placed respectful and challenging demands on him—while interpreting the curriculum through a social justice set of categories. Branch managers at Handelsbanken mull over their options and how they oversee their staff through the lens of local determination, the dominating coordinates of their cognitive cartography. And due to their ethical mission and organizing principles these firms cut and sharpen the interpretive lenses deployed, the constitutive rules of how work and social engagement gets done.

Both of these branches of thought—the culturally situated character of motivated action and the resilience of cognitive frames—stem from the so-called cognitive revolution, which sprouted in the 1950s. This conceptual break postulates that the individual's mind is driven by a biological impulse to be inquisitive, to learn how to become effective in a social context. What cultural psychology has added, along with the allied field of cognitive sociology, is to accent how one's milieu is so particular, so enveloping of the individual, and so situated in groups differing by gender, class, occupation, language, ethnicity, and local history. Decentralists start with the client's motivation in local context, rather than assuming that new knowledge or treatments can be beamed into the individual, sizzled and sealed without any agency exercised by the client in relation to their own memberships, scripts, and social motivations.

No longer is a context-free individual seen as simply maximizing (mysteriously arrived at) preferences, trying to shake dark Freudian hang-ups, or mindlessly jumping for Skinnerian-like incentives and carrots. Instead, the individual acts from a deep drive to interact, to become a member in good stead. And once embedded in these normative scripts, dislodging these behavioral habits is challenging—especially when the well-meaning practitioner fails to understand the client's context or that surrounding kith and kin may reinforce unhealthy or parochial behavior. Yet if an inquisitive practitioner can come to grasp the client's mental representation of the "problem" or task at hand, along with feasible courses of action, then together they are better able to mobilize necessary resources and social supports.

In these ways, cognitive representations become shared across actors—what psychologists have termed *distributed cognition*—both in how a client's issue is diagnosed and the co-constructed remedies that can be attempted cooperatively.[9] The trust and shared mores that we observed in Geisinger's roundtable reviews, or the collaborative decision making seen inside Handelsbanken branches, offer vivid examples of distributed cognition. Both the client's and the practitioner's engagement are seen as conditioned by, defined in relation to, one's immediate context.

Seeing the individual mind and one's perceptual lenses as embedded in particular contexts—along with the consequences for bending novel information—has spurred the past decade of work in behavioral economics as well.[10] But its roots go back to the 1980s and how social psychologists and sociologists illuminated cognitive bias, along with how culture bounds and opens motivating paths toward membership and efficacy within particular groups.[11] Behavior that looks "irrational" to the neoclassical economist—based on "misinterpreted" information or failing to pursue one's own interests—can be seen as quite rational by the individual embedded in his proximal structure of attainable opportunities. The decentered firms that we examined become acquainted with the immediate contexts known by clients, while attempting to open novel channels for learning, health, or altered behavior. Caring strangers who learn about the client's milieu without going native.

Clients Embedded in Local Contexts

Taken together, these conceptual tools rekindle curiosity about the strengths of *intermediate collectives*—the localized social networks and tribal ties in which clients and practitioners become embedded. The drive to personalize high schools, to call on patients at home in order to learn of their surroundings, to nurture long-term kinship with financial clients—make for a return to premodern social relations. We again see how the new decentralists reject the rationalized rules and strictly cast roles of hierarchy, as well as the atomistic nature of fleeting market ties. Neither modern form of cooperation is viewed as truly engaging or motivating for client or practitioner. Yes, contemporary localists focus on the complexities of each client. But that individual is rarely disconnected from an enveloping and supportive social context. This is not a constructed individual who "rationally" pursues pristine interests absent their own milieu. *Homo economicus*—if ever empirically spotted in the wild—is now viewed by many social scientists as a dying species.

How the distributed team around the table mulled over the case of Buck Strozzi, the trucker who had shot himself in the leg, offers another example.

Strozzi could see no other future; he had always been a long-haul trucker. Changing his diet was going slow, given his affection for burgers and fries at familiar truck stops. So case manager Kenda Danowsky went to work trying to understand the patient's own logic, the telling behavioral scripts and perceived opportunities, through Strozzi's eyes. She then devised a possible remedy that fit his cognitive frame, not the assumptions of medical technicians. Danowsky becomes the friendly stranger who hangs in there, works within his proximal world. It's Strozzi's "cognition in the wild" that's salient. By putting their heads together Danowsky helped to co-construct a credible course of action—with help from material tools, that smaller pump that would drain fluid from his pulsating calf.

Or take Rosetta Waychus in northern Iowa who just sits and listens at first, tenderly getting beneath the layers of loss and trauma, all the disorienting angst felt by veterans coming back from war. Her remedies flow from what's essential to her clients, whether it's helping to get a hunting license or finding a drinking buddy for Gunny Henagar, to finding a job in the nearby school cafeteria for Kim Marovets. Waychus avoids judgment or didactic guidance. She's neither trying to regulate behavior nor applying the salve of job markets or material incentives. Instead, she gently probes to understand her client's cognitive map, their conception of the problem and credible remedies, considering how to bring information, resources, and their own social supports to bear.

I couldn't pull from the shelves of Danowsky, Johnson, or Waychus any formal works of sociology or cultural psychology (I did look). But these advances in social science have crept into the discourse of the new decentralists over the past generation: how their organization plays within a wider field, keen attention to the client's own everyday context, and the interpretative lenses that color embedded realities—the situated cognition that sets tacit assumptions of client and practitioner alike.

Still, these firms are not in the business of reproducing the status quo; the client is to be moved or lifted, taken to a co-constructed future. Novel social behavior is required to get the blue-collar kid into college, to motivate the patient to lead a healthy lifestyle, to nurture greater confidence and efficacy inside the veteran's head and heart. We have seen how these local practices may be articulated and coached by managers at the center, or devised by practitioners on the ground. But they are preceded by that steady inquisitive quality, as the practitioner comes to understand how the client sees the problem or task at hand, then defines shifts in behavior that seem feasible within one's immediate milieu.

How the new decentralists see both clients and practitioners as embedded in particular contexts harks back to a long-running philosophical debate.

Hobbes argued that human beings are "primordially individualistic and that they entered into a society . . . only as a rational calculation that social cooperation was the best way for them to achieve their individual ends," as contemporary theorist Francis Fukuyama puts it.[12] Yet Hegel would counter that the individual's "struggle for recognition" is a far more powerful source of motivation, "it is the inter-subjective state of mind by which one human being acknowledges the worth or status of another human being or (their) gods, customs, and beliefs."

If Hegel is right, then local practice must not rely simply on some kind of contractual exchange with the client, but instead must scaffold up from her own intrinsic motivations and the sustaining tribes to which the client belongs and gains recognition. And this leads decentralists back to the facets of intermediate collectives—the features of the family, church, village, and peer group that offer a sense of belonging and competence in context. This is where language is acquired and shared rituals, humor, and spiritual beliefs are considered—becoming tacit and automatic, or consciously weighed and adjusted. And it's the ongoing negotiation between the firm's shared goals, situated with an organizational field, and the power of local context and human-scale motivations that mark the work of the new decentralists.

Once situated in the client's own milieu the individual's own interpretive schema come into play—sorting sensory experience into implicit categories or schema that hold situated meaning. This conceptual tool stems from the work of "pragmatic" American psychologists, like Mead and William James, from more than a century ago. But its application to the individual's learning and motivation inside formal organizations first arose in the 1980s, now galvanized by the new decentralists. They operate as pragmatists in their own right, not wide-eyed cultural relativists. That is, they aim to lift the learning of poor kids in ways envisioned by the humanists, to improve the health of patients, even to strengthen trusting relationships in markets. They aim to transport the client to another place, one that requires novel behavior, not cultural preservation. At the same time, they conform to Nietzsche's assertion that "there are no facts, only interpretations." To ignore the client's worldview only acts to limit the practitioner's understanding and influence.

Drawing on Earlier Social Forms

We discovered how the new decentralists reach back and borrow rather old social forms. The charter school's lateral camaraderie and reliance on student projects, along with public performances, takes us back to John Dewey's notion of hands-on education for democratic engagement. The recognition that learners construct their own understandings, anchored to their context, pulls forward constructivist precepts. We explored how Handelsbanken's version of decentralized management stems in part from a Lutheran tradition of trust and village-style familiarity. These earlier social forms or logics of action don't reappear overnight; they sprout up through the institutional concrete, take root, and then spread in contemporary organizational soil. That said, the new decentralists exercise agency in assembling these conceptual tools in ways that lift clients and advance the firm's position in their field.

These "innovations" are not necessarily revolutionary; they borrow from earlier social forms. But they now represent localized attempts by firms to connect more deeply and effectively with clients. Our theoretical counsel, Georg Simmel, emphasized how "forms of elementary social interaction" over time came to be "institutionalized structures," spreading more widely across a field.[13] And this process may operate reciprocally across levels of the firm or social networks that span organizations. For example, if Tomcavage's case managers find the tools and social motivations necessary to reduce chronic disease, this helps to validate the firm's shift toward prevention and behavioral change, which then spreads to other companies and medical associations.

The shifting demands pressed by organizational fields also percolate down to the work done by local practitioners. Theorists have long emphasized correspondence across field, firm, and practice at the grass roots. Vygotsky argued that "higher mental processes in the individual have their origin in social processes." And "tools and signs" often forged by central artisans may characterize how individuals cooperate at work locally.[14] Vygotsky highlighted how the shift from agricultural to factory production involved telling changes in the tools of production and the social signs that reshaped roles and newly legitimated forms of competence and status in groups. Children raised in agricultural societies, for instance, still learn to respect adult authority, how to cooperate closely with family members, and may not find literacy all that useful. In similar fashion, teachers at the San Francisco charter school didn't ignore the expressive features of youths' cultural forms—they scaffolded up from them. The client's own dominant context and social forms are not discounted by the new decentralists, they offer a platform from which to build.

The postulate that tacit scripts for how I should behave and perceive the world are acquired via social interaction—not inherited genetically or discretely rewarded through behaviorist mechanisms—was further advanced by Mead, the American pragmatist. "The social action is a precondition for consciousness," he asserted. That is, the "social formation of mind," as James Wertsch argued three decades ago. The new decentralists seek to persuade their clients to be like-minded, that is, to share the social world imagined by the practitioner.[15] It may be a world with more daily exercise, shared trust in a financial deal, or wider horizons for the developing adolescent. But it's a subtle negotiation of how to arrive at a common ground, respecting and extending out from the client's own social world, while not taking it as sacred.

Skilled practitioners in decentered firms get out of their own heads and seek to understand where their clients are coming from. They seek to reach an intersubjectively held agreement that cooperating to advance learning or shift behavior is mutually desirable. Note that it's consensus that's being sought: if tacit logics were already shared by practitioner and client alike, no intervention would be required. And the client, from a Meadian vantage point, must sufficiently trust the practitioner to attempt the novel behavior that's being nudged. The practitioner may be seen as a foreigner, but one who is respectful and curious about the client's own context and well-being. "Skilled social actors empathetically relate to the situations of other people and, in doing so, are able to provide those people with reasons to cooperate," as Fligstein and McAdam put it, drawing on Mead.[16] The client must also value the novel advice and gentle push offered by the practitioner. Decentralization of work practices may not be required, but our cases show how it shifts responsibility to the agile practitioner who can learn about and build from the client's own social foundations. The teacher, physician, or banker each nurtures a norm of mutual obligation, an ethic of collective responsibility.

After the State and Market—Cosmopolitan Organizing

The sociologist's emphasis on institutional logics—both how the firm adapts to its field and how practitioners construct legitimate (even productive) ways of working cooperatively—moves us beyond classical conceptions of what motivates the local individual or group under the press of hierarchy enforced by standard rules and coercion, or markets animated by individual utilities. And as hegemonic institutions give way to diverse kinds of local organizations—be they NGOs or for-profit firms—we have witnessed a pluralistic blossoming of institutional logics, while remaining nested in field-wide social forms and credible tools for how work gets done.

Across differing fields or sectors institutional logics also take on a rainbow of differing, at times contradictory forms. A charter school nurtures students to craft public presentations while prepping kids for standardized tests. An international bank proves highly profitable by radically decentralizing control to branch offices. A robust health-care firm experiments with new roles and power relations inside clinics while coping with reimbursement structures that work against prevention and innovation.

Indeed, one huge lesson is that the diversifying of logics, cultivated within decentering organizations, sprout with colorful regularity. Driven by the search for more robust forms of human cooperation, these firms do not express a parochial form of localism. Instead, the new decentralists experiment with how social ties can lift and advance their clients. This rainbow of ways in which work gets done between client and practitioner—infused with ethical verve—cannot be explained by engineered diversification from above, or by the discriminating wisdom of consumers who express tidy channels of discerning demand.

Rather, we are witnessing a poststructuralist process, in part, where shifting economic and institutional forces spark a variety of organizational adaptations. Some adjustments are shared and predictable, as I argue with the four distinct cornerstones of the new decentralism. But this contemporary localism spawns a thousand other organizational blossoms as well. Some will thrive; others will readily wilt.[17] What's key is that these varying ways of organizing work locally are not necessarily dedicated to advancing private interests or culled by any central authority. Our cases show how new forms of cooperation on the ground often seek to buoy the disadvantaged, offer alternative futures, and shape more fulfilling engagement among clients and practitioners alike.

The hierarchy and market of course will persist. The decentralizing forms advanced by Geisinger and Handelsbanken are sparked and sustained by their ability to compete in resourceful fields. Envision charter schools compete for families and funders; a weak organizational center inhibits the ability of Iowa NGOs to backstop troubled vets. Still, the everyday work and success of these firms unfold in quite local spaces on the ground. And their success stems from a maturing capacity to engage and move clients, to nurture a sense of trust and reciprocity. Together, they are taking the client to a more learned, healthier, or profitable place. That journey unfolds in particular local contexts.

The storyline of modernity long required stigmatizing the local, the parochial. Those intermediate collectives back in the village were defined as backward, since they resisted distant hierarchy and faceless market exchange, as Robert Wuthnow taught us back in chapter 1. Contemporary decentralists, instead, return to these viscerally felt communities, social networks that lend meaning and membership to our labor and everyday lives. And the new decentralists aim to create a cosmopolitan range of cooperative settings in which work gets done, not to segment or protect premodern tribes or isolating affiliations.

The riotous range of pluralistic organizational forms that has come to characterize America—rooted in nonprofit and for-profit fields—has yet to eclipse the duality between hierarchy and market. As sociologist Todd Gitlin argued a generation ago, we can't agree on how best to cooperate locally, since we remain split by two competing notions of society. "That of America as a force for individual freedom, and that of the Left as a force for equality [requiring public hierarchy]." The modern project and its focus on settling social ideals at a societal level weigh us down. "They are the two great heavily burdened ideas of the Enlightenment," Gitlin says.

What's so intriguing about the new decentralists is how they set aside such polemics, rejecting the idealized notions of hierarchy or market, opting instead to draw from the social foundations of intermediate collectives. They get to know individual clients. The focus is on how the client is situated within a particular context, be it set by relationships with family, peers, or an identity that's enmeshed in one's work. The focus is no longer on a treatment defined from above, targeted at an undifferentiated individual (as behavioral economists would have it). Instead, the new decentralists delve into the context surrounding the client, and how the individual's relation to implied scripts and expectations might be adjusted. If the human mind is a screen on which their everyday culture is projected, then changing the client's head and heart requires rethinking these surrounding contextual demands.

Inventive charter school leaders recreate small organizations and literally talk about "families" of students, arranged by pairs of grade levels. Geisinger's clinical case managers inquire about the surrounding kin members or partner that can lend a hand with the patient. Branch managers at Handelsbanken, still drawing from Swedish egalitarianism, reproduce participatory forms of consultation and decision making among local staff. Through such human-scale practices, central leaders and local practitioners create warmer, respectful, and inquiring organizational cultures, setting aside the formalized, role-bound ways of formal bureaucracy. In a sense, it's a return to Aristotle's pitch that the state should operate like a benevolent, if disciplined household.[18] Even the massive Gates Foundation spent $2 billion in the 1990s trying to "personalize" high schools—essentially to graft the warmer, lateral social relations of intermediate collectives onto the bureaucratic institution of high school.

As big institutions are disassembled they land locally amid a variety of nonprofits or storefront firms on the ground. The break-up of public education into charter schools, contracting-out to agencies that backstop veterans, even the decentering of finance banking all sift down into communities where small organizations and human associations already live. This kaleidoscopic array of civic groups or small-scale enterprises—what sociologist Gary Fine calls *tiny publics*—offer nodes of social cohesion to which decentralized institutions may adhere.[19] Health maintenance organizations now absorb private medical practices, charter school founders build from nonprofit groups or informal ties, first formed a century or so ago in many cities.

Together, these conceptual tools wielded by the new decentralists help to fashion new structures, forms of cooperation that energize novel action and social engagement in a variety of organizations. This contemporary discourse and material design of local organizations has departed from the old preoccupations of aging decentralists, the zeal to win "autonomy" from central bureaucracy or to bank on market devices. The politics of governance and regulation, once the priority issue of decentralists, recede into the background. Their contemporary descendants now focus on practices and social relations on the ground that account for a firm's efficacy and how a reflective and data-rich center can enhance local practice. It's a cosmopolitan vision of how experimentation can lead to cohesive forms of cooperation, not a parochial protection of maladaptive or uninspired means for working together.

New decentralists must organize at two levels simultaneously while recognizing the essential role of a lean and enabling center. The firm must position itself within a field in ways that reduce uncertainties around popular legitimacy and material inputs. Geisinger carefully advances its presence within its geographic region and presses its innovative character within the health-care field more broadly. Envision now tries to bottle its pedagogical magic and market it to traditional public schools. Even firms that decentralize authority, resources, and know-how out to local units must constantly negotiate their position in the wider organizational field.

Yet at the same time, decentralizing firms must attend to local practice, to small-scale methods for engaging clients and motivating frontline practitioners. The center plays a pivotal role, a fact once denied by first-wave decentralists. For Handelsbanken, Stockholm leaders continue to press the firm's culture and organizing principles, devise new products, and guide new forays into expanding markets. Such inventive centers at times deploy shared rules or individual incentives. But their robust tool kit relies more on commitments, data about clients, and evidence about what practices work under what conditions. So, local practitioners feel supported by the firm's center, rather than feeling ruled by it.

These novel tools are wielded less to fix individual clients and more to gently probe beneath the skin, to discover what makes them tick. The new decentralists remain curious about the individual, their own story, and their everyday motivations. But fixing the individual absent his particular milieu is no longer the task at hand. Students and patients are not lone individuals, isolated targets of didactic teaching or treatment. The individual is no longer regulated or merely incentivized. Instead, the individual is understood as an embedded actor, seeking membership, meaning, and everyday support among kith and kin, friends and peers.

The Local Architecture of Progressive Action

Let me close with a pragmatic pitch.

It's not only the recalcitrant corporate executive or right-wing conservative who might think more carefully about the strengths and risks of decentralization, or the inevitable ebbing of modern centralism, the failed rationalizing of everyday life. It's my progressive colleagues and fellow travelers—especially their penchant for burying their earnest heads in shifting sands—that worry me most. The political Left sorely needs a theory of decentralization that focuses on local capacity and democratic transparency, a model of social cooperation that blends economic justice and expressive variety. The Left's ancestry stems from the Enlightenment, a bundle of ideals that spoke not only of individual rights and central government, but also celebrated colorful expression and cultural pluralism. Secular centralism aimed to enhance civil rights and bring fairness, rather than building gray and mechanical institutions that too often resort to regulating the human spirit.

America's past half century of decentralizing drift tastes rather sour to many of my Left-leaning colleagues, being rooted in Berkeley after all. Don't you remember, they bemoan, that it was Ronald Reagan who pitched market competition and privatizing ailing public institutions. His allies would push the Supreme Court to approve publicly funded vouchers for parents who opted for parochial schools. Or what about George W. Bush who stood beside the deregulated corral of Wall Street cowboys who rode roughshod over millions of home buyers, then made billions by trading bundles of bad mortgages? Will unleashing market forces truly bring down health-care costs and result in higher quality care?

Why not instead simply rebuild the world of central regulation and hierarchical administration, many on the Old Left still argue. Would not a national curriculum and standardizing classroom life serve to narrow the dastardly achievement gaps that harden inequality? Why didn't President Obama opt for a universal-payer for health care? In other words, why not hold onto the illusion of a tightly packed nation-state, a unified Parsonian social system? Just like regulating meatpacking or flight safety, why can't the central state simply tell teachers or doctors how to best lift their clients? Should not corporate leaders more precisely specify how to stamp out burgers, decide on home loans, text or tweet in more uniform ways? One national group, drawn to such an Orwellian future, now lobbies to ensure that all three-year-olds in America learn the same bits of knowledge, enforced by federal intervention and a uniform national test.

Yet the past half century has taught us that the regulatory tools of government, just like the dusty industrial controls of abandoned factories, no longer speak to the kind of work that most Americans do. Nor do these graying forms of coordination and control sustain the rainbow of aspirations and lifestyles that diverse Americans now pursue. This is not to say that the state should not help to build a sustainable economy or lower the planet's rising fever in concerted fashion. But the forces that have transformed work and our colorful panoply of social ideals over the past half century do mean that government must decenter much of what the welfare state has historically tried to run. It already has.

I eagerly agree with my Old Left colleagues that our economic survival rests on an effective central government for essential civic projects. Selective regulation of the for-profit sector should and will persist as well. But die-hard centralists largely ignore the broad and unrelenting forces that have gained steam over the past half century. Organizations must adapt to these seismic economic and ideological shifts, and this rules out top-down management and the uniform moral norms that once lent order to a hegemonic society. Nor do cultural progressives desire the hegemonic routines pressed on *their* own work or the classrooms of *their* inventive children in the ways that elites on the Left often urge onto others.

Risks abound if the political Right comes to dominate civic discourse over decentralization and market remedies. Rather than regulating work and social life from above, elements of everyday life may become ever more commodified, priced and competed over—from the schools among which parents shop, to how we design (racially segregated) cities, to how barons trade on unhealthy forms of consumption. The quality and stratification that results from market relations comes to be seen as the natural result of individual character, not the province of civic debate and public accountability.

Instead, the cornerstones of decentralization advanced by firms like Envision, Geisinger, and Handelsbanken include an ethical commitment to trust and shared obligation, a prosocial focus on the quality of everyday relationships between client and practitioner. Local actors are not to be ruled by distant hierarchy or fleeting partners in momentary exchange. Instead, these decentralizing firms emphasize curiosity and respect for their client's motivations and immediate contexts. It's a social form that scaffolds up from what students, patients, and clients already know, how they glean meaning from their immediate worlds.[20] A portion of these firms operate in markets, some extract profit to further expand their work. But they host a democratic discourse on the ground that's mutual and cooperative, infused with professional tools and novel social forms that lift learning or shift behavior across a variety of clients and groups.

That is, friendly strangers do intervene into the worlds of others from decentered organizations—aiming to advance learning, more robust lifestyles, perhaps a more cosmopolitan recognition of human difference. The new decentralists push to devise a more thoroughly democratic way of organizing human-scale work and cooperation inside local organizations. It's an architecture that sets aside the standardizing, plain-vanilla taste of hierarchy while recognizing that we all yearn to be a respected and contributing member of a social community.

The new decentralists seek to improve how we work together, how we engage one another. They honor not the lone individual competing for status, but instead the wonder and intrinsic meaning that's tied to lifting others, learning from each other. Decentralizing firms will continue to negotiate with their local practitioners over who best holds authority, resources, and know-how. And these firms will struggle with regulatory and market pressures in their own particular field. But the new decentralists are repositioning their organizations within conditions that require local discretion and engaging social tools for getting work done. They put forward a compelling and respectful vision of human cooperation for how we labor together, how we find meaning in everyday life.

Methods Appendix: What Cases Tell Us, and Don't

> Every word that people use in telling their stories is a microcosm of their consciousness.
> —LEV VYGOTSKY

This study—like most inquiries—began with a puzzle. Ample empirical work had revealed that early attempts to decentralize large institutions often led to disappointing results. But at the same time, certain decentered firms, whether publicly funded or privately capitalized, showed encouraging results as detailed in chapter 2. So what distinguishes successful organizations from those that fail to benefit from the decentering of authority, resources, and know-how? What is it about the social organization of successful firms that host and sustain the magic?[1] As postindustrial currents gain force, bringing down hierarchy and revealing the limits of market relations, we better learn how to make decentralization work effectively.

This led to a terse mantra that my graduate students tire of hearing: your research design must flow from your empirical question, yielding the kind of knowledge that one hopes to uncover. This sacred tenet kept running through my mind as I mulled over where to best shine a bright light into how inventive decentralists organize work and social relations locally. We decided to go with in-depth case studies, requiring sustained fieldwork inside local units, or those situated in wider networks of community organizations. This was not an easy decision, at least not when one aims to influence the thinking of fellow scholars. The academy's own tribal ties often divide those who only believe inferences that stem from statistical modeling versus the anthropologically minded who uncover rich revelations and sketch causal mechanisms from a particular and less-generalizable corner of the world. After reading the growing literature and poking our heads inside a few organization, we surmised that little was known about the social and economic cornerstones of potent decentralized firms.

Given the paucity of evidence on *how*, or through *what forms of social action*, decentering firms display robust results, we decided to describe how work is organized and what animates social relations between practitioners and clients. We also hoped to advance a rudimentary theory-building question: Could a shared set of organizational features, a common structure of social cooperation, be observed in decentralized firms across differing sectors?

The scholarship of Anthony Bryk and Richard Ingersoll helped to shape our thinking at this juncture; these two sociologists have worked independently to identify social-organizational elements of schools that help to predict benefits for kids.[2] These features include the balance of coordination and autonomy afforded teachers' work, relational trust among staff members, and a keen focus on enriching the firm's "technical core," where human-scale work unfolds inside classrooms. These are observable dynamics at the local organizational level that lend material structure and normative cohesion for staff and clients alike. Yet we could not find similar, fine-grained literatures from inside other sectors, be it health care, the behavior of NGOs, or decentralizing reforms in the private sector. Nor was it clear from the prior sociology of organizations how the wider, postindustrial pressures to decenter authority, capital, and tools of practice might be causally tied to stronger forms of human cooperation on the ground.

This appendix sketches our thinking on the strength of case studies, as well as their inherent limitations, which methodologists have long debated. I cite earlier findings to illustrate these pluses and minuses regarding the case method. Building knowledge from living inside a case is more like a hike in the wilderness—marked by eye-opening and unexpected discoveries—rather than a plodding march through deductively arrived at hypotheses, then testing each with pristine mathematics.

Speaking to Three Questions

We first broke down our large quandary into three empirical questions, which guided our fieldwork. Each question grew from a frustration over the ideological claims of decentralists and market advocates, whether heard in endless ideological rallies and conferences, the popular media, or pseudo-academic journals like the *Harvard Business Review*. These voices pitch the virtues of separating from central institutions and letting a thousand flowers bloom locally. But these advocates often ignore mixed empirical results or fail to carefully examine *how* successful decentralists build inspiring organizations on the ground.

We began to ask, how is frontline work being organized in decentralizing firms, especially the character of social relations between clients and practitioners? Does a shared social architecture—what we came to call *organizational cornerstones*—emerge within effective firms across differing sectors of society?

As our work inside the four organizational settings proceeded, a third empirical question came to the fore: How do local practitioners interact with colleagues residing at the center to acquire resources and know-how to improve everyday practice? In short, we aimed to describe social relations inside decentralized firms, and then to identify the building blocks that may help to explain their success.

Given these empirical questions, case studies that drew from long-term fieldwork seemed most sensible methodologically. We then faced both the utility and limitations of the case method, the issues posed by qualitative methodologist Andrew Abbott: "What are (cases) trying to accomplish? What kinds of agents are they?"[3]

The case method first allowed us to *start afresh*, to shake off the first-generation literature that remains obsessed with breaking from the center, winning liberation from a bureaucratic apparatus, or naively searching for pure market dynamics. In turn, this is to spark unconstrained innovation and a drift toward higher quality, according to early proponents of decentralization or market remedies. I call it the Berlin Wall postulate of first-wave decentralists: shake off the oppressive center and robust civic and market organizations will automatically flourish. Instead, we pursued new vantage points, moving from what Zen philosophers call a "beginner's mind," or delving into a topic with an attitude of "astonishment and enquiry," as French philosopher Luc Ferry puts it.[4] We endeavored to enter field settings without predilection, instead learning how local actors subjectively see social action and human connection through their own eyes.

By circumscribing each case—at first bounded by the formal organization—we could easily locate core members who understood *how things worked inside*. It's their accounts, their salient episodes that revealed how their practice aimed to engage clients or customers. The local staff members whom you earlier met often spoke of their own theory of social action on the ground, which may or may not have been tied to governance and their relative position with the center. Their lay theories led to other empirical questions: How did local staff conceive of their work with clients and colleagues? Were job roles within local units fixed, at times experimental in nature, shifting, or becoming more laterally distributed? Did the organizational center help to infuse local work with ethical purpose or sturdier tools and know-how?

The teachers and bankers we met inside the Envision charter school and Handelsbanken branches articulated specific accounts of how decentering from the center was a necessary yet insufficient condition for inventive practice. Actors in the Geisinger and Mason City cases spoke differently about links between local practitioners and managers, along with the kinds of resources and rules that emanated from their central institutions. These internally valid accounts of decentralization and local practice could not have been deduced from prior theory while sitting in our university offices. Instead, theory building scaffolds up from the authentic narratives and locally rooted notions of how work and cooperation unfold in particular social contexts, as defined and enacted by local players.

In these ways, the case method prompted unanticipated discoveries that also inform theory building. This included how central managers may interact quite horizontally to improve the daily work of frontline practitioners. About a year into our fieldwork the key cornerstones of local organizing came into sight: the firm's ethical commitments, devising novel roles for practitioners, digging into the client's motivations, and rethinking the center's own work. The case evidence details how such abstracted features are brought to life by vivid and influential actors. At the same time, the underlying social structure can be discerned beneath the colorful particulars and local characters that enliven each organization.

The boundaries of the "case" became more elastic as we spent additional months—totaling between two and three years—in each setting. The center came into view, as did external firms that operated within each organization's wider network. This was seen most clearly with Geisinger's tight interplay between headquarters and local clinics. The fragmented Veterans Affairs offered a contrasting case, along with Iowa's loose archipelago of NGOs that struggled to serve vets. As Handelsbanken successfully expands in Britain and elsewhere, its reputation for decentralized management is positioned in sharp relief against American and other highly centralized banks within this organizational field. So the bounds of a particular firm and its identity relative to peers are revealed by the case method.

We also learned much about how individual practitioners and clients identify with the firm's ethical mission and goals, or come to feel alienated from them. These players frequently spoke of how they identify with the activity structures, norms, and supportive ties that animate cooperative work. So we saw how teacher Danielle Johnson's professional identity was interwoven with her relationships with students, as well as collaborating with curriculum designers residing at Envision's center. Or, Kim Marovets detailed how she identified with, and even adjusted her new identity in concert with, the care and support of certain practitioners inside local NGOs.

How these core actors draw resources from such social ties—and their success in doing so—points to the cohesion or fragmentation of local firms. And we saw how some clients remain on the edge of decentralized firms, not fully responding to the invitation to step inside, similar to what Henry Giroux calls "border identities."[5] Only long-term qualitative work can reveal these kinds of subtle social mechanisms and their causal consequences as experienced by clients or practitioners.

Seeing Causal Mechanisms

Digging deep into local settings yields vivid glimpses of social-organizational mechanisms that may account for downstream benefits. As Charles Ragin has argued, this method yields observational evidence on the "action, agency, and complex event sequences" that characterize the core work of actors in a social setting.[6] Until the researcher spends considerable time in a local setting it's impossible to discern consequential mechanisms, their prevalence, and how actors themselves understand these practices or social action. We focused on commonly observed activities or regular forms of social interaction through which work and expressive action occurred inside the organization's local units. Telling human interactions, backstopping or lifting clients, unfold in these daily *activity structures*.

Bigger samples and quantitative estimation are certainly required before claiming generalizable benefits from, say, Geisinger's monthly case briefings, enlivened through collective problem solving (one regular activity). Or whether the decentered discretion of an account executive at Handelsbanken nurtures more durable loyalty from customers also requires positivist science. Yet it's the illumination of consequential mechanisms on which our case studies focus, leading to testable hypotheses. While quantitative methods essentially test for the correlation between X and Y, the case method allows us to observe and discuss how actors in the situation understand simple chains of causality, what some call *grounded theory*, as anthropologist Joseph Maxwell has emphasized.[7]

These social mechanisms can be subtle until activity structures and less formal interactions for a key player begin to add up. Student Pablo Alba, for example, described which fellow pupils and teachers arrive into his sphere. We observe how he works with others, how his sense of belonging emerges, and how his teachers repeatedly attend to his writing, ideas, and contributions to curricular projects. Or Kim Marovets describes how just two people in formal organizations slowed down to listen and recognize her angst, then the specific activities that pulled her back from the precipice.

As these regularized forms of interaction or activities are observed over time, we begin to see which are set by organizational expectations and patterned forms of work, and which stem sporadically from individuals. That is, more foundational principles of action and social cooperation come into focus within a particular organization. This includes how the decentered firms we studied tended to express intense curiosity over clients, more lateral forms of respect and obligation, and so on. It is not simply the difficult-to-replicate inspiration or creativity of individuals at play; organizational foundations are laid that host core activities and social norms that precede and will outlast individual occupants.

As we inch toward causal accounts or theory, cases hold greater utility when they are representative of similar organizations or settings. What is one's case a case of? Law and medical faculties teach students through cases, fact sets, or similar diagnoses that lead to the application of a conceptual framework or remedy that proves useful across conditions. My research group arrived at four cases in which organizational leaders at the center had earlier decided to reshape the firm's goals, the roles enacted by key players, or the tools and know-how needed to implement more effective ways of engaging clients. We had plenty of organizations to choose from that had been deregulated or chosen to decenter surface-level governance. But we aimed to select cases where the engagement of clients was high on their organizational agenda. This implicitly moved us into service or white-collar sectors. We also gathered prima facie evidence that local units were having some success in lifting clients, then dug more deeply to gauge the evidence of effectiveness.

Within these scope conditions, we then selected quite variable settings—to include publicly funded units and those that depend upon private fees or capital—aiming to determine whether shared organizational practices were at play across these diverse sectors. That said, cases rooted in formal organizations, no matter how local or human in scale, pose the problem of not really knowing what it's a case of until we learn how key actors, given local particulars and situated meanings, define the cooperative work that's getting done. The boundaries and character of the case become more clear the deeper one's empirical dive.

Limitations of Case Evidence

These strengths of the case method yield evidence that's rich in what social scientists call *internal validity*. The researcher has lived so long inside the organization, and come to know key actors so well, that the inferences advanced likely hold robust validity or "truth"—but only for the particular case placed under the magnifying glass. It's *external validity* that we worry about, the limited ability to generalize beyond the modest count of particular organizational cases. Our draw of decentralizing firms across four sectors allows more confidence that the practices and organizational cornerstones uncovered will likely operate in other firms. Still, it's best to interpret our claims as working hypotheses that must be tested with larger samples of decentered organizations.

As our fieldwork progressed—visiting sites, observing, arranging for interviews, and informally chatting with members—another risk to validity arose. This deals with selective attention paid to a nonrandom set of actors or activities inside firms, which may not offer a representative picture of realities. For example, one compelling discovery across the four cases was how certain practitioners displayed such curiosity over the stories, immediate contexts, and motivations of their individual clients. This soon surfaced as one foundational cornerstone, a dynamic advanced by the decentralized orchestration of practice, one feature that strengthened cooperation with clients. In turn, leaders of local units or their central managers would recruit equally inquisitive staff, like Mark Cleary, Kenda Danowsky, or Danielle Johnson. And it's these enthusiastic adherents to the firm's culture and ethical mores that become most available to inquiring researchers.

These organizational members, in turn, seem so trustworthy, so intriguing that the researcher is drawn to their viewpoints, to how they describe the nature of work and social forms they claim typify life within the organization. To combat this possible bias we were careful to verify pivotal facts, the character of typical activities, and presence of organizational cornerstones. This required talking with a variety of actors, including members to whom we were not referred, and directly observing the inner workings and social interactions found within each organization. At times we pursued conversations with dissonant staff members who didn't hold the same perceptions or experiences of working in a local unit. Deep case studies aim to verify where there's intersubjective agreement on, say, how roles are being adjusted or social engagement with clients is crafted. And conversely, where do we see a normative or technical consensus when work begins to break down?[8] Despite our efforts, some degree of bias was likely introduced by hanging out with and learning through the eyes of members who made themselves more available, those more simpatico with the firm's public face.

A story told by physicist Stephen Hawking punctuates a final worry regarding the case method. A rather crotchety lady, listening to a lecture on the origins of the cosmos, suddenly interrupted to say that he was speaking rubbish. She claimed that the universe is actually a flat disk lying on the back of a turtle. He thought how to politely head her off, asking what the turtle was standing upon. The old woman quickly replied, "You're a very clever young man, but it's turtles all the way down."[9]

I recall this endearing episode when mulling over the knowledge that cases yield, and what they fail to pin down. Our ability to build theory that matches reality and yields practical advice depends on which turtle we start with. Social scientists hope to account for consequential phenomena. My team endeavored to discern social forms or elements of organizations that enrich how individuals cooperate to get work done. Yet as we enter complicated institutions, eagerly searching for pivotal drivers, we discover turtles residing on the backs of other turtles. And the originating level of human action, intersubjectively understood among actors in a particular setting, might not be the organizational level assumed by the investigator. So we need to understand which turtle the local actors stand upon, which defines their panorama.

We assumed that key social-organizational features or activity structures would be most telling when observed within the most local unit of the wider firm—the neighborhood charter school, the local medical clinic, the branch bank, and so on. But in central Pennsylvania we discovered that the turtles in the center were animating much of the innovative work and shifting to more lateral job roles for medical practitioners below. In northern Iowa we found several turtles inhabiting the village level, but they rarely spoke with each other to embrace detached clients. And the armored tortoise at the Department of Veterans Affairs in Des Moines exercised limited authority and few incentives to corral the smaller turtles out in the hinterlands.

One enters a case with an empirical objective in mind, assuming that the door you first enter to the social organization takes you to the most omniscient turtle. But maybe it's the intriguing creatures around the next corner, including how they cooperate via other networks and relationships, that more validly characterize or help to shape their work. Or perhaps these turtles bridge over to another firm or network, or seek to change norms, tools, and practices in the wider organizational field.

The case method—not to mention typical research budgets—don't allow us to follow every riveting turtle down every rivulet, or forever widen the borders of each case study. But qualitative methods offer multiple windows into what local practitioners are thinking, how they conceive of their work, and what core principles or cornerstones lend a resilient order to everyday social engagements. And this gets us closer to understanding the generalizable conditions under which decentralized organizations may effectively touch clients or customers and the social mechanisms that contribute to their local success.

Notes

Preface

1. M. T. Cicero (44 BC), *De Officis* (On rights and obligations), cited by Asma 2013.
2. Fogg and Harrington 2012.
3. Jong 2013.
4. Simon Price and Peter Thonemann offer vivid details of how spiritual pluralism marked the final centuries of the Roman Empire. Only in the early fourth century did the Christians finally move the state to legitimate Sunday as a holy day and civil authorities began to outlaw public festivals rooted in pagan beliefs. Our contemporary cultural pluralism is certainly not unprecedented, although tolerance for it in civic spaces and democratic political structures offers a rare historical episode. See Price and Thonemann 2011.
5. Cotter 2013.
6. Fukuyama 2011.
7. Orszag 2011.
8. Moore 2011.
9. Harrison 1994.
10. Paraphrased in Payne 2010.

Chapter One

1. Evans 1995.
2. Rorty detailed the widening split between the aging labor-led Left, still focused on material facets of inequality, and the youthful, post-1960s cultural Left, which centered their critique on moral tenets and lifestyle.
3. Rifkin 2011.
4. Dealbook 2013.
5. Delightfully examined in Kate Racculia's novel (2010).
6. Fuller 2000.
7. Economic indicators come from our analysis of data from the Census Bureau and the Bureau of Labor Statistics, along with reporting by Morris 2011, 6; Peck 2011.
8. Spence 2011.
9. US Census Bureau 2013.

10. Greenstone and Looney 2012.
11. Campbell 2011.
12. The predominance of women in service and professional jobs, stemming in part from their much higher college graduation rates, is detailed in Mundy 2012.
13. Income equality statistics come from Hacker and Pierson 2011; Pollin 2010.
14. Montopoli 2011.
15. Powell 2011.
16. Saez 2013.
17. Barboza 2011b.
18. A statement issued by China's official news agency, Xinhua, and reported by Barboza 2011a.
19. These dynamics are further detailed in *The Economist* 2010.
20. Congressional Budget Office 2010.
21. Hanushek 1997.
22. Estimate reported by Friedman and Mandelbaum 2011. More detailed cost projections under alternative federal policy scenarios appear in Congressional Budget Office 2010.
23. Emanuel 2013.
24. Munnell et al. 2012.
25. Data from the Organization of Economic Cooperation and Development, Paris, reported by Erlanger 2010.
26. Ferguson 2010.
27. Koval 2011. For other cases of immigrant groups filing into jobs that whites once occupied, see Morawska 2009.
28. Leonhardt 2011.
29. Economic indicators from Lanchester 2011, 35; Lyall and Cowell 2010.
30. Blow 2011.
31. Westen 2012.
32. Polling results draw from Gallup research, available at www.gallup.com/poll/27286/Government.aspx?version=print.
33. These data come from a Cable News Network (CNN) poll, available at www.pollingreport.com/institut_html#Government.
34. Bushaw and Lopez 2010.
35. Emanuel 2013.
36. Quoted by Reston and Blume 2011.
37. Paraphrased by Evans 1995, 29.
38. The finance agency, Sallie Mae, currently publishes an annual survey of how parents help to finance college costs. These data can be matched with earlier reports from the College Board of New York. See Sallie Mae 2013.
39. For example, see Smith 2012.
40. Zogby and Schiermeyer 2011.
41. Task 2011.
42. DeParle and Tavernise 2012; Portier et al. 2012.
43. US Census Bureau 2011.
44. Quoted by Ferry 2011, 153.
45. Ferry 2011, 58.
46. Simmel 1948.

NOTES TO PAGES 24-39

47. Quoted by Miller 2011. A rather erratic bohemian in his own right, Rousseau fathered several children with his lover, Thérèse Levasseur, who he refused to marry until late in life. Each time she became pregnant, their infant would be consigned to a foundling home in Paris. His postulated universals—largely focusing on the unlimited potentials of the individual—proved to be politically threatening. He believed that individuals, acting cooperatively, could pursue alternate destinies, rebelling against "the blindest obedience."

48. Quoted and paraphrased by Grogan 2013.
49. Farhi 2012.
50. Quoted in Goodstein 2012.
51. Wuthnow 1987.
52. Quoted by Asma 2013, 3.
53. Durkheim's contemporary in Germany, Georg Simmel, turned to the study of the New England village as he struggled to explain why and how nineteenth-century modernity was breaking off the individual as a reified entity, for the first time divorced from collectivities, be it the family or one's labor guild. Simmel observed that New Englanders "had a pronounced local orientation . . . in which the individual was tightly bound by his obligations to the whole, and although this whole was relatively small, it was also self-sufficient." Simmel 2012.
54. This argument has been developed by Marty 1997.
55. Asma 2013.
56. Florida 2002.
57. Quoted in Collins 2011; Smith 2011.
58. Smith 2009 [1759], 9.
59. Smith 2009 [1759], xiii, 29, 133.
60. Miller 2011, 61.
61. Hegel 1967.
62. Congressional passage of the federal income tax in 1913 allowed for deductions when individuals or companies donated to nonprofits. For details on the growth of NGOs, and the increasing role played by government contracting, see Smith and Lipsky 1993.
63. National Center for Charitable Statistics 2011.
64. The employment count is for 2007, from Salamon 2012.
65. The dramatic growth of NGOs and the off-loading of once government-run activities have spurred plenty of research on the nonprofit sector. See, for example, Powell and Steinberg 2006; Salamon 2012.
66. Wuthnow 2009; Miron and Urschel 2010.
67. Figures reported by the Giving USA Foundation and the Center on Philanthropy at Indiana University, reported and graphically displayed by Pearson 2011. For historical analysis of volunteering in Western societies, see Macmillan and Townsend 2006.
68. Sampson 2012.
69. This theoretical line of localized political theory is detailed in Clemens 2006.
70. Donahue 1989.
71. Blair 2010.
72. My earlier work details the forces that have recurrently moved political activists to nurture NGOs and nonstate organizations since the 1950s. See Fuller 1999.
73. Detailed in Schofer and Longhofer 2011.
74. For a review of the critique of a broadly conceived neoliberal movement, see Harvey 2005.
75. Fung 2004.

76. The contradictions inherent in the neoinstitutional or world culture line of thinking are examined in Anderson-Levitt 2003; Carney, Rappleye, and Silova 2012.

77. The push and pull between Rome and elites out in the city-states is detailed in Price and Thonemann 2011.

78. Greenblatt 2011.

79. *The Economist* 2012.

80. Cotter 2012.

81. Walzer 1983.

Chapter Two

1. The early education sector—informed by the research of developmental psychologists, sociologists, and economists—offers a notable exception. Child-care and preschool organizations, often run by NGOs, host many studies of how everyday relationships between caregivers and young children lead to gains in cognitive and social-emotional domains. How the decentralized character of this sector advances (and sometimes constrains) local practitioners' interest in relationships and the social-organization of classrooms is explored in Fuller 2007.

2. Schemo 2004.

3. Quotations and historical analysis of early bipartisan support of the charter school movement appears in Hess 2010.

4. National Alliance 2013.

5. Nelson, Rosenberg, and Van Meter 2004.

6. Stanford economist Martin Carnoy and colleagues provide a careful critique of the original charter school evaluation by researchers at the American Federation of Teachers, and place it in the context of state-level studies. Carnoy et al. 2006.

7. Braun, Jenkins, and Grigg 2006.

8. Raymond 2009. Also, see reviews of charter school evidence: Fuller 2009; Gleason et al. 2010.

9. Zimmer et al. 2003.

10. Hoxby, Murarka, and Kang 2009.

11. Such methodological critiques are key in carefully assessing the magnitude with which nontraditional public schools raise children's achievement, relative to peers remaining in conventional schools. See Reardon 2009.

12. Raymond 2014.

13. Lauen, Dauter, and Fuller in press.

14. Tuttle et al. 2013.

15. Miron, Urschel, and Saxton 2011.

16. Bloom and Unterman 2013.

17. Raymond et al. 2013.

18. Brookings analyst Tom Loveless emphasizes that Raymond's reported effect sizes for charter students ranged between 0.01 and 0.03 of a standard deviation. He equates this difference between the mean height of men at 5 feet, 10 inches and a man who is one-tenth inch taller; Loveless 2013.

19. Betts 2005.

20. Corcoran and Levin 2011.

21. Renzulli 2005.

22. Zimmer et al. 2012.

23. Buddin 2012.
24. Wolf 2012.
25. Hess 2010, 43.
26. Etheredge 1983.

27. Professor Scott's earlier study of organizational change in the health-care field emphasized the permanence of the taken-for-granted scripts that govern how practitioners assume work should be done, that reflect institutional logics. Scott et al. 2000. This construct has received considerable attention by sociologists in recent years. For review, Thornton, Ocasio, and Lounsbury 2012.

28. Orszag 2011; Starr 2011.
29. Organization of Economic Cooperation and Development (OECD) 2006.
30. Orszag 2011.
31. Starr 2011, 205.
32. Chapter appearing in Washington Post 2010.
33. For review of first-wave deregulation from Washington, see Rajan 2012.

34. The contemporary management literature is rife with empirical work that examines how decentralized operations or decision making is predictive of stronger productivity or even social responsibility inside large firms. For example, Wong, Ormiston, and Tetlock 2011.

35. Kaplan and Mikes 2012.
36. Details of IBM's history appear in Chesbrough and Teece 2002.

37. William Ouchi's notion of worker motivation and coordination went beyond the factory-like rational control of workers (Theory X) and the more recent human relations school, which had shifted managers' attention to intrinsic sources of staff motivation (Theory Y). Instead, Ouchi drew on East Asian thought and his observations inside work teams, where the collective's interests and dialogue over how to improve performance eclipsed the analytic assumption that each individual's source of motivation should be considered; Ouchi 1981. The following year two consultants working for McKinsey published *In Search of Excellence,* which advanced several principles for crafting more dynamic and innovative firms, including the idea of simultaneously advancing "loose-tight properties, autonomy in shop-floor activities plus centralized values." It sold over three million copies, and the loose-tight principle, by the early 1990s, would weave its way into thinking on how to improve the performance of publicly funded institutions, including education and health care.

38. Rockart and Short 1989.
39. Burrow 2003.
40. Malone 2004.
41. Exchange reported by Duhigg and Bradsher 2012.
42. Maslin 2011.
43. Harrison 1994.
44. Cited by Bottomore 1964, 169.
45. Appiah 2006, 57.

Chapter Three

1. Obama 2009.
2. For historical reviews of the social organization of health care, see Scott et al. 2000; Starr 2011. Data on the decline of private practices were compiled by the consulting firm Accenture, and were reported in Creswell and Abelson 2012.

3. Most recently, see Starr's 2011 analysis of health-care organizations and their policy environment.

4. Boyle et al. 2010.

5. Orszag 2011.

6. Evidence on the benefits of Geisinger reforms has appeared in several medical journals pertaining to various patient outcomes. Bloom, Graf, and Steele 2012; Weber et al. 2007; Johnson et al. 2010, 31; Slotkin et al. 2012, 33.

7. Kilo and Wasson 2010.

8. Ad Hoc Task Force 1992; Sia et al. 2004. A research consortium published in 2012 offering experimental evidence on the benefits of health navigators or "promoters" in terms of quicker and effective treatments for breast and other forms of cancer, reported across several cities: *Cancer Epidemiology Biomarkers and Prevention* 2012.

9. Again, pseudonyms are used for patients or staff members for whom consent was not obtained.

10. Editors 2010.

11. McCarthy, Mueller, and Wrenn 2009.

12. Steele 2009.

13. Data on end-of-life care and costs are reviewed in Gawande 2010.

14. One well-known research and development center is the Institute for Healthcare Improvement, based in Cambridge, Massachusetts. Their analysis of highly variable quality and costs across major health-care firms has received wide attention. The *New York Times* editorial board in 2011 and 2012 ran a series of articles that sketched a variety of organizational innovations undertaken by various firms. For example, see Martin et al. 2009.

Chapter Four

1. Milne 2013.
2. *The Economist* 2009, 16.
3. KPMG International 2012.
4. Kroner 2009, 101.
5. Wallander 2003.
6. Wallander n.d.
7. Wallander 2003, 27–29.
8. Wallander 2003, 36.
9. Wallander n.d., 15.
10. Kroner 2009, 93–94.
11. One explanation of Handelsbanken's sudden rise in Britain appears in Sibun n.d.
12. Wallender 2003, 141.

Chapter Five

1. Pseudonyms are used when a student or teacher did not consent to being identified by name.
2. Smith 2012.
3. Gawande 2011.

4. Smerdon and Means 2006.

5. Data on CAT enrollment patterns and teacher turnover are from authors' tabulations, based on information provided by school authorities and data reported to the California Department of Education.

Chapter Six

1. Kizer and Dudley 2009.
2. Kizer and Dudley 2009, 18.6.
3. National Center for PTSD 2006.
4. Hoge et al. 2004.
5. Tanielian and Jaycox 2008.
6. Statistics reported by Fitzpatrick 2010.
7. Data from Department of Veterans Affairs 2000.
8. Lilly 2009.

Chapter Seven

1. Iyer 2012, 16.
2. Jepperson 1991; Scott 2001.
3. Fligstein and McAdam 2012, 11.
4. Martin 2003.
5. Bourdieu and Wacquant 1992.
6. Holland and Quinn 1987, 22.
7. Shore 1998.
8. Frye 2012. On advances in cognitive sociology, also see Vaisey 2009.
9. Lave and Wenger 1991; Salomon 1993.
10. In behavioral economics, see a review by Etzioni 2009, 5–8; Ariely 2008; Thaler and Sunstein 2008.
11. On cognitive biases in decision making and judgment, see Tversky, Slovic, and Kahnemen 1982; Thaler 1994. On cultural psychology and sociology of social action in culturally bounded settings, see Wertsch 1985; Cole 1996; DiMaggio 1997; Holloway and Fuller 1996. For a review of these related threads, see Turiel 2012.
12. Fukuyama 2011.
13. Levine 1971, xxvii.
14. Paraphrased by Wertsch 1985, 14–15, 59.
15. For a review of these foundations of cooperation, see Fligstein 2001; Mead 1934.
16. Fligstein and McAdam 2012, 46.
17. For review, Sarup 1993.
18. Aristotle, *The Politics*, circa. 330 BC. Excerpt appearing in *Lapham's Quarterly* 2012.
19. Fine 2012.
20. The new decentralists focus on the specific features of formal organizations. But they may be seen as kindred spirits of communitarian thought in political theory. For recent discussion, see Dionne 2012.

Appendix

1. I also had recently completed a review in the education sector pointing to organizational elements that distinguished effective versus futile forms of decentralized firms, thanks to an invitation from David Plank, Barbara Schneider, and Gary Sykes. Fuller 2009.

2. Bryk et al. 2010; Ingersoll 2003.

3. Abbott 1992.

4. Ferry 2011.

5. Giroux 1992.

6. Ragin 1992, 12.

7. Maxwell 2004.

8. Sociologist Sara Lawrence-Lightfoot offers an instructive discussion of how the qualitative researcher can become drawn to the most enthusiastic members of an organization, often individuals who are most open to, and eager to share stories with, an outside analyst. See the methods appendix in Lawrence-Lightfoot 1983.

9. Told by Francis Fukuyama (2011).

References

Abbott, A. 1992. "What Do Cases Do? Some Notes on Activity in Sociological Analysis." In *What Is a Case? Exploring the Foundations of Social Inquiry*, edited by C. Ragin and H. Becker, 53–82. Cambridge: Cambridge University Press.
Ad Hoc Task Force. 1992. "American Academy of Pediatrics Ad Hoc Task Force on Definition of the Medical Home." Washington, DC: American Academy of Pediatrics.
Anderson-Levitt, Kathryn, ed. 2003. *Local Meanings, Global Schooling: Anthropology and World Culture Theory*. New York: Palgrave Macmillan.
Appiah, K. A. 2006. *Cosmopolitanism: Ethics in a World of Strangers*. New York: Norton.
Ariely, D. 2008. *Predictably Irrational: The Hidden Forces That Shape Our Decisions*. New York: Harper Collins.
Aristotle. 2012. "The Politics, Circa 330 B.C." In *Lapham's Quarterly*. Athens: True to Form, 5 (4): 162–63.
Asma, S. 2013. *Against Fairness*. Chicago: University of Chicago Press.
Barboza, D. 2011a. "China Strongly Condemns U.S. 'Addiction to Debts.'" *New York Times*, August 7, sec. A.
———. 2011b. "Endangered Dragon: As Its Economy Sprints Ahead, China's People Are Left Behind." *New York Times*, October 10, sec. A.
Berwick, D. 2011. "Launching Accountable Care Organizations: The Proposed Rule for the Medicare Shared Savings Plan." *New England Journal of Medicine* (April). doi: 10.1056/NEJMp1103602.
Betts, J. 2005. "The Competitive Effects of Charter Schools on Traditional Public Schools." In *Getting Choice Right: Ensuring Equity and Efficiency in Education Policy*, edited by J. Betts and T. Loveless. Washington, DC: Brookings Institution.
Blair, T. 2010. *A Journey: My Political Life*. New York: Knopf.
Bloom, F., T. Graf, and G. Steele Jr. 2012. "Improved Patient Outcomes in 3 Years with a System of Care for Diabetes." Learning Health System commentary series. Washington, DC: Institute of Medicine, National Academies.
Bloom, H., and R. Unterman. 2013. "Sustained Progress: New Findings about the Effectiveness and Operation of Small Public High Schools of Choice in New York City." New York: MDRC.
Blow, C. 2011. "Decline of American Exceptionalism." *New York Times*, November 19, sec. A.

Bottomore, T. B. 1964. *Karl Marx: Selected Writings in Sociology and Social Philosophy.* New York: McGraw-Hill.

Bourdieu, P., and L. Wacquant. 1992. *An Invitation to Reflexive Sociology.* Chicago: University of Chicago Press.

Boyle, J., T. Thompson, E. Gregg, L. Barker, and D. Williamson. 2010. "Projection of the Year 2050 Burden of Diabetes in the U.S. Adult Population: Dynamic Modeling of Incidence, Mortality, and Prediabetes Prevalence." *Population Health Metrics* 8. www.pophealthmetrics.com/content/8/1/29.

Braun, H., F. Jenkins, and W. Grigg. 2006. "A Closer Look at Charter Schools Using Hierarchical Linear Modeling." Washington, DC: Department of Education, National Assessment of Educational Progress.

Bryk, A., P. Bender Sebring, E. Allensworth, J. Easton, and S. Luppescu. 2010. *Organizing Schools for Improvement: Lessons from Chicago.* Chicago: University of Chicago Press.

Buddin, R. 2012. "The Impact of Charter Schools on Public and Private School Enrollments." Policy Analysis 707. Washington, DC: Cato Institute.

Burrow, P. 2003. *Backfire: Carly Fiorina's High-Stakes Battle for the Soul of Hewlett-Packard.* Hoboken, NJ: John Wiley.

Bushaw, W., and S. Lopez. 2010. "A Time for Change: 42nd Annual Phi Delta Kappa/Gallup Poll of the Public's Attitudes toward the Public Schools." *Phi Delta Kappan Magazine*, September.

Cable News Network (CNN). n.d. www.pollingreport.com/institut_html#Government.

Campbell, D. 2011. "Ration Care with Medicare Credits." *USA Today*, August 10, sec. A.

Cancer Epidemiology Biomarkers and Prevention. 2012. University of California, Berkeley. Volume 21, October.

Carney, S., J. Rappleye, and I. Silova. 2012. "Between Faith and Science: World Culture Theory and Comparative Education." *Comparative Education Review* 56 (3): 366–93.

Carnoy, M., R. Jacobsen, L. Mishel, and R. Rothstein. 2006. "Worth the Price? Weighing the Evidence on Charter School Achievement." *Education Finance and Policy* 1 (1): 151–61.

Chesbrough, H., and D. Teece. 2002. "Organizing for Innovation: When Is Virtual Virtuous." *Innovative Enterprise*, August, 127–35.

Clemens, E. 2006. "The Constitution of Citizens: Political Theories of Nonprofit Organization." In *The Nonprofit Sector: A Research Handbook*, edited by W. W. Powell and R. Steinberg, 207–20. New Haven, CT: Yale University Press.

Cole, M. 1996. *Cultural Psychology: A Once and Future Discipline.* Cambridge, MA: Harvard University Press.

Collins, L. 2011. "England, Their England." *New Yorker*, July 4.

Congressional Budget Office. 2010. "Federal Debt Held by the Public under Budget Scenarios (August Revision)." Washington, DC: Congress of the United States.

Corcoran, S., and H. Levin. 2011. "School Choice and Competition in New York City Schools." In *Education Reform in New York City: Ambitious Change in the Nation's Most Complex School System*, 199–224. Cambridge, MA: Harvard Education Press.

Cotter, H. 2012. "Racial Redefinition in Progress." *New York Times*, December 1, sec. D.

———. 2013. "A Constellation of Identities, Winking and Shifting." *New York Times*, June 14, sec. C.

Creswell, J., and R. Abelson. 2012. "A Hospital War Reflects a Bind for U.S. Doctors." *New York Times*, December 1, sec. A.

REFERENCES

Dealbook. 2013. "Avis to Buy Zipcar for $500 Million." *New York Times*, January 2. http://dealbook.nytimes.com/2013/01/02/avis-to-buy-zipcar-for-500-million/?hp.

Denby, D. 2012. "Animal Instincts." *New Yorker*, November 26.

DeParle, J., and S. Tavernise. 2012. "For Women under 30, Most Births Occur Outside of Marriage." *New York Times*, February 17, sec. A.

Department of Veterans Affairs. 2000. "FY08 Geographic Distribution of Veterans Affairs Expenditures." Des Moines and Washington, DC: National Center for Veterans Analysis and Statistics.

DiMaggio, P. 1997. "Culture and Cognition." *Annual Review of Sociology* 23: 263–87.

Dionne, E. J. 2012. *Our Divided Political Heart: The Battle for the American Idea in an Age of Discontent*. New York: Bloomsbury.

Donahue, J. 1989. *The Privatization Decision: Public Ends, Private Means*. New York: Basic Books.

Duhigg, C., and K. Bradsher. 2012. "How U.S. Lost Out on iPhone Work: Apple's Experience Shows Why Jobs Are Flowing to China." *New York Times*, January 22, sec. A.

The Economist. 2009. "Back at the Branch: More Swedish Lessons for the Banking Industry." May 16.

———. 2010. "China Buys Up the World." September 13.

———. 2012. "Junk Food: Recycling in Mexico." October 27.

Editors. 2010. "Rapid Cycle Innovation." *Health Affairs* 29: 2047–53.

Emanuel, E. 2013. "Health Care Reform and the Future of American Medicine." Lecture at the Ohio State University School of Medicine, Columbus, October 4.

Erlanger, S. 2010. "Crisis Threatens Liberal Benefits of European Life." *New York Times*, May 23, sec. A.

Etheredge, L. 1983. "Reagan, Congress, and Health Care Spending." *Health Affairs* 1: 14–24.

Etzioni, A. 2009. "Adaptation or Paradigm Shift?" *Contemporary Sociology* 38: 5–8.

Evans, P. 1995. *Embedded Autonomy: States and Industrial Transformation*. Princeton, NJ: Princeton University Press.

Farhi, P. 2012. "The Boss Rocks Out with a Teleprompter: Can You Roll with It?" *Washington Post*, March 31, sec. C.

Ferguson, N. 2010. "Complexity and Collapse: Empires on the Edge of Chaos." *Foreign Affairs* (April 21).

Ferry, L. 2011. *A Brief History of Thought*. New York: Harper Collins.

Fine, G. A. 2012. *Tiny Publics: A Theory of Group Action and Culture*. New York: Russell Sage Foundation.

Fitzpatrick, L. 2010. "How We Fail Our Female Vets." *Time Magazine*, July 12.

Fleuran, M., K. Wiefferink, and T. Paulussen. "Determinants of Innovations within Health Care Organizations." *International Journal for Quality Health Care* 16: 107–23.

Fligstein, N. 2001. "Social Skill and the Theory of Fields." *Sociological Theory* 19: 105–25.

Fligstein, N., and D. McAdam. 2012. *A Theory of Fields*. New York: Oxford University Press.

Florida, R. 2002. *The Rise of the Creative Class*. New York: Penguin Books.

Fogg, N., and P. E. Harrington. 2012. "The Employment and Mal-Employment Situation for Recent College Graduates: An Update." Philadelphia: Drexel University, Center for Labor Markets and Policy.

Friedman, T., and M. Mandelbaum. 2011. *That Used to Be Us: How America Fell Behind in the World We Created and How We Can Come Back*. New York: Farrar, Straus and Giroux.

Frye, M. 2012. "Bright Futures in Malawi's New Dawn: Educational Aspirations as Assertions of Identity." *American Journal of Sociology* 117: 1565–624.

Fukuyama, F. 2011. *The Origins of Political Order: From Prehuman Times to the French Revolution.* London: Profile Books.

Fuller, B. 1999. *Government Confronts Culture: The Struggle for Local Democracy in Southern Africa.* New York: Garland.

———. 2000. *Inside Charter Schools: The Paradox of Radical Decentralization.* Cambridge, MA: Harvard University Press.

———. 2007. *Standardized Childhood: The Political and Cultural Struggle over Early Education.* Stanford, CA: Stanford University Press.

———. 2009. "Policy and Place: Learning from Decentralized Reforms." In *Handbook of Education of Education Policy Research*, edited by G. Sykes, B. Schneider, D. N. Plank, with T. G. Ford, 855–75. New York: Routledge.

———. 2010. "We'd Better Learn It: Will Americans Really Learn Chinese?" *New York Times*, February 7. roomfordebate.blogs.nytimes.com/2010/02/07will-americans-really-learn-chinese/#bruce.

Fung, Archon. 2004. *Reinventing Urban Democracy.* Princeton, NJ: Princeton University Press.

Gallup. n.d. Polling Results Drawn from Gallup Research. www.gallup.com/poll/27286/Government.aspx?version=print.

Gawande, A. 2010. "Letting Go: What Should Medicine Do When It Can't Save Your Life?" *New Yorker*, August 2.

———. 2011. "Personal Best: Top Athletes and Singers Have Coaches. Should You?" *New Yorker*, October 3.

Giroux, H. 1992. *Border Crossings: Cultural Workers and the Politics of Education.* New York: Routledge.

Gleason, P., M. Clark, C. Tuttle, and E. Dwoyer. 2010. "The Evaluation of Charter School Impacts: Final Report." Washington, DC: National Center for Education Evaluation and Regional Assistance.

Goodstein, L. 2012. "Nuns Weigh Response to Scathing Vatican Rebuke." *New York Times*, July 29, sec. A.

Greenblatt, S. 2011. *The Swerve.* New York: Norton.

Greenstone, M., and A. Looney. 2012. "The Importance of Education: An Economics View." *Education Week*, November, 32.

Grogan, J. 2013. *Encountering America: Humanistic Psychology, Sixties Culture, and the Shaping of Modern Self.* New York: Harper Collins.

Hacker, J., and P. Pierson. 2011. *Winner-Take-All Politics: How Washington Made the Rich Richer—and Turned Its Back on the Middle Class.* New York: Simon and Schuster.

Hanushek, E. 1997. "Assessing the Effects of School Resources on Student Performance: An Update." *Education Evaluation and Policy Analysis* 19: 141–64.

Harrison, B. 1994. *Lean and Mean: The Changing Landscape of Corporate Power in the Age of Flexibility.* New York: Basic Books.

Harvey, David. 2005. *A Brief History of Neoliberalism.* Oxford: Oxford University Press.

Hegel, G. W. F. 1967. *Hegel's Philosophy of Right.* Translated by T. M. Knox. London: Oxford University Press, x–xi.

Hess, F. 2010. "Does School Choice 'Work'?" *National Affairs* 5 (Fall).

Hoge, C., C. Castro, S. C. Messer, D. McGurk, D. I. Cotting, and R. L. Koffman. 2004. "Combat Duty in Iraq and Afghanistan, Mental Health Problems, and Barriers to Care." *New England Journal of Medicine* 351: 13–22.

Holland, D., and N. Quinn. 1987. *Cultural Models in Language and Thought*. Cambridge: Cambridge University Press.

Holloway, S., and B. Fuller. 1997. *Through My Own Eyes: Single Mothers and the Cultures of Poverty*. Cambridge, MA: Harvard University Press.

Hoxby, C., S. Murarka, and J. Kang. 2009. "How New York City's Charter Schools Affect Achievement." New York City Charter Schools Evaluation Project.

Ingersoll, R. 2003. *Who Controls Teachers' Work? Power and Accountability in America's Schools*. Cambridge, MA: Harvard University Press.

Iyer, P. 2012. *The Man within My Head*. New York: Knopf.

Jepperson, R. 1991. "Institutions, Institutional Effects, and Institutionalism." In *The New Institutionalism in Organizational Analysis*, edited by W. W. Powell and P. J. DiMaggio. Chicago: University Of Chicago Press.

Johnson, D., G. Divine, G. Alexander, S. Rolnick, J. Calvi, M. Stopponi, J. Richards, J. McClure, V. Strecher, and C. C. Johnson. 2010. "C-A3-04: The Role of Family Disease History and Perceived Risk of Disease in Change in Fruit and Vegetable Intake over 12 Months." *Clinical Medicine and Research* 8 (1): 31.

Jong, Erica. 2013. "Unzipped." *New York Times Book Review*, October 6.

Kaplan, R. S., and A. Mikes. 2012. "Managing Risk: A New Framework." *Harvard Business Review* 90 (6): 48–60.

Kilo, C., and J. H. Wasson. 2010. "Practice Redesign and the Patient-Centered Medical Home: History, Promises, and Challenges." *Health Affairs* 29 (5): 773–78.

Kizer, K., and R. Dudley. 2009. "Extreme Makeover: Transformation of Veterans Health Care System." *Annual Review of Public Health* 30: 18.1–18.27.

Koval, J. 2011. "The Latino Labor Force in Metro Chicago: Growth, Mobility, and Future Prospects." Berkeley: Institute of Human Development, Notre Dame University.

KPMG International. 2012. "Optimizing Banking Operating Models: From Strategy to Implementation." London.

Kroner, N. 2009. *A Blueprint for Better Banking: Syenska Handelsbanken and a Proven Model for Post-Crash Banking*. Hampshire, England: Harriman House.

Lanchester, J. 2011. "Euro Science." *New Yorker*, October 10.

Lave, J., and E. Wenger. 1991. *Situated Learning: Legitimate Peripheral Participation*. Cambridge: Cambridge University Press.

Lauen, D., L. Dauter, and B. Fuller. n.d. "Positioning Charter Schools in Local Fields: How Organized Segmentation Conditions Student Achievement." *American Journal of Education*. In press.

Lawrence-Lightfoot, S. 1983. *The Good High School: Portraits of Character and Culture*. New York: Basic Books.

Leonhardt, D. 2011. "The Gridlock Where Debts Meet Politics." *New York Times*, November 5, sec. A.

Levine, D., trans. 1971. *Georg Simmel on Individuality and Social Forms*. Chicago: University of Chicago Press.

Lilly, R. 2009. *Health Care for Rural Veterans: The VA Strategy*. Togus, MN: Veterans Rural Health Resource Center—Eastern Region.

Loveless, T. 2013. "Charter School Study: Much Ado about Tiny Differences." Washington, DC: Brookings Institution.

Lyall, S., and A. Cowell. 2010. "Britain Plans Deepest Cuts to Spending in 60 Years." *New York Times*, October 21, sec. A.

Macmillan, R., and A. Townsend. 2006. "A 'New Institutional Fix'? The 'Community Turn' and the Changing Role of the Voluntary Sectors." In *Landscapes of Voluntarism: New Spaces of Health, Welfare, and Governance*, edited by C. Milligan and D. Conradson, 15–32. Bristol: Policy Press.

Malone, T. 2004. *The Future of Work*. Boston: Harvard Business School Publishing.

Martin, J. 2003. "What Is Field Theory?" *American Journal of Sociology* 109: 1–49.

Martin, L., C. Neumann, J. Mountford, M. Bisognano, and T. Nolan. 2009. *Increasing Efficiency and Enhancing Value in Health Care: Ways to Achieve Savings in Operating Costs per Year*. Cambridge, MA: Institute for Healthcare Improvement.

Marty, M. 1997. *The One and the Many: America's Struggle for the Common Good*. Cambridge, MA: Harvard University Press.

Maslin, J. 2011. "Steve Jobs by Walter Isaacson." *New York Times*, November 25, sec. C.

Maxwell, J. 2004. "Causal Explanation, Qualitative Research, and Scientific Inquiry in Education." *Educational Researcher* 33: 3–11.

McCarthy, D., K. Mueller, and J. Wrenn. 2009. "Geisinger Health System: Achieving the Potential of System Integration through Innovation, Leadership, Measurement, and Incentives." *Commonwealth Fund Publications* 9 (1233).

Mead, G. 1934. *Mind, Self, and Society*. Chicago: University of Chicago Press.

Miller, J. 2011. *Examined Lives: From Socrates to Nietzsche*. New York: Farrar, Straus and Giroux.

Milne, R. 2013. "Sweden's Back-to-the-Future Banker." *Financial Times*, January 13. www.ft.com/intl/cms/s/0/4f4d6894–5a82–11e2-b60e-00144feab49a.html.

Miron, G., and J. Urschel. 2010. "Profiles of Nonprofit Education Management Organizations, 2009–2010." Boulder, CO: National Education Policy Center.

Miron, G., J. Urschel, and N. Saxton. 2011. "What Makes KIPP Work? A Study of Student Characteristics, Attrition, and School Finance." New York: National Center for the Study of Privatization in Education, Teachers College.

Montopoli, Brian. 2011. "Poll: Most Want Taxes on Millionaires Increased." *CBS News*. October 3. www.cbsnews.com/8301–503544_162–20114988–503544.html.

Moore, L. 2011. "In the Life of 'The Wire.'" *New York Review of Books* 57 (October). www.nybooks.com/articles/archives/2010/oct/14/life-wire/?page=2.

Morawska, E. 2009. *A Sociology of Immigration: (Re)Making Multifaceted America*. New York: Palgrave Macmillan.

Morris, C. 2011. "The New Normal? Why So Many Americans Remain Unemployed." *Commonweal*, September 23.

Mundy, L. 2012. *The Richer Sex: How the New Majority of Female Breadwinners Is Transforming Sex, Love, and Family*. New York: Simon and Schuster.

Munnell, A., J. Aubry, J. Hurwitz, M. Medenica, and L. Quimby. 2012. "The Funding of State and Local Pensions, 2011–2015." Boston: Center for Retirement Research, Boston College.

National Alliance. 2013. "A Comprehensive Data Resource from the National Alliance for Public Charter Schools." Washington, DC. http://dashboard.publiccharters.org/dashboard/schools/page/overview/year/2012.

REFERENCES

National Center for Charitable Statistics. 2011. "Quick Facts about Nonprofits and Number of 501(c)(3) Public Charities by NTEE Activity or Purpose." Washington, DC: Urban Institute. nccs.urban.org/statistics/quickfacts.doc.
National Center for PTSD. 2006. *Returning from the War Zone: A Guide for Families of Military Members.* Washington, DC: United States Department of Defense.
Nelson, H., B. Rosenberg, and N. Van Meter. 2004. "Charter School Achievement on the 2003 National Assessment of Educational Progress." Washington, DC: American Federation of Teachers.
Obama, B. 2009. Remarks by President Obama at a Town Hall Discussion of Health Care Reform. Green Bay, Wisconsin, Green Bay Southwest High School, June 11.
Organization of Economic Cooperation and Development (OECD). 2006. "OECD Health Data 2006: How Does the United States Compare." Paris.
Orszag, P. 2011. "How Health Care Can Save or Sink America." *Foreign Affairs* (August): 42–56.
Ouchi, W. 1981. *Theory Z: How American Business Can Meet the Japanese Challenge.* Reading, MA: Addison-Wesley.
Payne, C. M. 2010. *So Much Reform, So Little Change.* Cambridge, MA: Harvard Education Press.
Pearson, M. 2011. "Giving and Volunteering in America." *USA Today*, November 20, sec. D.
Peck, D. 2011. "Can the Middle Class Be Saved?" *The Atlantic*, September.
Pollin, R. 2010. "It's Not the Party—It's the Policies." *The Nation*, September 27.
Portier, W., N. Dallaville, C. Roberts, T. Beattie, R. Reno, P. Hampl, L. Johnson, L. Woodcock, and P. Baumann. 2012. "A Modus Vivendi? Sex, Marriage, and the Church." *Commonweal*, January, 12–19.
Powell, Walter, and Richard Steinberg, eds. 2006. *The Nonprofit Sector: A Research Handbook.* New Haven, CT: Yale University Press.
Powell, M. 2011. "Profits Are Booming, Why Aren't Jobs?" *New York Times*, January 9.
Price, S., and P. Thonemann. 2011. *The Birth of Classical Europe: A History from Troy to Augustine.* New York: Viking.
Racculia, K. 2010. *This Must Be the Place.* New York: Henry Holt.
Ragin, C. 1992. "Cases of 'What Is a Case.'" In *What Is a Case? Exploring the Foundations of Social Inquiry*, edited by C. Ragin and H. Becker, 1–18. Cambridge: Cambridge University Press.
Rajan, R. 2012. "The True Lessons of the Recession: The West Can't Borrow and Spend Its Way to Recovery." *Foreign Affairs* (June).
Raymond, M. 2009. "Multiple Choice: Charter School Study in 16 States." Stanford, CA: Center for Research on Education Outcomes.
———. 2014. "Charter School Performance in Los Angeles." Stanford, CA: Center for Research on Education Outcomes.
Raymond, M., E. Cremata, D. Davis, K. Dickey, K. Lawyer, Y. Negassi, and J. L. Woodworth. 2013. "National Charter School Study, 2013." Stanford, CA: Center for Research on Education Outcomes.
Reardon, S. 2009. "Review of 'How New York City's Charter Schools Affect Achievement.'" Boulder, CO: Think Tank Review. www.greatlakescenter.org/docs/Think_Twice/TT_Reardon_NYCCharter.pdf.
Renzulli, L. 2005. "Organizational Environments and the Emergence of Charter Schools in the United States." *Sociology of Education* 78: 1–26.

Reston, M., and H. Blume. 2011. "Mayor's State of the City Speech Focuses on Education." *Los Angeles Times*, April 14. http://articles.latimes.com/2011/apr/14/local/la-me-mayor-speech-react-20110414.

Rifkin, J. 2011. *The Third Industrial Revolution: How Lateral Power Is Transforming Energy, the Economy, and the World*. New York: Palgrave Macmillan.

Rockart, J., and J. Short. 1989. "IT in the 1990s: Managing Organizational Interdependence." MIT-Sloan Management Review. http://sloanreview.mit.edu/article/it-in-the-s-managing-organizational-interdependence/.

Ruef, M., and W. Scott. 1998. "A Multidimensional Model of Organizational Legitimacy: Hospital Survival in Changing Institutional Environments." *Administrative Science Quarterly* 43: 877–904.

Saez, E. 2013. "Striking It Richer: The Evolution of Top Incomes in the United States." Berkeley: Department of Economics. http://elsa.berkeley.edu/~saez/saez-UStopincomes-2012.pdf.

Salamon, L. 2012. *The State of Nonprofit America*. 2nd ed. Washington, DC: Brookings Institution.

Sallie Mae. 2013. How America Pays for College, 2013. Newark, Delaware. September 17. http://news.salliemae.com/research-tools/america-pays-2013.

Salomon, G., ed. 1993. *Distributed Cognition: Psychological and Educational Considerations*. Cambridge: Cambridge University Press.

Sampson, R. 2012. "Chapter 8." In *The Great American City: Chicago and the Enduring Neighborhood Effect*. Chicago: University of Chicago Press.

Sarup, M. 1993. *An Introductory Guide to Post-Structuralism and Postmodernism*. Athens: University of Georgia Press.

Schemo, D. J. 2004. "Charter Schools Trail in Results, U.S. Data Reveals." *New York Times*, August 17, sec. A.

Schofer, E., and W. Longhofer. 2011. "The Structural Sources of Association." *American Journal of Sociology* 117: 539–85.

Scott, W. R. 2001. *Institutions and Organizations*. 2nd ed. Thousand Oaks, CA: Sage.

Scott, W. R., M. Ruef, P. Mandel, and C. Caronna. 2000. *Institutional Change and Healthcare Organizations: From Professional Dominance to Managed Care*. Chicago: University of Chicago Press.

Shore, B. 1998. *Culture in Mind*. New York: Oxford University Press.

Sia, C., T. Tonniges, E. Osterhus, and S. Taba. 2004. "History of the Medical Home Concept." *Pediatrics* 113: 1473–78.

Sibun, J. N.d. "'Old' or 'New' Fashioned, People Want a Different Approach to Banking." *Telegraph*, July 18. www.telegraph.co.uk/finance/comment/9410491/.

Simmel, G. 1948. *Social Sciences III: Selections and Selected Readings*. Translated by E. A. Shils. 14th ed. Vol. 2. Chicago: University of Chicago Press.

———. 2012 [1908]. "Group Expansion and the Development of Individuality." In *Contemporary Sociological Theory*, 3rd ed., edited by Craig Calhoun, Joseph Gerteis, James Moody, Steven Pfaff, and Indermohan Virk, 371. Malden MA: John Wiley.

Slotkin, J., A. Casale, G. Steele Jr., and S. Toms. 2012. "Reengineering Acute Episodic and Chronic Care Delivery: The Geisinger Health System Experience." *Neurosurgical Focus* 33 (1). http://thejns.org/doi/pdf/10.3171/2012.4.FOCUS1293.

Smerdon, B., and B. Means. 2006. "Evaluation of the Bill and Melinda Gates Foundation High School Grants Initiative: 2001–2005, Final Report." Washington, DC: American Institutes for Research. http://www.gatesfoundation.org/learning/Documents/Year4Evaluation AIRSRI.pdf.

Smith, A. 2009 [1759]. *The Theory of Moral Sentiments*. New York: Penguin Books.

Smith, P. D. 2012. *City*. London: Bloomsbury.

Smith, S. R., and M. Lipsky. 1993. *Nonprofits for Hire: The Welfare State in the Age of Contracting*. Cambridge, MA: Harvard University Press.

Smith, Z. 2011. "Monsters." *New Yorker*, September 12.

———. 2012. "Permission to Enter." *New Yorker*, July 30.

Spence, M. 2011. "The Impact of Globalization on Income and Employment." *Foreign Affairs* (August).

Starr, P. 2011. *Remedy and Reaction: The Peculiar American Struggle over Health Care Reform*. New Haven, CT: Yale University Press.

Steele, G. 2009. "Reforming the Healthcare Delivery System." Testimony to the Committee on Finance, United States Senate. Danville, PA: Geisinger Healthcare System.

Swayne, L., W. Duncan, and P. Ginter. 2008. *Strategic Management of Health Care Firms*. 6th ed. San Francisco: Jossey-Bass.

Tanielian, T., and L. Jaycox. 2008. "Invisible Wounds of War: Psychological and Cognitive Injuries, Their Consequences, and Services to Assist Recovery." Santa Monica, CA: Rand Corporation.

Task, A. 2011. "41% of People Say American Dream Is Lost." *Yahoo News—Daily Ticker*, November 15. Finance.yahoo.com/blogs/daily-ticker/41-people-american-dream-lost-63-economy-getting-144604132.html.

Thaler, R. 1994. *Quasi-Rational Economics*. New York: Russell Sage Foundation.

Thaler, R., and C. Sunstein. 2008. *Nudge: Improving Decisions about Health, Wealth, and Happiness*. New Haven, CT: Yale University Press.

Thornton, P., W. Ocasio, and M. Lounsbury. 2012. *The Institutional Logics Perspective: A New Approach to Culture, Structure, and Process*. Oxford: Oxford University Press.

Turiel, E. 2012. "Social Science as Fiction." *Human Development* 54: 408–22.

Tuttle, C., B. Gill, P. Gleason, V. Knechtel, I. Nichols-Barrer, and A. Resch. 2013. "KIPP Middle Schools: Impacts on Achievement and Other Outcomes." Princeton, NJ: Mathematica Policy Research.

Tversky, A., P. Slovic, and D. Kahnemen. 1982. *Judgment under Uncertainty: Heuristics and Biases*. Cambridge: Cambridge University Press.

US Census Bureau. 2011. "America's Families and Living Arrangements: 2011." February 1, 2012. http://www.census.gov.

———. 2013. "Mean Household Income Received by Each Fifth and Top 5 Percent, All Races: 1967 to 2012 (Table H-3)." www.census.gov/hhes, www/income/data/historical/household/.

Vaisey, S. 2009. "Motivation and Justification: A Dual-Process Model of Culture in Action." *American Journal of Sociology* 114: 1675–715.

Wallander, J. 1999. "Budgeting—An Unnecessary Evil." *Scandinavian Journal of Management* 15: 404–21.

———. 2003. *Decentralization—Why and How to Make It Work: The Handelsbanken Way*. Translated by M. Knight. Stockholm: SNS Fölag.

———. N.d. *Budgeting—An Unnecessary Evil (monograph)*. Stockholm: Svenska Handelsbanken.

Walzer, M. 1983. *Spheres of Justice: A Defense of Pluralism and Equality*. New York: Basic Books.

Washington Post. 2010. *Landmark: The History of America's New Health Care Law and What It Means for All of Us*. Washington, DC: Public Affairs Press.

Weber, V., F. Bloom, S. Pierdon, and C. Wood. 2007. "Employing the Electronic Health Record to Improve Diabetes Care: A Multifaceted Intervention in an Integrated Delivery System." *Journal of General Internal Medicine* 23: 379–82.

Wertsch, J. 1985. *Vygotsky and the Social Formation of Mind*. Cambridge, MA: Harvard University Press.

Westen, D. 2012. "How to Get Our Citizens Actually United." *New York Times*. Campaign Stops Blog. http://campaignstops.blogs.nytimes.com/2012/07/14/how-to-get-our-citizens-actually-united/.

Wolf, P. 2012. "The Comprehensive Longitudinal Evaluation of the Milwaukee Parental Choice Program." Fayetteville: University of Arkansas, Department of Education Reform.

Women of Color and Violence, ed. 2007. *The Revolution Will Not Be Funded: Beyond the Non-Profit Industrial Complex*. Cambridge, MA: South End Press.

Wong, E., M. Ormiston, and P. Tetlock. 2011. "The Effects of Top Management Team Integrative Complexity and Decentralized Decision Making on Corporate Social Performance." *Academy of Management Journal* 54: 1207–28.

Wuthnow, R. 1987. *Meaning and Moral Order: Explorations in Cultural Analysis*. Berkeley: University of California Press.

———. 2009. *Boundless Faith: The Global Outreach of American Churches*. Berkeley: University of California Press.

Zimmer, R., R. Boudin, D. Chau, B. Gill, C. Guarino, and L. Hamilton. 2003. "Charter School Operations and Performance: Evidence from California." RAND Corporation.

Zimmer, R., B. Gill, K. Booker, S. Lavertu, and J. Witte. 2012. "Examining Charter Student Achievement Effects across Seven States." *Economics of Education Review* 31: 213–24.

Zogby, J., and C. Schiermeyer. 2011. "Zogby Poll: Faith in American Dream Sinking as U.S. Adults Become Split over Whether or Not They Can Achieve It." *Forbes*, July 21.

Index

Abbott, Andrew, 217
accountability: demanded by actors on the Left, 39; in early health-care reforms, 61; hierarchy and, 70; at local bank branches, 119; of local organizations, 41; market competition and, ix–x
activity structures, 219, 222
Adami, Peg, 80–82, 92, 93
advisory periods, 129–30, 131, 135, 136, 140, 155
Affordable Care Act. *See* Obama health-care reforms
aging population, 6, 11, 14, 33, 38, 187
Alba, Pablo, 43, 44, 129–30, 133–34, 135–38, 149, 151–52, 153–54, 197, 203, 219
Alda, Alan, 27
Allen, Daniel, 154, 155
Allport, Gordon, 28
alternative schools, 27, 56. *See also* charter schools
Altman, Robert, 27
American Dream, 15, 20, 188
American Friends Service Committee, 35
American Legion, 163
Amtrak, 17
Appiah, Kwame Anthony, 72
Apple Computer, xix, 9, 17, 66–67, 68, 189, 194
Aristotle, 210
Asma, Stephen, 30
AT&T, 47, 65
authenticity, xiii, 26, 27–28, 31

Baez, Joan, xiii, 28
banking: American environment in, 122, 124; centralization trend in, 106, 197–98. *See also* Handelsbanken; Wall Street
Beat Generation, 3, 6, 25, 26, 31
Beckett, Samuel, 47
behavioral economics, 17, 204, 210

behavior change: bureaucratic principles unsuited for, xiv; client context and, 192, 205; health conditions and, 85, 86, 94, 95, 97, 100, 207; lateral relations with clients and, 197, 214. *See also* motivation
Benoza, Noel, 138
Berne, Eric, 27
Betts, Julian, 56
Bill and Melinda Gates Foundation, 34, 151, 210
black community: American pluralism and, 21; charter school students from, 54; empowering, 47; Great Society and, 34
Blair, Tony, 8, 36–37
Bloom, Fred, 91, 97
Bloomberg, Michael, xix
border identities, 219
Bourdieu, Pierre, 200
Bouvin, Anders, 121
Brown, Jerry, 68
Bryk, Anthony, 216
Buddin, Richard, 57–58
bureaucracies: of American banks, 117; first-generation decentralists seeking liberation from, xvii, 49; vs. human-scale practices of decentralists, 210; of postwar economic boom, 25; of public schools, xiv, 47, 130, 132, 156; subverted by economic and institutional forces, xiv, 185. *See also* government bureaucracy; hierarchies
Bush, George H. W., 48, 52, 162
Bush, George W., 15, 19, 52, 167, 212

Cage, John, xiii
Cameron, David, 30, 102
Cárdenas, Miguel, xiv
career academies, 56

Carlin, George, 28
case managers, 60, 62, 64
case managers, in Geisinger Health System, 74, 76, 77–78, 79, 80, 81, 82, 91–93; allied local organizations and, 99; caseloads of, 90, 92; curiosity about patients, 74, 80–81, 103, 192, 193, 210; distributed problem solving and, 86–90, 192; in lateral form of cooperation, 197; "medical home" model and, 85, 191, 196; negotiation over authority and resources and, 193; physicians' dependence on, 90–91; Proven Health Navigator initiative and, 84; providing information to central managers, 97, 102, 103; spreading to other companies, 207. *See also* Danowsky, Kenda
case managers, of Veterans Administration, 174, 183
case method, xix–xx, 192, 215–22, 230n8; external validity of, xx, 100, 127, 221; internal validity of, 220–21
CAT (City Arts and Technology High School): adjustments in, going forward, 155–56; advisory periods at, 129–30, 131, 135, 136, 140, 155; building community in, 142, 150; building culture in, 135; college attendance rate from, 129, 130, 152; "critical friend" assigned to teacher at, 142, 150; evening exhibitions at, 143–44, 149, 155; job applicants at, 142; leadership meetings at, 135–36, 150; lessons from experience of, 151–56; number of students in, 130; relationships in, 131, 132, 136, 140, 148, 152, 155, 156; standardized testing at, 144–45, 146, 147, 152, 155, 200; state's official curriculum at, 139, 145; students not finishing at, 129, 136, 152–53, 154; teacher burnout at, 148, 155; teacher on the edge of culture at, 145–48; teachers' roles in, 141–43 (*see also* warm demanders); teacher turnover at, 153. *See also* charter schools; Envision Charter Schools
Catholic Church: attack on Rousseau by, 24; marriage rates within, 21; protection of abusive priests in, 20; women's issues in, 28–29
Catholic Relief Services, 35
causal mechanisms, 192, 219–20
center, organizational: charter schools without regulation by, 52; data on clients compiled by, 43, 192, 211; enabling effective practice locally, 70–71, 217; essential role of, 43–44, 191, 211; ethical principles from, 44, 70–71, 191, 193, 198, 218; lateral relation with local practitioners, 196; loose coupling between local practitioners and, 201; rethinking, 193, 218. *See also* data about clients; ethical principles
Center for Medicare and Medicaid Innovation (CMMI), 101
central authority: cultural subversion of, 6, 27; dichotomy between market freedom and, xviii; economic inequality leading to cynicism about, 12; erosion of, xiii–xiv, 2–4, 20, 186, 187–88; factors leading to decline of, 33; modern notions of progress and, ix, xv, 18–19; need for, xix, 9, 33; subverted by authenticity, 28; today's advocates of, x, xv. *See also* hierarchies; state, the
charter management organizations (CMOs), 53, 54, 71. *See also* education management organizations
charter schools: African American students in, 54; benefit-cost ratio for, 53; between-state variability of, 57; breaking free from education bureaucracies, xiv; built from existing groups, 211; diversity as issue in, 71; dramatic differences among, 54; factors affecting demand for, 57; forces constraining efficacy of, 190–91; number of, 52; organizational field of, 201; politicians' promotion of, 17, 42, 48, 188; popularity in poor communities, 7–8; as possible sorting mechanism, 56; pulling students out of private and Catholic schools, 57–58; teacher turnover in, 50; uneven results of, 49, 51–59, 69, 188; warm, respectful cultures of, 210. *See also* CAT (City Arts and Technology High School); charter management organizations (CMOs); education; Envision Charter Schools
Chavez, Cesar, 28
child care: gaps in quality of, 49; studies of cognitive and social-emotional gains in, 226n1; vouchers for, x, xiv, 38, 48, 188. *See also* preschool organizations
chronic health conditions: costs of treating, 62, 77, 94; in Geisinger Health System, 64, 73, 74, 75, 76, 78, 80, 82, 83, 84, 92, 93, 97, 207 (*see also* diabetes, in Geisinger Health System); lower reimbursement for primary care and, 95; practices for managing, 63; preventable, 77, 93; preventing, 64 (*see also* health care, prevention in)
church-tower principle, 106, 117, 122
Cicero, viii, 32
civil rights movement, 34
civil society: fractured by local associations, 29; individual dedicated to advancing, 24, 32; learning critical thinking for, 134; nonprofits offering social cohesion in, 35–36; not incorporated into the state, 33; of secular state, 23, 24; strengthened by NGOs, 37
Cleary, Mark, 105, 114, 116, 117, 118, 121, 124–25, 185, 192, 221
clients. *See* curiosity about clients; data about clients; local context of clients; motivation; tribal ties
Clinton, Bill: as centrist Democrat, xii; charter schools and, 37, 48, 51; ethical lapses of, 19;

holding educators accountable, 16; on personal responsibility, x, 18, 135; promoting decentralization, 37; public incentives and, 17, 18; Veterans Administration reforms and, 159
cognitive sociology, 203
collaborative economy, 7
collective efficacy, 36
college: high cost of, 20; portable aid for, 42, 188 (*see also* Pell Grants)
Colonel, The, 86–88
community: humanistic forms of, 31; membership in, 45. *See also* tribal ties
community action agencies, 34
concentration without centralization, xix
conformity of 1950s, 25–27, 187
Congress, lack of confidence in, 15, 16
conservatives, pressing for market competition, xiv, 7, 35, 47, 102, 212. *See also* Right, the
consumer choice: mixed results of, 69; not leading to effective organizations, 70. *See also* demand-side forces; market competition
cooperation: cognitive psychology and sociology of, 202–4; in decentralized organizations, 1, 2, 29, 69, 70, 185, 191, 211, 214; distributed cognition and, 193, 204; in education and health care sectors, 11; empathic skills of practitioner and, 208; in humanistic forms of community, 31; institutional logics and, 208, 209; long-running philosophical debate on, 205–6; as long-standing human problem, 1, 40, 185–86; in postindustrial organizations, 4–5, 9–10, 216; Wallander's approach to workers and, 111, 113; in work of global economy, 5. *See also* social cooperation
cooperative student projects, 139
Corcoran, Sean, 57
cornerstones of second-wave decentralists, xviii, xx, 43–45, 191–94; in CAT charter school, 130, 131–32, 133, 152–53, 155; emerging from case evidence, 218; in Geisinger Health System, 78–79, 80–82, 85, 93–94, 101, 103; in Handelsbanken, 107, 125–28, 192; summary of, 190; in veterans' safety net, 159, 160, 166, 182. *See also* center, organizational; curiosity about clients; data about clients; job roles, new or recast; laterally arranged work roles
corporations: decline of hierarchy in, x; liberation from bureaucracy in, 189; positive results of decentralization in, 227n34; scandals of, 20. *See also* banking
Cotter, Holland, 43
critical friend, 142, 150
cultural Left, xi, 6, 223n2
cultural pluralism, xiii–xiv, 3, 6, 21–22, 30, 187; historical precedents for, xiv, 212, 223n4

cultural psychology, 203
curiosity about clients, 43, 191, 192, 204, 208, 211–12, 213–14, 220; at CAT charter school, 131, 133, 140, 146, 152; in Geisinger Health System, 74, 78–79, 80–82, 103, 192, 193, 210; at Handelsbanken, 118, 122, 124, 125; validity of case method and, 221; in veterans' services, 169. *See also* data about clients; local context of clients

Danowsky, Kenda, 44, 81, 85, 86–90, 92–93, 111, 192, 205, 221
Darwin, Charles, 29
data about clients, 43–44, 192, 211; in Geisinger Health System, 79, 84, 86, 90, 94, 102, 103; in Handelsbanken, 114, 125; in Veterans Administration bureaucracy, 173. *See also* curiosity about clients
Dauter, Luke, 54
Davis, David, 30
Davis, Duane, 95
Death of a Salesman (Miller), 26
decentralization: benefits of, xix, 48–51, 67; case method for studying, xix–xx, 192, 215–22, 230n8; demand-driven approaches to, 49, 168, 182–83, 195; drivers of, 3–4, 5–7, 38–39, 187–88, 199; field-specific dynamics of, xvi–xvii, 11, 194–95; interest groups coalescing around, 47–48; long human history of, 40–41; risks of, xix, 213; unprecedented scope of, 41; Wallander's theory of, 111–14. *See also* localism; nongovernmental organizations (NGOs)
decentralization, first-wave, 4, 17–18, 42; focused on first step of liberation, xvii, 4, 49, 70, 189, 191, 211, 217; lessons from, xvii, 48–51, 69–72, 188–91
decentralization, second-wave, xviii–xx, 42–43; coaching role in, 142; focus of, 211; in health care, 63–64; summary of, 213–14. *See also* cornerstones of second-wave decentralists
deinstitutionalization, viii, x–xi
DeLay, Dorothy, 142
demand-side forces, 49; ineffective for veterans, 168, 182–83; organizational field and, 195. *See also* supply response
demographic moment, 14, 187. *See also* aging population
Denby, David, 185, 186
DeParle, Jason, 21
depression, in returning veterans, 161, 169, 176, 177. *See also* suicide among veterans
deregulation: charter school oversight lacking due to, 52; 1970s federal push for, 65; of Wall Street, 65, 212. *See also* government regulation
Dewey, John, 112, 132, 196, 206
diabetes, in Geisinger Health System, 77, 78, 83–84, 86, 88–89, 95

diagnosis related group (DRG), 75
discharge summaries, 85, 91
distributed cognition, 86, 193, 204
diversity. *See* pluralism
Douglas, Josh, 169
Durkheim, Émile, 29

education: advocates of national standardization in, 212–13; breaking free from bureaucracies in, xiv, 47; choice often seen as panacea in, 58; equalization of opportunity in, 9; as growing economic sector, xvi; lessons for decentralists in, 49–51, 58–59; market competition in, x, 59 (*see also* vouchers); mixed markets in, 16–17; nonprofit sector in, 35; policies benefiting the affluent in, 71; of poorly educated labor force, 14; rise in public spending on, 13–14; vouchers for, x, xiv, 7–8, 38, 58, 59, 70, 188, 212. *See also* charter schools; schools
education management organizations, 35. *See also* charter management organizations (CMOs)
electronics industry. *See* high-tech industry
Ellsberg, Daniel, 28
El Museo del Barrio, New York, xiv
employment, growing sectors of, 11. *See also* unemployment
empowerment zones, xiv
energy costs, 7
Enlightenment, 23, 26, 31, 123, 210, 212
Envision Charter Schools: coaches from, 131, 138, 141–42; community-building guide used by, 142; culture building by, 149–51; curricular handbook of, 148–49; developing leadership skills in, 132, 133, 134, 137, 141; ethical principles of, 44, 131–32, 148–51; founding of, 132; four R's of, 132, 144, 148; funding challenges for, 153; lack of well-honed incentives in, 195; limited government requirements for, 130; marketing its strategy and materials to public schools, 155, 199, 211; organizational center of, 130, 131–32, 148–51, 152, 156, 218; pedagogical tools of, 131, 132, 139, 148–49, 152, 199; principals hired by, 151, 193; recruitment of teachers for, 142, 149, 150. *See also* CAT (City Arts and Technology High School); charter schools
ethical principles: decentralization with commitment to, xviii, 213; of Envision Charter Schools, 44, 131–32, 148–51; of Geisinger Health System, 44, 74, 93–94, 103, 198; of Handelsbanken, 111, 117, 125, 126, 127; individuals' identification with or alienation from, 218–19; from the organizational center, 44, 70–71, 191, 193, 198, 218; veterans' services and, 175
Evans, Peter, 5
evidence-based medicine, 16, 94, 96, 97, 103

experimentation with roles. *See* job roles, new or recast
external validity of cases, xx, 100, 127, 221

factory model of production, x, 1, 4, 18–19, 38, 42. *See also* manufacturing
farmers' markets, 7, 21, 42
Farrell, Pat, 29
federalism, 41
Ferguson, Niall, 14
Ferry, Luc, 23, 217
Fetters, Robert, 75
field theory in sociology, 190. *See also* organizational fields
fieldwork. *See* case method
Figueroa, Josefa, 138
financial collapse of 2008, 6, 10; Handelsbanken and, 106, 109, 114, 116, 127; Wall Street deregulation and, 212. *See also* Great Recession; Wall Street
Fine, Gary, 211
Finn, Checker, 52
Fiorina, Carly, 67
Fligstein, Neil, 198, 200–201, 208
Florida, Richard, 30
food-cart movement, 8
for-profit firms pursuing public projects, xvi, 7, 33, 35, 188; of Veterans Administration, 160. *See also* market competition
foundations, 34. *See also* Gates Foundation
freedom of the individual, vs. hierarchical control, 22, 23–24, 26, 29, 31–32, 42–43, 210
freedom of the market, vs. central control, xviii–xix
Friedan, Betty, 26
Frye, Margaret, 203
Fukuyama, Francis, xv, 23, 206
Fung, Archon, 39

Games People Play (Berne), 27
Gates Foundation, 34, 151, 210
Gawande, Atul, 142
Geisinger Health System: case reviews in, 86–90, 91, 93, 96, 97, 101, 219; centrally collected data in, 79, 84, 86, 90, 94, 102, 103; chronic health conditions in, 64, 73, 74, 75, 76, 78, 80, 82, 83, 84, 92, 93, 97, 207; ethical focus of, 44, 74, 93–94, 103, 198; facilities of, 74, 76, 79; improved outcomes in, 78, 82; incentives in, 64, 73, 82, 94, 98, 101, 102, 103–4, 113, 199; insurance arm of, 73, 80, 82, 90, 92, 94, 95; lessons learned from, 100–104; local organizations as context of, 99–100; negotiation between center and local unit in, 193; number of patients served by, 80; patient's role in, 93; profitability of, 101; promoting its reputation in health-care field, 211; protocols

of, 75, 82, 94, 96, 97, 98, 101, 103; Proven Health Navigator initiative of, 84; seeking to influence federal policy, 199; shift to HMOs and, 60, 77. *See also* case managers; Tomcavage, Janet
Gibbs, Nancy, 17
Gilfillan, Rick, 84, 101
Ginsberg, Allen, 26, 28
Giroux, Henry, 219
Gitlin, Todd, 210
Glazer, Nathan, xiii
global economy: America's position in, xii, 9–11; concentration of capital in, 69; as decentralizing force, 3, 5–6; exploitation in, 69; faith in markets associated with, 38–39. *See also* manufacturing: moving offshore
Goffman, Erving, 144
Gore, Al, xii, 17, 36, 51, 159
Gould, Elliot, 27
government: decentralization model used in, 189; declining fiscal capacity of, 6, 9, 13–14, 38, 187; ethical lapses beginning in 1960s in, 19; loss of popular legitimacy of, 6, 13, 14, 20, 27, 187; reinventing, xii, 17, 36, 51, 159, 188. *See also* central authority; state, the
government bureaucracy: Jerry Brown on decentering and, 68; first-wave decentralists winning liberation from, 189; in mid-twentieth-century America, ix; successful through 1950s, 19. *See also* bureaucracies; government regulation
government regulation: early decentralists breaking free from, 189; efforts to dismantle, in 1990s, xii; efforts to rekindle trust by using, 16; of health care, 61, 191; in lightly regulated mixed markets, 50; necessary role for, 213; Old Left ideals and, 212–13; of schools, 130, 132, 152; strain on government associated with, 9. *See also* deregulation; government bureaucracy
Graduate, The, xii, 27
Graf, Tom, 91, 98
Grateful Dead, xiii
Great Rationalization Project, 28
Great Recession: corporate profits rebounding from, 12; employment lost since, 10–11; Handelsbanken's refusal of bailouts during, 106. *See also* financial collapse of 2008
Great Society, 34, 59, 74. *See also* Medicare
Green, Isis, 139
Greenblatt, Stephen, 40
Greene, Graham, 197
grounded theory, 219
Gunny. *See* Henagar, Roy "Gunny"

Handelsbanken: center of, 114, 117–18, 120, 123, 125–26, 211; cognitive schema of branch managers at, 203; competition among branches and regions in, 113; cornerstones of decentralization in, 107, 125–28, 192; cost consciousness in, 122–23; culture of, 123, 124–25, 126, 210; customer relationships in, 106, 107–8, 110, 111, 112–13, 114, 117, 118, 121, 124, 125, 219; decentralized management model of, 105–7, 108, 111–14, 126–27; history of, 109–10; job roles in, 117, 121, 123–25, 126, 192–93; material incentives in, 113–14, 119, 199; mentoring of staffers in, 124–25; negotiating decentralization in, 119–20; questions for future research on, 127–28; Swedish branches of, 108, 110; in United Kingdom, 121–22, 123, 126, 200, 218
Harrison, Bennett, xix, 68
Hartung, Kyle, 135
Havel, Václav, 37
Hawking, Stephen, 221
Hawthorne Electric experiment, 111
Head Start, 34, 48
health care: central regulation of, 59, 60, 61, 62, 63, 76–77; consolidation in, 48, 59, 77, 79, 188, 211; employment in, 11; European nations' outcomes in, 14; as growing economic sector, xvi; lessons for decentralists in, 49–51; market competition in, x, 47, 59–60, 64, 77; nonprofit sector in, 35; segregated by class, 71. *See also* Obama health-care reforms; *and specific patient entries*
health care, prevention in: costs and, 62–63, 77, 201; discouraged by reimbursement practices, 90, 95, 209; emergence of focus on, 83; employer tax advantages for, 64; in Geisinger Health System, 75, 78, 79, 81, 82, 83, 84–85, 91, 94, 96, 101, 102, 103, 198, 207; historical neglect of, 197; managed care and, 59–60; Medicare and, 90; stronger within decentered HMOs, 64; variety of institutional strategies for, 201
health care costs: central regulation of, 59, 61, 62, 64; for chronic or terminal conditions, 62, 77, 94, 99; discussed by charter students, 146–47; in Geisinger Health System, 74, 76, 82, 84, 89–90, 92, 94, 102, 103; in HMOs, 60; increased by specialization, 77, 95; increased by technology, 77; lowered within decentered HMOs, 64; rising levels of, 14, 45, 59, 62, 188
Health Care Financing Administration, 75
health maintenance organizations (HMOs): absorbing many small practices, 79, 188, 211; diversity of patients and practitioners in, 71; erratic quality and performance of, 49, 69; federal centralization and, 75, 76–77; federal push for development of, 47, 48, 59, 61, 188; large successful examples of, 60; in mixed markets, 103. *See also* Geisinger Health System; Kaiser Permanente
Hegel, G. W. F., 29, 33, 206

246 INDEX

Henagar, Roy "Gunny," 162–64, 165, 168, 175, 181, 184, 205
Hess, Fred, 58
Hewlett Packard, 42, 66, 67
hierarchies: advantages of, xix; breaking apart, xiv, 2–5; duality of markets vs., 25, 69, 70, 189, 204, 210; as force for equality, 210; freedom of the individual and, 22, 23–24, 26, 29, 31–32, 42–43, 210; in health care, 79, 85; institutional logics compared to, 208; mass production based on, 19; mixed results of liberation from, 69, 185; not usefully regulating practitioners or clients, 195, 196; of public education, 130; traditional American skepticism about, 1; waning faith in, x, xi, xii, 67. *See also* bureaucracies; central authority
high-tech industry, x, xii, 2, 47, 49–51, 65–69, 187, 199
high schools, small, 55, 56, 71
HMOs. *See* health maintenance organizations (HMOs)
Hobbes, Thomas, 206
Hoffman, Dustin, xii, 27
Hoffman, Sonia, 85
Holbrook, Steve, 165, 166–67, 168–69, 172, 173, 174, 178, 181, 183
holistic health care, 82, 83, 94, 102
Holland, Dorothy, 202
Holly, Buddy, 160
Holman, Konnie, 165, 180, 181
horizontal set of roles, 44–45, 197, 218; in Envision Charter Schools, 149; in Geisinger Health System, 78, 90; in Handelsbanken, 125. *See also* laterally arranged work roles
hospice, 62, 99
house calls, in Geisinger Health System, 76, 84
household income, decline in, xii–xiii, 7, 10, 187–88. *See also* inequality, economic; upward mobility
housing: high cost of, 20; market competition in, x; vouchers for, x, xiv, 17, 70, 188
Hoxby, Caroline, 53–54
Huerta, Elena, 140–41
Huffman, David, 172, 173, 174
humanist agenda of emancipation, 29, 42, 69–70
humanistic psychologists, 28

IBM, 66, 189, 194
incentives: under Affordable Care Act, 63–64; delivered by government, 17–18; economics of organizational fields and, 194–95; evidence of effectiveness and, 195; first-wave decentralization and, 70; lacking in centralized banking model, 106; success of decentralized organizations and, 194–95, 199. *See also* Geisinger Health System: incentives in

income. *See* household income, decline in
individual, the, 22–25; in context, 30–33, 43; rewarded in the hierarchy, 69; rights of, advanced by the state, 23, 24–25, 42, 69; Rousseau on, 24, 69, 225n47; second-wave decentralists and, 43; Simmel on, 225n53. *See also* freedom of the individual, vs. hierarchical control
industrial revolution, 23. *See also* factory model of production; postindustrial societies
inequality, economic, 3, 10, 11–12; Geisinger Health System and, 78. *See also* household income, decline in; upward mobility
Ingersoll, Richard, 216
innovation: charter schools and, 56, 131, 132, 152; in decentralizing organizations, 50; from local practitioners, 201; offshoring of manufacturing and, xix; politicians' promotion of, 17; in technology industry, xii, 4, 65, 66, 67, 68, 189
innovation, health care, 60, 61, 62, 63; in Geisinger Health System, 82, 90, 94, 96–97, 100, 101; rapid cycle, 96–97; research on, 101
institutional logics: concept of, 197, 208, 227n27; diversifying of, 208–9; Geisinger Health System and, 82–83, 85, 90, 100, 101–2, 103, 198–99, 200; recrafting, 62, 197–200
intermediate collectives, 45, 204, 206, 209, 210–11
Intermountain Healthcare, 95, 100
internal validity, 220–21
Iyer, Pico, 197

James, William, 112, 206
Jefferson, Thomas, xiii, xvii, 2, 24, 41
job roles, new or recast, 44–45, 192–93, 198, 218; in CAT charter school, 131, 139–40, 141–43, 152; in Geisinger Health System, 79, 85, 95–96, 191; in Handelsbanken, 117, 121, 123–25, 126, 192–93; in Mason City veterans' services, 184. *See also* laterally arranged work roles
Jobs, Steve, 68
Johnson, Danielle: conceptual foundations for, 196, 197, 198; cornerstones of decentralist organization and, 130, 185; identification with firm's goals, 132, 135, 218, 221; interactions with students, 129, 136–38, 140, 144–45, 146, 152, 192, 197; status of the school and, 154–56; working with other teachers, 142, 149, 150, 153, 198
Johnson, Elizabeth A., 29
Johnson, Lyndon B., 34, 38
Johnson, Richard, 107, 118–20, 122, 125–26, 198
Jong, Erica, xiii

Kaiser Permanente, 60, 64, 77, 80, 97, 100
Kang, Jenny, 53–54
Kant, Immanuel, 37
Kennedy, John F., 17, 34
King, Martin Luther, viii

Knowledge Is Power Project (KIPP), 35, 55
Kobylinski, Susie, 86, 90–91, 103
Koval, John, 14

labor-led Left, xi, 223n2
labor unions: charter school teachers not belonging to, 149, 156; in conflict with corporate hierarchies, xi; government regulation in support of, 19; Handelsbanken staff belonging to, 122; of teachers, xvi, 130, 132; undercut by offshore production, xix
Larsson, Stieg, 106
lateral forms of discourse, 131, 141, 152, 192, 220
laterally arranged work roles, 192, 193, 196–97, 217; in Geisinger Health System, 95, 104. *See also* horizontal set of roles; job roles, new or recast; lateral forms of discourse
Latino communities, 21, 34, 47, 54
Lauen, Doug, 54
Lawrence-Lightfoot, Sara, 230n8
Left, the: British, 37; decentralist achievements of, 42; as force for equality, 210; labor-led vs. cultural, xi, 6, 223n2; need for decentralist theory for, 212; public institutions and, x, xiv, 39, 48, 210, 213
Lennon, John, xiii
Lenz, Bob, 132, 139, 144, 152, 156
Leonhardt, David, 14
Levin, Henry, 57
lifestyles: diversity of, xiii–xiv, 3, 6, 21, 187, 213; prevention of illness and, 77, 83, 85
Littlewood, Diane, 81, 91
local context of clients, 32, 189–90, 195, 203–6, 207–8, 209, 210, 213. *See also* curiosity about clients; tribal ties
local government, Americans' confidence in, 16
localism: constraints on, 190–91; renewed vitality in, xiii, xiv, 1, 2–4, 38, 186; social organization in, 21–22. *See also* decentralization
Locke, John, xiii, xvii, 2, 42
Loveless, Tom, 226n18
Luther, Martin, 109
Lutheran culture, and Handelsbanken, 111, 123, 126, 207

MacGillis, Alec, 63
magnet programs, 56
Malone, Thomas, 67
managed care, 59–60, 76, 83. *See also* health maintenance organizations (HMOs)
Mandela, Nelson, 37
Manning, Bradley, 134
Manufacturers Hanover Trust, 108, 117
manufacturing: America's successes in, ix, 1; job losses in, 6, 10, 11, 21, 78, 187; moving offshore, x, xii, xix, 2, 3, 9, 65–66, 68

market competition: in charter school market, 52, 56, 57; conservatives pressing for, x, xiv, 7, 35, 47, 102, 212, 213; eighteenth-century advocates of, xv; Handelsbanken's success in, 127; in health care, 47, 59, 60, 61, 63, 102; in initial round of decentralization, xvii, 49, 189; neoliberal faith in, 38–39; new decentralists not well served by, 196; other motivations for decentralizing vs., 7–8; political leaders' faith in, x, xi; rewarding quality, 195; risks of domination by political Right and, 213. *See also* for-profit firms pursuing public projects; vouchers
markets: declining relevance of, 5, 186; duality of hierarchies vs., 25, 69, 70, 189, 204, 210; first-wave decentralists and, 42; freedom associated with, xviii; institutional logics compared to, 208; lack of naive faith in, xv, 12, 185; scandals undermining trust in, 20. *See also* market competition; mixed markets
Marovets, Kim: family problems of, 166, 176, 179–81, 184; interactions with agencies, 159, 160, 163, 168, 173–78, 180–82, 184, 205, 218–20; interactions with other veterans, 164–65, 176, 177, 178, 180, 202; life story of, 157–58, 175–76
Martensson, Arne, 121
Martin, John Levi, 199
Marx, Karl, 26, 70
Maslin, Janet, 68
Maslow, Abraham, 111
Mason City. *See* veterans' safety net, in Mason City, Iowa
materialism, xiii, 20, 25, 187
Maxwell, Joseph, 219
May, Rollo, 28
Mayo Clinic, 60, 77, 80, 95, 100
McAdam, Doug, 198, 200–201, 208
McCormick, Bernadette, 144–45
Mead, George Herbert, 202, 206, 207, 208
medical home, 83, 85, 101, 191, 196
Medicare: centralized control of physicians under, 76; choice under, 61; cost containment in, 74–75; creation of, 74; federal center for innovation in, 101; Geisinger Health System patients in, 84; most expensive subsets of beneficiaries in, 62, 77; prevention and, 90; reimbursement under, 16
medicine. *See* health care
Mellbin, Elisabeth, 108–9
meritocracy, 20, 23, 187
Merton, Robert, xx
metacognition, 149, 154
Meyer, John W., 28
Microsoft, 66
middle class: central management of production and, 18–19; declining incomes of, 3, 10, 187–88; of mid-twentieth-century America, ix; nineteenth-century rise of, 1

Miller, James, 32
mixed markets, xvi, 3, 7, 13, 16–17, 38; ethical issues in, 71; of health care in America, 103; new forms of work in, 187; quality issues in, 50; unprecedented size of, 41, 188
modernity, xv, xvii, 22, 23, 33, 37, 209, 225n53
Mogiano, Dr., 81
Moore, Lorrie, xvii
Morales, Ron, 136, 137, 140, 152
Morgan, Robin, 28
Morgan, Ted, 145–48
motivation: of clients, 191, 193, 195, 197, 203, 206, 213, 218; Maslow on, 111; of patients, 74, 79, 82, 84–85, 86, 90, 93, 95, 101, 102, 104; of practitioners, 67, 69, 70, 71, 111; of students, 131, 136, 140. *See also* behavior change; curiosity about clients
Muenchrath, Beth, 172–73
multiculturalism, xiii, 30. *See also* pluralism
Murarka, Sonali, 53–54
mutual obligation: in CAT charter school, 135, 138, 139, 144; Cicero on, 32; between practitioner and client, 208

National Guard, returning members of, 161, 167, 182; Kim Marovets, 157, 158, 164, 175, 176, 177
Nee, Siv, 107–8, 109, 112, 117, 119, 120
Neilsen Andrew, Erika, 148–51, 152
Nelson, Ronald L., 7
neoclassical economics, 29, 31, 42, 70, 202, 204
neoinstitutional theorists, 39, 198
neoliberalism, xi, 6, 7, 38–39, 48, 70
New Public Management, 39
Nietzsche, Friedrich, 20, 22, 206
Niewoehner, Lisa, 165–66, 174, 178, 183, 184
Nixon, Richard, 47, 134
No Child Left Behind Act, 52, 70
Nomu Kollager, 108–9
nongovernmental organizations (NGOs), xvi, 7, 33–38; contracting with Veterans Administration, 160, 166, 172–73, 183, 218; serving National Guard veterans, 167
nonprofit sector, xiv, 7, 8, 34–35, 36
nurse navigator, 81
nurse practitioners, 60, 62, 64, 83
nurses: in Geisinger Health System, 76, 78, 79, 83–84, 85, 91, 98; medical home concept and, 83. *See also* case managers
nursing homes, 98, 99

Obama, Barack: education policies of, 16, 37, 48, 70; income taxes on millionaires and, 12; overseas manufacturing and, 68
Obama health-care reforms: identifying best practices in, 73–74; institutional reforms seeded under, 101; not universal-payer, 212; overview of, 60–61, 63–64; press for efficiency in, 59; shift to prevention in, 63, 198; state-level insurance exchanges in, 17
obesity: behavioral causes of, 95; childhood, 77, 99; type-2 diabetes and, 77, 86
Occupy Wall Street movement, 12
offshoring of labor, x, xii, xix, 2, 3, 9, 65–66, 68
Oktogonen Foundation, 113, 119
organizational cornerstones. *See* cornerstones of second-wave decentralists
organizational fields, 190, 194–95, 196, 197, 198–202, 207, 211
Organization for Economic and Community Development (OECD), 39
Osborne, David, 51
Ouchi, William, 67, 227n37

Parker, Lynette, 153
patient-centered medical home, 83. *See also* medical home
patients. *See* behavior change; curiosity about clients; data about clients; local context of clients; motivation
patient support networks, 74, 76, 80, 83, 84, 86, 94, 98, 100, 101, 203, 212. *See also* tribal ties
Pell Grants, 38, 47
pension liabilities of state governments, 14
Pentagon Papers, 134
performance: centrally defined targets for, xii, 61; need to gather evidence of, 195; rewards for, 194–95. *See also* incentives; quality
Perlman, Itzhak, 142
perpendicular organizing strategy, 103–4. *See also* laterally arranged work roles
Peterson, Paul, 58
physicians: changes from traditional authority of, 60, 61–62, 74–75, 90; diminishing time with patients, 50; federal regulation of, x, xvi, 76; fraction working from independent practices, 77; under Obama reforms, 63; recasting role of, 62–63, 90–91, 93–96. *See also* primary care physicians
Plato, 32
pluralism: cultural, xiii–xiv, 3, 6, 21–22, 30, 212, 223n4; moral, 187, 199; organizational, 32–33, 50; political, xiii, 6; spiritual, of late Roman Empire, xiv, 223n4. *See also* local context of clients
Postal Service, US, 7, 17
postindustrial societies: cultural pluralism of, xiii–xiv, 21–22; decentering shift of, xv, xix, 2, 7, 199; elusive promise of upward mobility in, 20; shifting nature of work in, xii, 187, 195; social cooperation in, 195

INDEX

posttraumatic stress disorder (PTSD), 161, 166
poverty: chronic health conditions and, 62; Geisinger Health System and, 78, 79, 102; loss of manufacturing jobs and, 21; of many CAT students, 130, 150, 152
power, flattening hierarchical relations of, 28, 79
pragmatists, 206, 207
preschool organizations: cognitive and social-emotional gains in, 191, 226n1; Head Start, 34, 48; Left's support for public funding of, xiv. *See also* child care
prevention. *See* health care, prevention in
Price, Simon, 223n4
primary care: costly specialists vs., 77; in Geisinger Health System, 64, 74, 79, 83, 85, 86; in HMOs, 64; learning about the patient in, 86; "medical home" concept in, 85
primary care physicians: Britain's conservative proposal for, 102; in Geisinger Health System, 92, 95; government reimbursement for, 77, 201; struggling economically, 94; for veterans, 174
prisons, for-profit, x, 7
private sector, decentralization in, 188–89. *See also* corporations; Handelsbanken; high-tech industry
productivity: faltering worker education and, 14; in Hawthorne Electric experiment, 111; in high-tech industry, xii; improved by decentralization, 227n34
Protestant work ethic, 12, 15
Proven Health Navigator, 84. *See also* case managers, in Geisinger Health System
public housing, xiv, 188

quality: need for measurement of, 194–95; not guaranteed by decentralization alone, 49–51; rewards for, 194–95. *See also* incentives; performance
quality of health care: in Geisinger Health System, 74, 78, 82, 84, 92, 94, 100, 102, 103; under Medicare DRG system, 75; mixed results of decentralization for, 71, 188; in regulated market, 60–61, 62
Quinn, Naomi, 202

Ragin, Charles, 219
rapid cycle innovation, 96–97
Raymond, Margaret, 53, 54–56, 226n18
readmissions to hospitals, 84, 85, 86, 91, 96, 97, 98
Reagan administration: confidence in, 15; health care costs and, 14, 59, 61, 62, 63; market competition and, x, 17, 47, 212
reciprocity, in CAT charter school, 135, 138
regulation of local work, xv. *See also* government regulation

reinventing government, xii, 17, 36, 51, 159, 188
relationships between client and practitioner, 213–14, 216, 217; at CAT charter school, 131, 132, 136, 140, 148, 152, 155, 156; at Geisinger Health System (*see* case managers); at Handelsbanken, 106, 107–8, 110, 111, 112–13, 114, 117, 118, 121, 124, 125, 219. *See also* curiosity about clients
religious institutions, 19. *See also* Catholic Church
religious pluralism, of late Roman Empire, xiv, 223n4
Renzulli, Linda, 57
Richards, Keith, xiii
Riesman, David, xii, 26
Rifkin, Jeremy, 7
Right, the: decentralist reforms coming from, 42; market competition and, 7, 48; public institutions and, x; risks associated with domination by, 213. *See also* conservatives, pressing for market competition
Rogers, Carl, 28
Roman Empire: decentering forces in, 40–41; spiritual pluralism of, xiv, 223n4
Rorty, Richard, 6, 223n2
Rousseau, Jean-Jacques, 2, 16, 24, 26, 30, 69, 225n47
Rowland, Allison, 131, 133, 135–36, 139, 142, 147, 149–56
Russo, Kristin, 153

Sampson, Robert, 36
Sandberg, Monika, 106, 114–17, 118, 119
Schemo, Diana Jean, 51
schools: citizens' levels of confidence in, 16; late twentieth-century changes affecting, x; mid-twentieth-century, ix, 19; portfolio management of, 156; small high schools, 55, 56, 71; sociological research on, 216; standardized tests in, 16, 17. *See also* charter schools; education
Scott, W. Richard, viii, 62, 82, 227n27
Sen, Amartya, 31
Shore, Brad, 202
Sicko (Moore), 146–47
Silicon Valley, xix, 14, 68
Simmel, Georg, 23, 80, 197, 207, 225n53
Skanska USA, 105–6, 113, 114–17, 118, 123, 125, 192
Smith, Adam, xvii, 31, 42, 104
Smith, Zadie, 139
smoking cessation, 64, 73, 84; taxes on cigarettes and, 17
Smothers Brothers, 27
Snyder, Gary, 26
social capital, 30, 36
social cohesion: local practitioners and, 70, 201; new decentralists and, 22; nonprofits offering, 35–36; offered by existing small groups, 211

social contract, 24, 30; human-scale, at CAT charter school, 135
social cooperation, 195–96, 198, 212, 220. *See also* cooperation
socialist thought, Swedish, 122, 126–27
Springsteen, Bruce, 28
standardized tests, 16, 17; at CAT charter school, 144–45, 146, 147, 152, 155, 200
Starr, Paul, 63
state, the: Aristotle on benevolence of, 210; civil society not incorporated into, 33; declining legitimacy and trust in, 187–88; as exit from tribalism, xv, 29; federalist model of, 41; hospitals managed by, 76; modernist presumption of authority of, 37; modern rise of, xv, 18, 23; no longer master institution, 5; protecting rights of the individual, 23, 24–25, 42, 69; reversing flow of authority back to community, 29–30. *See also* central authority; government
state health insurance exchanges, 17
Steele, Glenn, Jr., 78, 80, 94, 97
Stewart, Jon, 28
strategic action fields, 199
Strozzi, Buck, 43–44, 88–89, 204–5
Stuflick, William, 169–71, 174, 178, 181–82, 184
suicide among veterans: attempted by Kim Marovets, 158, 165, 177, 178, 179, 182; preventive services for, 173. *See also* depression, in returning veterans
supply response, 49, 50, 70; constrained by local capacity, 190. *See also* demand-side forces
Swoop, D. J., 158, 165, 175, 176, 177, 178, 182, 184

Tavernise, Sabrina, 21
tax credits, 50, 71
teachers: balance of coordination and autonomy for, 216; central regulation of, x; evaluation of, 16; labor union model for, xvi, 130, 132. *See also* CAT (City Arts and Technology High School); education; schools
Theory Z, 67
"think globally, act locally," 2, 71
Third Way, 8, 36–37
Thompson, John, 75
Thompson, Tommy, 52
Thonemann, Peter, 223n4
tight-loose management, 67, 227n37
Time-Warner, 117
tiny publics, 211
Tocqueville, Alexis de, 41
Tomcavage, Janet: activating patients, 84, 85, 93; case managers recruited by, 76, 77–78, 81, 84–85, 90, 97, 103 (*see also* case managers, in Geisinger Health System); on childhood obesity, 77, 99; on chronic care, 83; decentralizing principles advanced by, 78, 79, 82, 185; diabetes management and, 73, 83–84; distributed problem solving and, 86, 87–88, 89, 104; end-of-life care and, 99; incentives for physicians and, 94; innovation and, 100, 101; job responsibilities of, 73, 76; prior nursing career of, 73; on supporting nursing-home staff, 98; tracking costly procedures, 94–95; on treatment bundles, 98. *See also* Geisinger Health System
Tönnies, Ferdinand, 22
treatment bundles, 74, 97–98
tribalism: concern over segmentation associated with, 30, 71; modernists' exit from, xv, 29
tribal ties: acculturation into, 203; behavior change and, 192; defined, 45; of Geisinger patients, 192, 197; in Handelsbanken, 121, 125; the individual free from context of, 22; of intermediate collectives, 204; motivated action situated within, 196; new decentralists and, 30, 32, 45; revival of, across postindustrial societies, 29, 33; in social context of client, 32, 206; of veteran Kim Marovets, 176, 177, 178. *See also* intermediate collectives; patient support networks
trust: at CAT charter school, 131, 132, 138, 140, 151, 152, 156; of client for practitioner, 208; ethical decentralization and, 213; in Geisinger's roundtable reviews, 204; in Handelsbanken culture, 111, 114, 116, 117, 118, 119, 121, 123, 125, 127; required for veterans' healing, 166, 174, 175, 177, 178; among staff members of schools, 216

Uggla, Magnus, 110, 113, 121–23, 124, 125–26
unemployment, 10–11; among college graduates, xiii, 20. *See also* manufacturing
upward mobility: declining capacity for, xii, 3, 15, 20; through first half of twentieth century, 19; secular state and promise of, 23. *See also* household income, decline in; inequality, economic
US Postal Service, 7, 17

Valens, Richie, 161
veterans: brain injury among, 161; debriefed on difficulties of returning home, 159, 168; deep ties among, 165; homeless, 160, 169; with stress or trauma from original families, 166, 174, 176; Vietnam-era, 166
Veterans Administration (VA): as huge, centralized organization, 158–60, 171; Office of Rural Health, 172–74; push to decentralize services in, 160
veterans integrated services networks (VISNs), 159
veterans' safety net, in Mason City, Iowa: caseloads of, 164, 174, 178; central office in Des Moines and, 159, 165, 166–67, 171–75, 178, 182–83, 184; county office of Veterans Affairs, 163–65 (*see also* Waychus, Rosetta); lessons from, 182–84, 193; loose structure of, 160, 167, 168, 171, 174–75, 178, 181–82, 183; outpatient clinic in,

163, 165–67, 168, 174, 183, 184; state employment office and, 169–71. *See also* Marovets, Kim
Vietnam War, xiii, 6, 19, 26
Villaraigosa, Antonio, 17
Virginia Mason Medical Center, 97
volunteerism: amount of, 35; serving National Guard veterans, 167, 168; Tocqueville on, 41
Volvo, 123
vouchers: for child care, x, xiv, 38, 48, 188; for education, x, xiv, 7–8, 38, 58, 59, 70, 188, 212; for health care, 61, 70, 102; for housing, x, xiv, 17, 70, 188; not necessarily leading to effectiveness, 50, 70
Vygotsky, Lev, 202, 207, 215

Wallander, Jan, 107, 110–14, 116, 117, 122, 123–24, 126–27
Wall Street: deregulation of, 65, 212; influence on government, 15; meltdown in 2008, 106, 114; moral lapses of, 2, 20, 212; rising inequality and, 12. *See also* banking; financial collapse of 2008; Handelsbanken
Walzer, Michael, 45
warm demanders, 131, 135, 140, 141, 155
Watergate, xiii, 6, 15, 19
Waychus, Doug, 162
Waychus, Rosetta, 162, 163–65, 168, 169, 170, 171, 174, 176, 177–78, 180–82, 183–84, 205
Weber, Max, 15, 19, 24, 26, 39, 123–24
welfare state, 213
Wertsch, James, 207
Whyte, William, xii, 26
Williams, William Carlos, 73
Willson, Meredith, 160
Wilson, Pat, 167–68, 174, 177, 183–84
Wolf, Patrick, 58
World Bank, 37, 39
World Trade Center Hub, 105
Wuthnow, Robert, 29, 42, 69–70, 209

Yerke, Chris, 154

Zimmer, Ron, 53, 57
Zipcar, 7